D1568950

Spirits, Shamans, and Stars

World Anthropology

General Editor

SOL TAX

Patrons

CLAUDE LÉVI-STRAUSS
MARGARET MEAD†
LAILA SHUKRY EL HAMAMSY
M. N. SRINIVAS

MOUTON PUBLISHERS · THE HAGUE · PARIS · NEW YORK

Spirits, Shamans, and Stars

Perspectives from South America

Editors

DAVID L. BROWMAN
RONALD A. SCHWARZ

MOUTON PUBLISHERS · THE HAGUE · PARIS · NEW YORK

ISBN 90–279–7890–5
Indexes by Society of Indexers, Great Britain
Jacket photo by De Spaarnestad, Haarlem, The Netherlands
Cover and jacket design by Jurriaan Schrofer
Phototypeset in V.I.P. Times by
Western Printing Services Ltd, Bristol
Printed in Great Britain

General Editor's Preface

This is one of two complementary volumes describing aspects of the populations and cultures of South America. The present volume deals mainly with their thought and the symbolic and expressive aspects of their cultures; the other (*Peasants, primitives, and proletariats*) looks primarily at the interrelations of the people and their social institutions. Both volumes, and the two together, have as their major organizing principle a place: South America; and a time; the post-conquest period. They honor the tradition in anthropology of deriving theory from data located in particular time–space frameworks. Specialists on different geographical areas appreciate the differences when they meet for comparison and discussion. In the present case this was especially so because among the scholars were many native to the continents being studied.

Like most contemporary sciences, anthropology is a product of the European tradition. Some argue that it is a product of colonialism, with one small and self-interested part of the species dominating the study of the whole. If we are to understand the species, our science needs substantial input from scholars who represent a variety of the world's cultures. It was a deliberate purpose of the IXth International Congress of Anthropological and Ethnological Sciences to provide impetus in this direction. The *World Anthropology* volumes, therefore, offer a first glimpse of a human science in which members from all societies have played an active role. Each of the books is designed to be self-contained; each is an attempt to update its particular sector of scientific knowledge and is written by specialists from all parts of the world. Each volume should be read and reviewed individually as a separate volume on its own given subject. The set as a whole will indicate what changes are in store for anthropology as scholars from the developing countries join in studying the species of which we are all a part.

The IXth Congress was planned from the beginning not only to include as many of the scholars from every part of the world as possible, but also with a view toward the eventual publication of the papers in high-quality volumes. At previous Congresses scholars were invited to bring papers which were then read out loud. They were necessarily limited in length; many were only summarized; there was little time for discussion; and the sparse discussion could only be in one language. The IXth Congress was an experiment aimed at changing this. Papers were written with the intention of exchanging them before the Congress, particularly in extensive pre-Congress sessions; they were not intended to be read aloud at the Congress, that time being devoted to discussions — discussions which were simultaneously and professionally translated into five languages. The method for eliciting the papers was structured to make as representative a sample as was allowable when scholarly creativity — hence self-selection — was critically important. Scholars were asked both to propose papers of their own and to suggest topics for sessions of the Congress which they might edit into volumes. All were then informed of the suggestions and encouraged to re-think their own papers and the topics. The process, therefore, was a continuous one of feedback and exchange and it has continued to be so even after the Congress. The some two thousand papers comprising *World Anthropology* certainly then offer a substantial sample of world anthropology. It has been said that anthropology is at a turning point; if this is so, these volumes will be the historical direction-markers.

As might have been foreseen in the first post-colonial generation, the large majority of the Congress papers (82 percent) are the work of scholars identified with the industrialized world which fathered our traditional discipline and the institution of the Congress itself: Eastern Europe (15 percent); Western Europe (16 percent); North America (47 percent); Japan, South Africa, Australia, and New Zealand (4 percent). Only 18 percent of the papers are from developing areas: Africa (4 percent); Asia-Oceania (9 percent); Latin America (5 percent). Aside from the substantial representation from the U.S.S.R. and the nations of Eastern Europe, a significant difference between this corpus of written material and that of other Congresses is the addition of the large proportion of contributions from Africa, Asia, and Latin America. "Only 18 percent" is two to four times as great a proportion as that of other Congresses; moreover, 18 percent of 2,000 papers is 360 papers, 10 times the number of "Third World" papers presented at previous Congresses. In fact, these 360 papers are more than the total of *all* papers published after the last International Congress of Anthropological and Ethnological Sciences which was held in the United States (Philadelphia, 1956).

The significance of the increase is not simply quantitative. The input of scholars from areas which have until recently been no more than subject matter for anthropology represents both feedback and also long-awaited theoretical contributions from the perspectives of very different cultural, social, and historical traditions. Many who attended the IXth Congress were convinced that anthropology would not be the same in the future. The fact that the Xth Congress (India, 1978) was our first in the "Third World" may be symbolic of the change. Meanwhile, sober consideration of the present set of books will show how much, and just where and how, our discipline is being revolutionized.

Persons interested in this volume should note not only its companion, but also a score of others which include substantial material on South America. Among these are two volumes edited by the senior editor alone, on the Maya and Andean civilizations, as well as others on facets of culture and on social, psychological, and medical problems. David Browman has also edited a fifth volume in the series, on American archaeology, while Ronald Schwarz has collaborated with Justine Cordwell on a volume about costume, cosmetics, and ornamentation.

Chicago, Illinois   SOL TAX
September 21, 1979

Preface

The papers in this volume are an extension of the session Sociocultural Development and Economic Patterns in the Andes, held during the IXth International Congress of Anthropological and Ethnological Sciences, September 1973. Most of the sessions at the Congress were organized around themes and topical areas. Geographical or regional considerations were involved in less than twenty percent of the symposia and normally were used to set the context for a research problem (for example, Changing Ethnic Identities in Modern Southeast Asia). For several of us with research and professional interests in South America, the scattering of information concerning the region throughout many sessions was viewed as inefficient and frustrating. It was obvious that, unless the scope of the original symposium could be expanded and the disparate articles brought together within a single geographic framework, only a small percentage of the material on South America would be readily available to scholars and students. It would be an even greater handicap for individuals residing outside North America, for whom libraries, books, and journals are very scarce resources. Moreover, we believed that the potential cross-fertilization of ideas, the very essence of such congresses, would bloom in such a mix of diverse approaches and would make these volumes exceptionally powerful.

These concerns were expressed to Dr. Sol Tax, president of the Congress, and Ms. Karen Tkach, Mouton editor. With their encouragement and permission, we reviewed all the Congress papers which dealt with South America and added a number of them to the core material presented in Browman's session. This has resulted in two volumes: *Peasants, primitives, and proletariats: the struggle for identity in South America,* and *Spirits, shamans, and stars: perspectives from South America.* This preface and the first portion of our general introduction have been correspondingly generated in tandem to cover both volumes.

We wish to express our appreciation to Sol and Karen for the encouragement they gave us. We hope that this effort will make the results of the Congress more accessible to students and professionals who share with us an interest in the anthropology of South America. We would also like to thank Alejandro Camino, who served as cochairman with Browman of the original session in Chicago, through whose aid the sessions came to fruition.

DAVID L. BROWMAN
RONALD A. SCHWARZ

Table of Contents

General Introduction:
"A Little Glass of Rum"

DAVID L. BROWMAN and RONALD A. SCHWARZ

> In Martinique I went over certain rusticated, half-abandoned rum distilleries where neither methods nor apparatus had been changed since the eighteenth century. In Puerto Rico, by contrast, the factories of the company which enjoys a quasi-monopoly of cane-sugar were agleam with white-enamelled tanks and chromium-plated faucets. And yet in Martinique, where the ancient wooden barrels are silted up with sediment, the rum was like velvet on the palate and had a delicious scent; in Puerto Rico it was brutal and vulgar.
> CLAUDE LÉVI-STRAUSS, *Tristes Tropiques*,
> p. 381

The continent of South America is as elusive and perplexing to its inhabitants as it is to the outsider. Few generalizations can be satisfactorily made about a single republic, and characterizations of the continent as a whole are as misleading as they are informative. In the present world situation caricature and ignorance of the complexity of South America, which contains three hundred million people and a major portion of the world's yet unexploited resources, is unfortunate and dangerous. The rate of population growth in several of the nations is among the world's highest, yet the region has vast expanses of fertile land which could be exploited to reduce world food problems; and South America contains some of the largest reserves of unexploited mineral wealth so necessary for modern industrial economies. These factors — the high rate of population growth, and the large reserves of unexploited resources — suggest that events on the continent will increasingly have worldwide importance.

The pressures for modernization and change are today felt by millions of South Americans who are culturally and politically isolated from the decision-making processes. This powerlessness is not restricted to marginal aboriginal populations, but also characterizes the vast majority of rural and urban dwellers who share a common cultural framework with the political elite. For those who formulate policy, demographic and economic problems receive the most attention and, in this context, sociocultural diversity is often transformed into an obstacle for development.

While the theme of both this volume, and its companion, *Peasants, primitives and proletariats*, is the anthropology of South America, not its politics or economics, it is not always possible or desirable to separate them. Though more than three decades have passed since Lévi-Strauss first visited the Antilles, the undercurrent of social and cultural conflict persists. While today there are more white-enamelled tanks, some still prefer their rum from silted wooden barrels.

PARAMETERS OF DIVERSITY

The native societies of South America had their beginnings at least twenty-five thousand and possibly more than forty thousand years ago. Descendants of the immigrants who crossed the Bering land bridge from Siberia drifted south, crossed the Darien region of Panama, and entered Colombia. Archeologists are beginning to pick up their trail as far south as Peru some twenty to twenty-five thousand years ago. These early inhabitants moved into zones whose ecological resources were unfamiliar, and the early prehistory of the continent is basically one of people slowly discovering the riches of the new lands and experimenting with techniques to exploit available resources (Browman 1978).

Approximately eight to ten thousand years ago, man in South America reached a new level of achievement, a level which his fellows in Mesoamerica, Mesopotamia, China, and other areas of the world were also just reaching — a stage characterized by the first tentative experiments in the domestication of plants and animals. The next half dozen millennia of man's prehistory in South America are characterized by the development of such major modern crops as potatoes, beans, sweet potatoes, and manioc, and by an increasingly sophisticated agricultural technology in those areas where it was appropriate for exploiting natural resources. Llama pastoralism also developed during the period and spread over the high central Andes. Only in later times as population pressure increased do archeologists see a shift from the pastoral life-styles to the more efficient and intensive exploitative techniques of plant agriculture. These epochs also see the stabilization of the sea level following the postglacial variations due to climatic warming. With this stabilization, new fishing cultures sprang up, exploiting an incredibly rich marine resource base and giving rise on the Pacific coast to the first settlements to achieve the level of cultural complexity referred to as "civilization."

With shifts from nomadic life-styles to more sedentary ones, ethnic groups began accumulating material possessions in greater abundance and constructed more permanent dwellings. The material remains of these groups provide the basis for archeological investigation and analysis, and have enabled scholars to reconstruct many patterns of cultural-ecological adaptation. More recently, some archeologists have turned to more complex questions regarding boundary maintenance, economic organization, and the cosmology of prehistoric peoples. For example, it can now be argued that the dual structures which fascinated Lévi-Strauss (1964), in his analysis of South American societies, are a widespread trait with a time depth of at least five thousand years. Similarly, *mita*-type tax duties, still used and abused by modern political elites to coerce the rural populations into public labors, may be shown to have been practiced for more than two thousand years. Finally, the basic grist of archeology, the self-statements of ethnic identity, are preserved for the prehistorians in terms of ceramic vocabularies, settlement patterns, and motif inventories. In short, thousands of years of sociocultural and technological evolution, trade, migration, and conflict have resulted in an indigenous cultural kaleidoscope the dimensions of which we are just beginning to explore.

When the Spanish arrived, peoples such as the gold-working Quimbayas, the San Agustin sculptors, the Tiwanaku merchant-missionaries, and the Mojos mound builders, societies that had once flourished and achieved great cultural wonders, had already perished. Along the western slopes of the Andes, many previously autonomous tribal groups had recently been conquered and incorporated into the Inca empire. Spread over the rest of the continent were hundreds of societies at various levels of technological and sociocultural development.

The impact of the conquest and subsequent colonization by the Spanish and Portuguese, coupled with epidemic diseases and social dislocation, had a devastating effect on the native cultures. Immediate mortality in areas of first contact ran as high as seventy to ninety percent of the local groups with depressing regularity, and the ripple effect of the diseases was felt deep into Amazonia in areas not penetrated by colonists until decades or centuries later. Severe cultural loss and social disorganization occurred among the indigenous societies, no matter whether they collaborated with or violently opposed the conquistadores. Subsequent domination, followed by widespread epidemics, frequently led to the collapse of the substance and autonomy of the native groups and the incorporation of their impoverished relics into the colonial empire.

The patterns of conquest and control varied with ecological conditions and, more frequently, according to the local gold and silver supply. The willingness or capability of the indigenous groups to adapt to foreign rule also played a part in determining the postconquest settlement pattern.

Thus in the highlands of Bolivia, Peru, and parts of Ecuador and Colombia, where the cultural level of the native peoples was roughly comparable to that of the Hispanic conquistadores, the shift from imperial Inca or Chibcha rule to imperial Spanish rule was relatively swift. In other areas, such as the upper Cauca valley in Colombia, the Napo in Ecuador, or the upper reaches of the Rio de La Plata, resistance to the conquistadores was fierce, and effective control was established only after decades of skirmishing, usually after the resisting population was largely destroyed or pushed back into a more remote region.

For Indians in isolated territories not directly affected by the initial military conquest, church missions and later economic interests were the vehicles of exploitation and control. Within fifty years of the landing of the first conquistadores, the majority of Indian leaders and their resources were subordinate to colonial European governments. As the politically dominant culture, Iberian cultural forms were relatively rapidly implanted in the Americas. Interaction between the two groups was in part reciprocal; Iberian ways were modified by indigenous customs, and Iberian technology and cultural forms were in turn woven into the native social fabric. The cultural unity found from northern Mexico to southern Chile is clear testimony to the effectiveness of Iberian tradition in bringing a measure of constancy and stability to a continent divided by geography, language, culture, and warfare.

The independence of the South American colonies, framed in the rhetoric of the French and American revolutions, did little to change the hierarchical structure inherited from colonial society. A native-born aristocracy replaced the Iberian administrators. The feudal structure of society remained but quickly fragmented to the independent republics of the continent. There was little desire and even less action on the part of the new ruling elite to share power with their fellow citizens. For much of the indigenous population, the situation remained unchanged; and for some, whose rights and territory had been partially protected under the empire, a bad situation became worse. Liberal ideas embodied in new constitutions and laws sought to remove the Indians from their third-class status, but these were mainly declarations on paper since it remained economically advantageous for the ruling elite to retain their subordination. In the independence and postindependence periods, the exploitation of Indian labor, expropriation of Indian lands, and deculturation of their societies continued and slowly expanded into the more isolated regions.

In the twentieth century, technological, social, and ideological changes have had a profound effect on the culture and organization of South American societies. Hispanic tradition, still strong throughout the continent, now competes with Marxist doctrine and a range of more moderate social philosophies. Industrialization, population growth, and technological developments, especially those in communication and transportation, have contributed to dramatic changes from the Brazilian interior to the Bolivian highlands to the Colombian coast. They have accelerated, almost simultaneously, processes of integration and separation at a number of social levels. On the one hand, there is a growing sense of cultural nationalism in contrast to a previous European orientation, while on the other hand, there is a growing pattern of "internal colonialism" with respect to the indigenous groups whose members still struggle to maintain a measure of social and cultural autonomy. Ironically, both cultural nationalism and internal colonialism are related to a reevaluation and reaffirmation of the indigenous heritage. This has been accompanied by a wave of programs and agencies designed to "integrate" the Indian groups into national political and economic structures on a more egalitarian basis. While the motives of many involved in such programs may be liberal or revolutionary, their ability to achieve political and economic goals while allowing for and maintaining individual cultural integrity is open to serious doubt.

The extent to which acceleration of the integration process is generating strategies designed to maintain or reinforce cultural and social boundaries is difficult to estimate. While information presented by some of the papers reveals the difficulty or inability of traditional peoples to maintain their way of life, others suggest that indigenous groups have made some successful compromises to defend their ethnic identity.

Anthropological fieldwork by both national and foreign scholars has dramatically increased in South America in the last fifteen years. The earlier emphasis on research projects in Peru and Brazil is being balanced by investigations in other regions. The current pace and scope of research does not easily lend itself to classification and summary. In fact, it is the diversity of problems, methods, and theories, and the range of cultural-ecological settings, that distinguishes the present fieldwork from that of previous decades. Research on the continent as reflected in this and the companion volume (Browman and Schwarz 1979) is a microcosm of that being carried out throughout the world.

SPIRITS, SHAMANS, AND STARS

"Anthropology is what anthropologists do" is sometimes cited as a definition to underscore our eclectic approach to the study of man. While the subject matter of this volume is primarily native peoples, the diversity of theoretical and methodological orientations of the contributors provides additional evidence of the open-ended, multidisciplinary character of anthropology. Taken collectively, the perspectives and investigative techniques of anthropologists are those of the humanities and the social, biological, and physical sciences. The questions we raise lead us to consider fields such as genetics and geology, proxemics and politics, medicine and madness, history and humor, art and artifacts. As anthropologists we share a concern for understanding the species *Homo sapiens*, but as scholars and field-workers we frequently intrude into domains of other disciplines and into the lives of individuals of other cultures.

The reason for restating this "holistic" and what Hughes (1972:14–15) calls the "species-centered character of anthropology" is because it provides one frame of reference for understanding the diversity of problems and approaches used by the contributors to this volume. Furthermore, it can be used as the basis for considering some parallels between shamanism and anthropological query. Such parallels come into sharper focus if we restrict ourselves to the general concerns of this volume and what in recent years has come to be included under the rubric of "medical anthropology."

"Medical anthropology," like "shamanism," refers not to a specific set of beliefs and practices but to a wide range of concepts and methods which attempt to integrate phenomena at various levels of abstraction. Both the shaman and the medical anthropologist are concerned with the patterning of health and illness within and between psychobiological and sociocultural frameworks. Situations in which something has "gone wrong" — misfortune, illness, disease — are matters which both seek to understand through a pragmatic, open-ended, and systematic process of inquiry. While the parallel stops when we consider the direct intervention of the shaman in healing compared with the normally passive role of the anthropologist, they share a holistic orientation which links them on the grid of mankind, perhaps not as brothers, but possibly as distant cousins.

The origin of shamanism may be closely coeval with that of humankind. While we should seek evidence for religious consciousness, and by inference, shamanism, in archeological remains, the activities and mode of thought associated with shamanism are rooted in the human condition. As Furst (1972:ix) notes: "The striking similarities between the basic premises and motifs of a shamanism the world over suggest great antiquity as well as the universality of the creative unconscious of the human psyche."

Anthropologists use the term "shaman" to refer to persons encountered in nonliterate cultures who are actively involved in maintaining and restoring certain types of order. Individuals who have political authority are also involved in maintaining order, and shamans sometimes have political status. While boundaries of this sort are difficult to delineate in small-scale societies, we use "shaman" to refer to those persons who mediate relationships between man and the supernatural, and intervene in specific cases of misfortune and illness to determine a cause and to administer a cure. Compared with others of their society, shamans frequently have more extensive knowledge of the natural world (ranging from plants to stars), a keener grasp of the subtleties of interpersonal and psychic phenomena, and a clearer understanding of and more intimate involvement with the world of spirits. Depending on the specific cultural context, shamans are involved in consulting, propitiating, and manipulating supernatural beings; divining the causes of thefts, fevers, and deaths; curing illnesses ranging from fractures to psychotic episodes; and guiding members of society in economic pursuits, political activities, and religious ceremonies. When viewed collectively, shamans combine, in varying degrees in different cultures, the roles of physician, pharmacologist, psychotherapist, sociologist, philosopher, lawyer, astrologer, and priest — and aspects of other statuses which in our society have become highly specialized.

Consideration of the shaman's role and activities related to the maintenance of health in non-Western settings should not, however, be viewed solely as a matter of intellectual interest and scholarly pursuit. They may also be examined for their relevance in helping us understand our own situation, since problems of ecological balance, population control, physical and spiritual well-being are ones we share with our primitive contemporaries. As we extend our highly technological and bureaucratic culture, we might give some consideration to their solutions, as we force them to share our problems.

This volume is organized into three sections. The first uses psychotropic plants as a common theme. The second covers a wide range of issues in medical anthropology that partially reflect the diversity of conceptual problems and methodologies currently employed in the cross-cultural study of illness and disease. Articles in the last section focus on the content and structure of relationships between man, nature, and the supernatural. They remind us again of the intimacy and complexity of humankind's experience with spirits, shamans, and stars.

REFERENCES

BROWMAN, DAVID L., *editor*
  1978 *Advances in Andean archeology.* World Anthropology. The Hague: Mouton.
BROWMAN, DAVID L., RONALD A. SCHWARZ, *editors*
  1979 *Peasants, primitives, and proletariats: the struggle for identity in South America.* World Anthropology. The Hague: Mouton.
FURST, PETER, *editor*
  1972 *Flesh of the gods: the ritual use of hallucinogens.* New York: Praeger.
HUGHES, CHARLES C., *editor*
  1972 *Make men of them: introductory readings for cultural anthropology.* Chicago: Rand McNally.
LÉVI-STRAUSS, CLAUDE
  1964 *Tristes tropiques.* Translated by John Russell. New York: Atheneum.

PART ONE

Perspectives on Psychotropic Drugs

Introduction

DAVID L. BROWMAN and RONALD A. SCHWARZ

During the past decade anthropologists have become increasingly involved in research on the role of psychotropic plants and other mind-altering substances in both nonliterate and modern societies (see Furst 1972; Harner 1973). Much of this investigation has occurred in South America, especially, but not exclusively, in the interior tropical zones that contain numerous species of hallucinogenic plants. The ritual use of psychotropic plants among indigenous groups on the continent is related to the shaman's role as a mediator between the observable world and the culturally constructed world of spirits. The importance of the drug-induced state of consciousness for the shaman and those who follow his guidance is that it facilitates their ability to "see" more clearly, to transcend the limits of the natural world, and to "travel" through various domains and levels of the supernatural.

Research in this area is an exciting one for anthropologists and involves the investigator in a wide range of questions and disciplines. There are linguistic and historical issues, and a need for integration of information from pharmacology, chemistry, human biology, and cosmology. Papers in this section reflect a small but representative sample of the problems and methods used by anthropologists and extend our understanding of the role of hallucinogens in the cultures of South America.

In the first article, Wilbert presents a comprehensive description and analysis of the role of tobacco in the "magico-religious" activities of South American Indian groups. He describes several methods of preparation and consumption of tobacco and discusses their differential physiological and psychological effects. He presents ethnographic data on the ritual use of tobaccos and shows why it has such an important role in maintaining relations between man and the supernatural.

Gagliano presents a description of uses and attitudes towards coca in

Peru from the time of the conquest to the present day. He discusses many medical and ritual aspects of coca consumption and analyzes the controversies surrounding its use in different historical periods. Wassén considers the various uses of *espingo* (*ispincu*) by shamans in Peru. He traces its use to the sixteenth century and discusses some of the difficulties confronting the researcher in an interdisciplinary study involving methodological issues ranging from interpretation of historical data to proper botanical identification.

Langdon's contribution, based on her extensive fieldwork among the Siona of southern Colombia, deals with the relationship of *yagé* (*Banisteriopsis*) to cultural beliefs and aspects of social structure. She presents a detailed analysis of "culturally expected visions" experienced under the influence of *yagé* and discusses the role of the Siona shaman in ritual and secular contexts.

FURST, PETER T., *editor*
   1972   *Flesh of the gods: the ritual use of hallucinogens.* New York: Praeger.
HARNER, MICHAEL J., *editor*
   1973   *Hallucinogens and shamanism.* New York: Oxford University Press.

Magico-Religious Use of Tobacco Among South American Indians

JOHANNES WILBERT

Few plants have attracted more scholarly attention, or from a greater variety of disciplines, than tobacco. As early as the eighteenth century, von Schloezer (1775–1781) suggested that in order to deal adequately with tobacco, its historian had to consider it from religious, therapeutic, medicinal, sociological, economic, commercial, and financial points of view. To these Putnam (1938:47–48) added archeology, philology, linguistics, ethnography, chemistry, and theology. Today, of course, no writer on the subject could afford to ignore the important input of such fields as botany and pharmacology, not to mention geography. Indeed, even this would not exhaust the entire spectrum of professional interest in this most nearly universal of psychodynamic substances employed by man.

The present paper will limit itself to the magico-religious dimension, specifically among South American Indians. Inasmuch as what may appear to the casual observer to be purely medicinal or pharmaceutical use of tobacco more often than not involves a vital magico-religious component (and vice versa), I will also touch occasionally on ethno-medicinal beliefs and practices.

Tobacco (*Nicotiana* species) is a native of the New World, derived from a variety of different species. Of paricular interest to us are the two principal cultivated species — *Nicotiana tabacum* and *N. rustica* — that achieved greater dissemination throughout Indian America as ritual nar-costimulants than any of the others. *N. tabacum*, a hybrid formed from *N. tomentosum* and *N. sylvestris*, probably had its origin in the eastern valleys of the Bolivian Andes. It remained closely associated with Arawakan, Cariban, and Tupian tropical forest planters, in the flood plains of the Amazon, in Guyana, and in the West Indies. It may also have spread through portions of coastal Brazil, although like the Brazilian highlands this area of the continent was never typically a part of tobacco dissemination. At the time of European discovery, the northernmost extension of *Nicotiana tabacum* did not reach beyond the tropical lowlands of Mexico.

By contrast, *Nicotiana rustica*, the hardier of the two cultivated species, diffused far beyond tropical America almost to the very limits of New World agriculture. It was the Indian tobacco of the eastern woodlands of North America, the *piciétl* of the Aztecs, and probaby also the *petún* of Brazil. In fact, in its dispersal *Nicotiana rustica* rivaled even maize, and along with such cultigens as cotton and the *Lagenaria* gourd extended farthest into the North American continent. Possibly a hybrid between the progenitors of *Nicotiana paniculata* and *N. undulata*, *Nicotiana rustica* most likely originated on the western slopes of the Andes in the border region between Ecuador and Peru, where the Mochica and Cañari cultures once flourished.

Since man's historic interest in tobacco focused exclusively on the narcotic properties of its principal alkaloid, nicotine, one might conjecture that *Nicotiana rustica* outdistanced *N. tabacum* mainly because of the considerably higher nicotine content of the former. This came to be of special significance in connection with the widespread practice of ritual smoking, especially in South America. Still another consideration may be that after planting, *N. rustica* requires far less attention than *N. tabacum*, a characteristic that surely facilitated its rapid adoption from one tribe to another (Goodspeed 1942; Sauer 1950:522–523; 1969:128–129).

In the light of the extensive distribution area of both kinds of tobacco in the Americas, it is safe to say that the Indians made use of the plant thousands of years before Columbus. Likewise, on the basis of its close association with indigenous ideology and ritual at the time of the conquest and since, it is reasonable to assume that the use of tobacco was always largely confined to magico-religious purposes. Thus the extraordinary geographical distribution of domesticated tobacco in pre-European times and the exclusively ritual use of the plant in Indian America can both be seen as evidence for the great antiquity of the plant as an integral element of American Indian culture.

In the early centuries after discovery and even more in recent times, tobacco experienced an ever greater tribal and territorial expansion through North and South America, so that today there is virtually no native population, from Canada to Patagonia, that does not know or use tobacco. Especially in northern South America, on the one hand, and the extreme southern area on the other, this phenomenal expansion was increasingly accompanied by the secularization of its once wholly ritual functions. Clearly this profanization was largely due to European influence. The Europeans, to whom tobacco was, of course, completely unknown before the first voyage of Columbus, were slow to recognize the plant as anything more than a new ornamental with certain medicinal properties. Its profound religious significance remained largely concealed to them, and if they referred to it as "divine" or "holy" it was mainly as a euphemism, not because they had somehow assimilated Indian attitudes. Likewise, the miraculous properties that were early ascribed to tobacco by the Europeans were based on its allegedly curative powers as a panacea. Once that had been proved a fallacy, a purely hedonistic interest in its effects obviously provided sufficient impetus for its swift assimilation into European culture and its wide geographical dissemination throughout the Old World.

Among the Indians, however, secular or hedonistic use continued to be the exception rather than the rule. No doubt there were sporadic instances, for one of the earliest chroniclers, Benzoni (1565:96–98) found the Indians of Haiti smoking cigars "simply because it gave them pleasure." On the other hand, we are told, the priests and doctors among them also smoked ritually to procure dream visions and to consult with their *zemi* deities concerning the sick. As Purchas (1626:57–59), another early writer, put it, they esteemed tobacco not only "for sanetie also for sanctitie" (Plate 1).

De cómo los médicos curan a los enfermos

Plate 1.   Woodcut published by Benzoni (1565) showing Indians of Haiti smoking tobacco from a cigar or pipe. One smoker has dropped his cigar and lies on the ground intoxicated by the smoke he has consumed. A shaman cures a sick person in his hammock

Probably there were other indigenous groups that came to use tobacco for pleasure in the early colonial period. Notwithstanding these exceptions, however, it can be stated as a general rule that "during the period from first Discovery to about 1700, over most of the tobacco area, use was, it seems, exclusively or chiefly magico-religious and/or medicinal" (Cooper 1949:526–527). And indeed, the further we travel away from civilization into the early distribution area of tobacco in the tropical forest, the more we find tobacco still to be closely associated with its ancient ritual meanings. Here at least the native species continue to be employed mainly in a magico-religious context. Smoking for pleasure does occur, but when it does it is commonly restricted to the white man's imported "Virginia tobacco," as it is often called, while the tobacco cultivated by the Indians themselves is reserved for ceremonial occasions.

To summarize, from the combined chronological and spatial evidence bearing on the near universality and cultural functions of tobacco among South American Indians, we conclude the following:

1. In prehistoric and early historic times tobacco achieved a fairly extensive distribution throughout large parts of the tropical forest, the Andes, and the Caribbean, mainly as a psychotropic agent. As such it constituted an integral element of the intellectual culture and ritual practices of tribal South America. Among many Central and North Andean groups tobacco was also or even primarily employed hygienically and therapeutically.

2. During recent historic times, and especially since 1700, tobacco diffused practically throughout the remainder of the continent, down to its extreme southernmost region, the Tierra del Fuego, while at the same time the manner and ideological foundations of its use shifted increasingly from the magico-religious to the profane.

The Indians of South America employ tobacco in many different ways, of which smoking (in cigarettes, cigars, or pipes) is the most common. Of techniques other than smoking, the best known are drinking, licking, chewing, and snuffing. Which of these is the oldest is difficult to say. However, inasmuch as we lack archeological or historic evidence for smoking in either area of original tobacco domestication, Sauer (1969:48) may well be right when he suggests that "tobacco may have been used first as a ceremonial drink, next in chewing and snuff, and perhaps last, by smoking."

Tobacco is sometimes used in combination or association with true botanical hallucinogens, such as *Coca, Datura, Banisteriopsis caapi* (*ayahuasca*) or (especially in Peru) such psychotropic cacti as *Trichocereus pachanoi*. Often it serves its primary sacred function as the supernatural purifying, mortifying, and revitalizing agent during life-crises ceremonies, particularly during the long and arduous initiatory training of neophyte shamans who subsequently begin to use other psychotropic plants as well (e.g. *Banisteriopsis caapi*) (Plate 2).

Finally, tobacco is one of several vehicles for ecstasy in South American shamanism; it may be taken in combination with other plants to induce narcotic trance states or it may, as it does among the Warao of the Orinoco delta, represent the sole psychoactive agent employed by shamans to transport themselves into the realm of the metaphysical. Unfortunately, largely due to the aforementioned failure to comprehend the profound ideological and ritual significance of tobacco, we lack to this day a systematic study of its magico-religious use in South America. Nevertheless, at least some insight into this complex area of inquiry may be had even from its sketchy treatment in the ethnographic literature.

Plate 2.   A Yupa Indian smoking the pipe. Courtesy Luis T. Laffer

TOBACCO DRINKING AND LICKING

As Cooper (1949:534) has shown, there exist in South America two major distribution areas of tobacco use in liquid form — the montaña region and Guyana. In both areas tobacco infusions are of great magico-religious significance. Among the Jivaro of the montaña ritual tobacco drinking became especially elaborated and formalized. These Indians prepare the liquid either by boiling the leaves in water or by spitting the chewed leaves into their hands or into a container before further macerating them in spittle or water. In Guyana, such Indians as the Barama River Caribs or the Akawaio simply squeeze and steep the leaves in water.

Tobacco juice may be either drunk or taken through the nose. Among the Jivaro the application varies according to sex: women in the main drink it, whereas men inhale it through the nostrils. Some tribes of the tributaries of the upper Amazon (Jivaro, Witoto, Bora, Campa, and Piro) boil down tobacco leaves in water to a concentrate. An even thicker paste (*ambil*) is made by adding some thickened cassava starch to the soaked and mashed tobacco leaves. In pre-Columbian times this was also the practice among tribes of the Venezuelan Andes and adjacent Colombia. I saw the Ica of the Sierra Nevada still employing small calabashes for this purpose; similarly, the Kogi continue to adhere to this old custom. Interestingly enough, a specially prepared tobacco paste known as *chimó* is also still taken "by a large segment of the modern, non-Indian population" of western Venezuela (Kamen-Kaye 1971:1). In general, however, Indian tobacco concentrates are sufficiently liquid to be drunk in most instances. Licking of liquid tobacco from one or two fingers or from a short stick that is dunked into the syrup is also known. Sometimes *ambil* and coca are taken together. Whatever the manner of preparation or ingestion, however, the liquid tobacco quickly puts the user into a state of somnolence. The effect of the nicotine is usually felt soon after drinking two or three doses: the face turns pale and the body starts to tremble. Vomiting may occur at this stage, a physiological reaction considered indispensable in initiation and certain life-crises rituals, when the body has to be purged of all impurities. Repeated drinking of large doses of tobacco juice or syrup eventually brings on extreme nausea, especially in women, and produces the desired comatose state with its intensive dream-visions.

Among the narcotic plants cultivated by the Jivaro of Ecuador, tobacco occupies first place. The Indians consume most of their tobacco in liquid form, although occasionally it is also smoked in the form of big cigars. As a narcotic beverage tobacco fulfills a very specific magico-religious function in the Jivaro ideational universe, a role that is clearly differentiated from that ascribed to the hallucinogenic *ayahuasca* (*Banisteriopsis*) beverage or to *Datura*.

The Jivaro imbibe tobacco juice on many different occasions and for different purposes. But the common objective they all share is magico-religious. This is true to some degree even when tobacco juice is taken prophylactically against general symptoms of indisposition, colds, or chills. In case of the latter, the shaman holds his sacred rock crystal into the calabash filled with tobacco water and utters a blessing over it before the patient drinks the medicine. Similarly, when used as a remedy for snakebites, the therapeutic value of tobacco juice is mainly magical. When imbibed in large quantities or, for that matter, even when applied externally as body paint, tobacco infusions are believed to fortify a person against evil spirits. Not only does it invigorate his own body but the magical power of tobacco also radiates outward from the drinker and predisposes in his favor the elements of his entire environment.

Finally, as with other psychotropic beverages, the Jivaro consume tobacco water in order to acquire an *arutam* soul (Harner 1972:136) and to be enlightened by a particular spirit concerning their fortune in warfare and life in general. This spirit can appear to them under the influence of the customary ritual hallucinogens. Young men in particular often leave their villages in small bands to retire into the solitude to a special "dreaming-hut" that has been constructed for that purpose away from the village in the immediate vicinity of a waterfall. For several days the young men restrict themselves to a diet of tobacco, daily drinking it in considerable quantities. In the mornings they exchange their dream experiences and interpret their visions. Only after several days do they rejoin the community as a whole, physically emaciated but psychically reinvigorated.

The Witoto Indians of Colombia also perform group ceremonies of tobacco licking, when the council of warriors and elders meets to discuss hunting, warfare, and those that have offended the ethical standards of the community. The men are seated on the ground around a vessel filled with tobacco syrup, from time to time dripping their index and middle fingers into the concentrate and licking it off. By their participation in the ceremony the men seal any agreements reached during the session (Koch-Grünberg 1923:329). Padre Gabriel (1944:58) confirms that in 1936 this same population considered the tobacco concentrate to be sacred. Wrongdoers had to lick it standing up and subsequently had to leave the house. During the ceremony "god" would come to provide nourishment for the good and remedies for the sick. In former times gifts of tobacco concentrate and coca were given on the occasion of such life-crises ceremonies as childbirth and marriage (Whiffen 1915).

Tobacco juice that is intended for use during any of the major Jivaro festivals must be especially macerated with saliva. The juice is absolutely indispensable for the nuptial feast for women, the initiation feast for men, and the great victory feast. Preparations for these feasts are invariably elaborate. For instance, only after general preparations and food taboo restrictions that may last for as much as two or three years has the time for the four-day tobacco feast for women finally arrived. The principal purpose of this fertility rite is the initiation of the Jivaro girl into womanhood through the intercession of the tobacco spirit. In the course of a series of elaborate ceremonies of dancing, chanting, and the frequent drinking of tobacco water, this spirit enters the woman's body to confer upon her a magic power. Her body impregnated and sometimes externally anointed with the liquid tobacco, the life-giving force radiates out from the young woman, permeating her present and future crops as well as animals. At night she converses with the Great Earth Mother, experiences dream-visions of flourishing gardens and growing flocks, and receives the supernatural promise of fertility and longevity.

An equivalent feast of initiation for boys follows upon an equally prolonged period of preparation, partial fasting, and tobacco drinking. The general purpose of the ceremony — to guarantee an abundant life and fertility — is the same as that for girls. However, there is a difference in the administration of tobacco, in that boys not only take it in liquid form but also swallow it as smoke. The latter is accomplished by the ritual leader, who blows the smoke from a bamboo tube into the mouth of the youngster. Another technique is for the leader to take the lighted end of a cigar into his mouth and blow the smoke through it into the mouth of the initiate, until the entire cigar has been consumed. Immediately after the smoke swallowing, which occurs about six to eight times daily on each of two successive days, the novice has to drink tobacco juice prepared with much saliva by the ritual leader.

Great quantities of tobacco juice are also drunk on the occasion of the Jivaro victory feast, especially during the ceremony of the washing of the trophy head. This ceremony is performed to protect the slayer and his kin from revengeful evil spirits and to endow him with life-giving forces through his *tsansa* [shrunken trophy head].

Among the tribes of the Peruvian and Ecuadorean montaña, the shaman drinks tobacco whenever he seeks to communicate with the spirit world. Any shaman may use his power negatively or positively, in that he has the ability to not only cure his kinsmen but cause sickness to enemies by magical means. "Dark" shamans preparing to shoot a magic projectile that will bring sickness or misfortune to the victim diet for several days on tobacco water. The juice is also efficacious in producing the actual magical pathogen from the practitioner's body and in manipulating the "thorns" that cause illness. However, in his positive or "light" role the shaman also takes large quantities of tobacco water through the nose in order to summon the tobacco spirit and ask him to diagnose and treat sicknesses caused by hostile sorcerers, evil spirits, or other supernatural agencies, (e.g. on the Jivaro see Karsten 1920, 1935).

Among the Campa, another montaña tribe, the *sheripiari*, or "tobacco shaman," prepares concentrated tobacco juice of the consistency of syrup. He drinks the syrup (and also beverages of *Banisteriopsis caapi* and *Datura*) to achieve ecstatic trance states, in the course of which he negotiates with the spirit forces to procure health and sustenance for his kinsmen and to retrieve souls that might have strayed or been stolen by demons ("rape of the soul"). The tobacco syrup allows him to alleviate the suffering of those that have been struck by the sickness projectiles of dark shamans, forest spirits, and demonic bees and ants. In his tobacco narcosis the healer is able to diagnose such sicknesses and to treat the patient by anointing him with tobacco concentrate and by blowing on the affected area.

Those who would take on the enormous responsibility of becoming shamans in future years must begin to take tobacco syrup when still tender adolescents. Later, as novices, on the day of their initiation into the company of spirits, future shamans of the Campa are first given an infusion of *Banisteriopsis*, followed by a large quantity of tobacco concentrate. Elick (1969:206–207) quotes the experience of one such neophyte shaman as follows:

Suddenly the room became very brightly lit and after a while Tsori [novice's name] felt that he was slowly withdrawing from his body through the crown of his head. He watched the *sheripiari* [shaman] and his body for a while then found himself walking through the semi-dark forest. He heard a noise and looking in its direction he saw a great jaguar bounding toward him through the trees, but felt no real fear. The jaguar grabbed him tightly with his claws and acted as though it were going to close its mouth over his face and neck. Just at this point the jaguar disappeared and a young woman stood there holding his shoulders with her hands. This was the "Mother of Tobacco," the principal tobacco spirit. He had been told this would happen if he were acceptable as a shaman. Suddenly he was in the hut again, seated on the ground, with the young woman before him. She repeated over and over a new and different song that he realized would thereafter be his own. He sang the song with her until he had it perfectly memorized. This was the only time the new shaman saw the Mother of Tobacco. After this his own tobacco spirit would come to him.

The next night the novice embarked upon a second ecstatic journey to receive the spirit stones of light and/or dark shamanism. The Campa shaman also owns a third sacred stone to which he feeds a daily portion of tobacco syrup. This sacred rock metamorphoses into a jaguar "daughter" when the shaman blows on it. He himself is capable of changing into a jaguar with the assistance of his spirit wife or female spirit helper, who lives in the tubular bamboo syrup container.

In order to summon their supernatural tobacco wives, daughters, and nieces, neophyte shamans must imbibe great quantities of tobacco juice. But as they become more experienced, shamans only need to lick the stopper of their tobacco containers in order to accomplish comparable ends. Female shamans employ the same methods as their male counterparts to summon their tutelary "daughters" and "sons" (Elick 1969).

In Guyana, especially among Cariban tribes, the drinking of tobacco juice is fundamental to shamanic healing practices and the ecstatic trance experience. Here as elsewhere "a man must die before he becomes a shaman" (Wavell, Butt, and Epton 1966:43). For the apprentice preparing to become a so-called tobacco shaman, the initiatory crisis is brought on by prolonged fasting and tobacco drinking. Only thus will he be enabled to gain entrance to the spirit world and use tobacco as do its supernatural denizens. Tobacco belongs to the order of mountain spirits; wild tobacco is searched out and gathered by Akawaio shamans high up in the hills by virtue of their special powers. Since the mountain tobacco was originally received from a spirit only shamans are permitted to use it. This recalls the Jivaro shaman, who also seeks out patches of semiwild tobacco for ritual purposes.

In order to summon the "old man" tobacco spirit for a healing séance, the shaman first consumes a large quantity of tobacco juice:

The tobacco spirit then comes and can be heard making characteristic whistlings: "pwee, wee, wee." He is thought of as an old man. The whistling is shortly followed by the noise of a spirit coming to drink the juice, through the medium of the shaman, who has a cupful by him. A succession of spirits comes during the séance, each in turn seeking to drink the tobacco juice, and every time when one arrives for this purpose there is a loud and elaborate gurgling, sucking and spitting noise, which denotes the fact that the spirit which is possessing the shaman is sipping its share of tobacco. The tobacco spirit has the power to entice other spirits because no spirit can resist the attraction of tobacco, just as, the Akawaio confess, they themselves are unable to resist it either. Once a spirit has drunk tobacco juice then it is "glad" and satisfied and can be induced to help the shaman by allowing itself to be interrogated (Wavell, Butt, and Epton 1966:54).

To enter into the ecstatic trance state the shaman takes tobacco through the nostrils. On his supernatural journey he finds himself accompanied by his spirit wife and helper, the clairvoyant bird-woman. Together they join the company of spirits who might assist the shaman in curing the patient. The shaman's flight is made possible through the combined effort of the tobacco spirit and the spirit-bird helper (the swallow-tailed kite), who provide the shaman with magic wings. Upon returning from his cosmic journey, the shaman returns his wings to the bird spirit and once more adopts his everyday human form.

There are also practicing female shamans among Guyana Indians who employ tobacco as a medium of communication with the spirit world. Lacking, however, in this northeastern area of the tobacco-drinking complex, are the communal tobacco-drinking rituals found elsewhere in South America.

TOBACCO CHEWING

The chewing of tobacco has a rather sporadic distribution among South American Indians. It is found mainly in central Guyana and the Caribbean, in the upper Amazon region, and among several tribes of the Gran

Chaco. It was formerly a custom also among the ancient Chibcha and Goajiro of Colombia. As Zerries (1964:99–100) and other writers have pointed out, the scattered distribution of the practice and its occurrence mainly among "marginal" and "submarginal" populations are indications of the great antiquity of this custom.

In tobacco chewing the narcotic juice is swallowed and the nicotine absorbed into the system through the lining of the stomach. Users commonly mix the minced or rolled tobacco leaves with such alkalinic substances as wood ashes, black-niter earth, or pulverized shell. These are either simply added to a pinch of chopped tobacco leaves or sprinkled into a roll made of green or dried tobacco which the chewer holds in his mouth, usually in front of the lower or upper gum:

Before using them [the tobacco leaves], they put them in a cuia [pot] with a little water; then, near the fire, they mix the leaves with ashes until they are dry again. Generally they take three leaves, beat them to remove the ashes and then roll them one over another. If the leaves are very long, they double them over several times, until they make a big long sausage which they put under their lower lip (Biocca 1970:135).

The psychotropic effect of chewing tobacco appears to vary from light to severe. Among the Yanoama of the Upper Orinoco, for example, men and women chew with great frequency and for prolonged periods of time, but I have never noted any acute tobacco intoxication to result from this practice. On the other hand, a Tukano shaman was observed by Nimuendajú (1952:104) falling over backwards with shaking knees after sucking on a wad of cut tobacco that he had placed in each cheek.

In what might be the first recorded observation of tobacco chewing in the New World, Amerigo Vespucci reported in a letter of 1504 to his friend Piero Soderini that the Indians of Margarita Island "each had his cheeks bulging with a certain green herb . . . and each carried hanging from his neck two dried gourds, one of which was full of the very herb that he kept in his mouth; the other full of a certain white flour like powdered chalk" (Brooks 1937:189).[1] The mystified explorer was soon to learn that on this island where water is scarce the Indian fishing folk chewed to quench their thirst (Plate 3).

Among the Yanoama of Guyana, where both sexes, adults as well as children, chew (or better, suck) tobacco almost incessantly, the practice appears to be largely hedonistic. However, dying Indians also receive a final roll of tobacco under their lower lip so that Thunder and the spirits of the other world will recognize them. But even apart from this obviously ritual practice, there is ample evidence that elsewhere magico-religious ideas are closely associated with the chewing of tobacco. Even where

---

[1]   Some scholars suspect, however, that Vespucci's account, published by Waldseemüller (1507), actually referred to coca chewing rather than tobacco.

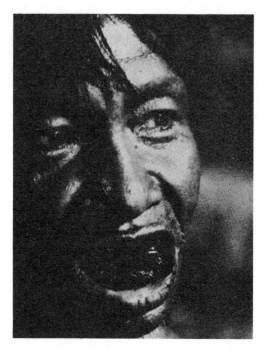

Plate 3. Yanoama Indian sucking on a wad of tobacco (Photograph courtesy Barbara Braendli)

masticated tobacco is medicinally applied, it is often intended to ward off the evil spirits that had caused the patient's illness. Patients among the Páez of Colombia also provide their shamans with chewing tobacco and coca which, when taken together, produce dream visions that reveal future events, and especially the patient's likely fate (Bernal Villa 1954:237). These shamans employ chewed tobacco to blow away the rainbow, so that children may not be afflicted with scabies. Among some tribes — the Tukano, for example — tobacco chewing is mainly practiced by the dark shaman who seeks to be possessed by the spirit helpers that supplied him with his magic sickness projectiles (Nimuendajú 1948:723).

TOBACCO SNUFFING

The inhaling of narcotics is a peculiarly New World custom that spread to the Old World only in post-Hispanic times, specifically with powdered tobacco. In the Americas, the snuffing of pulverized tobacco was largely restricted to the western regions, especially the humid Amazon valley. Powdered tobacco as a magic repellent against hostile demons and disease spirits is also employed by the shamans of the Tukano of the Bolivian

Andes, who blow the narcotic powder at their supernatural adversaries (Hissink and Hahn 1961). (Rare occurrences of tobacco snuffing have also been reported from Mexico and North America; in Mexico, also, at the time of the Conquest, pulverized *piciétl* [*Nicotiana rustica*] was externally applied to the patient's body rather than inhaled.)

In South America, tobacco snuffing is mainly practiced on the Guaporé, by Arawakan tribes of the montaña, and by Panoan-speakers of the Jurua-Purús. However, the distribution area also reaches out toward the south, to include Quechua-speakers of central and southern Peru as well as Aymara groups of Bolivia. Outside this main region the snuffing of tobacco seems to have been restricted to only a few tribes of the Orinoco basin and the West Indies (Zerries 1964:96).

Powerful hallucinogenic snuffs were (and still are) prepared in many areas of South America from such species as *Virola* and *Anadenanthera* (Schultes 1972:24–31), but as Schultes noted in an earlier paper (1967:292), powdered tobacco was certainly a widely used narcotic. There are also several cases on record where tobacco snuff is mixed with coca, *Erythroxylon coca*, or *Anadenanthera peregrina*, but generally speaking tobacco was used either by itself or side by side, rather than mixed, with other psychotropic snuffing preparations.

The fairly extensive distribution of tobacco snuffing and its typical association with ecstatic and divinatory shamanistic techniques again suggest considerable antiquity for this custom. In any event, it is likely to antedate the rise of the Andean civilizations rather than to have originated with them and to have subsequently diffused to the less complex populations of the montaña.

In early contact times Peruvian Indians are reported to have sometimes prepared tobacco snuff from the roots rather than the leaves. Generally, however, the snuff is made by pulverizing the dried leaves. Plant ashes are occasionally mixed with the powdered tobacco, possibly for the same pharmocological reason that ashes are mixed with *Anadenanthera* or *Virola* snuff and lime is taken with coca. Some peoples snuff tobacco without the use of special snuffing instruments, others use single or bifurcated tubes to suck the narcotic powder into their own noses or to blow it into the nostrils of others. These techniques and instruments closely resemble those employed in the use of *Anadenanthera* and other hallucinogenic snuffs (Plate 4).

Like tobacco juice, snuff is sometimes taken prophylactically, for reasons of hygiene, or to forge alliances during peacemaking ceremonies. But its main function is in connection with shamanizing, when the practitioner blows it into the patient's nose as a magic remedy, or administers it to participants in ceremonies. Otomac shamans are reported to have taken tobacco snuff (possibly mixed with *Anadenanthera*) in order to experience prophetic dream-visions in the company of the supernaturals.

Plate 4.   Witoto Indians taking snuff by blowing powder up into the nostrils of a partner
(After J. Crévaux, *Voyages dans L'Amérique du Sud*. Paris 1883)

The tobacco snuff of the Tukano included six different ingredients, mainly the bark ashes of several trees but not *paricá* (*Anadenanthera*). It will be recalled that among these Indians the chewing of tobacco is a mark of dark shamans. Snuffing, however, is practiced only in connection with the ceremony of the sacred musical instruments. The sacred trumpet that is sounded during a girl's initiation ceremony to ward off demons and invisible "immortals" can only be blown by men and boys over seven years of age who have been initiated into the use of tobacco snuffing.

The snuff is taken within the compound where the sacred instrument is kept hidden from the girls and the women. It is here also that men enter into ecstatic trance communication with the protective spirits of the sacred instruments, thereby assisting in assuring magical protection for the pubescent girls and the women. The boys are traditionally initiated into this fertility complex when their voices change and when, in the course of formal puberty observances, they are secluded from the community in order to be admitted to the secrets of the sacred trumpet under the influence of the narcotic tobacco snuff (Nimuendajú 1948:718).

Among the tribes of the Guaporé tobacco snuff is commonly used with *Anadenanthera* powder, either in combination or sequentially. Shamans blow it into their patient's nose and take it themselves by means of two to three-foot-long bamboo tubes. The snuffing tube is sometimes decorated at its mouth with the head of a bird. This avian head may be provided with a pair of eyes which, among the Aikana, for example, facilitate the shaman's vision in the supernatural sphere. Tupari shamans communicate in their trances with ancestral shamans who appear to them "up there" as half-man, half-animal (Caspar 1952; 1953:158).

SMOKING

As mentioned earlier, smoking is the most common and most widespread mode of tobacco use. The dried leaves are smoked either as cigars and cigarettes or in a pipe. According to Cooper (1949:527–528):

In earlier times, shortly after and sometime before the period of Discovery — and in large measure at present as well — cigars-cigarettes prevailed over the great northern focal area of the continent and adjacent Antilles and Middle America, pipes over a roughly crescent-shaped belt peripheral thereto on the southeast, south, southwest, and west, a tobaccoless zone peripheral in turn to the pipe zone.

Both cigars and pipe smoking were the first forms of tobacco use witnessed by the Europeans. Two sailors whom Columbus had sent to scout the island of Haiti found the natives there smoking tobacco rolled in dried leaves of maize. Benzoni (1565:81), whose experiences go back to 1541–1555, reports the following:

When these [tobacco] leaves are in season, they pick them, tie them up in bundles and suspend them near their fireplace till they are very dry; and when they wish to use them, they take a leaf of their grain (maize) and putting one of the others into it, they roll them round tight together; then they set fire to one end, and putting the other end into the mouth, they draw their breath up through it, wherefore the smoke goes into the mouth, the throat, the head, and they retain it as long as they can, for they find a pleasure in it, and so much do they fill themselves with this cruel smoke, that they lose their reason. And there are some who take so much of it, that they fall down as if they were dead, and remain the greater part of the day or night stupefied. Some men are found who are content with imbibing only enough of this smoke to make them giddy, and no more.

Other islanders took smoke through the nose. Of this "very pernicious" custom of inhaling smoke from burning tobacco leaves through the nostrils by means of a straight or forked tube, Oviedo y Baños said in 1526 that the Indians persisted until they became stupefied (Oviedo y Baños 1940).

While it was the physical effects of tobacco smoking that struck the Europeans first and foremost, Benzoni (1565:82) did note some of its magico-religious functions:

In La Española and the other islands, when their doctors wanted to cure a sick man, they went to the place where they were to administer the smoke, and when he was thoroughly intoxicated by it, the cure was mostly effected. On returning to his senses, he told a thousand stories of his having been at the council of the gods, and other high visions (Plate 5).

Shamanic healing with tobacco smoke continues to be an almost universal technique through the South American tobacco area and beyond. This is

Plate 5.   Roucouyenne Indian is treated by tobacco smoke blowing shaman (After J. Crévaux, *Voyages dans L'Amérique du Sud*. Paris 1883)

related to the belief that the shaman's breath is charged with magic energy which is reinforced through tobacco smoke. The very "power of the shaman is often linked with his breath or tobacco smoke, both of which possess cleansing and reinvigorating properties which play an important part in healing and in other magic practices" (Zerries 1969:314). "Receive the power of the spirit," exclaims the Tupi shaman when he blows over his people (De Léry 1592:281). The Mbyá-guaraní call the smoke of tobacco "life-giving mist," because they consider it to be the source of vitality, an attribute of the god of spring, the patron of shamans (Cadogan 1958:93).

Generally speaking, the blowing of tobacco smoke by the light shaman, whether over patients and others in different kinds of life-crises situations, or over objects, foodstuffs, gardens, rivers, and the forest, invariably has as its principal purpose the purification of what is unclean or contaminated, the reinvigoration of the weak, and the warding off of evil of whatever kind or form.

Thus, the light shaman of the Warao presides over an ancient cult of fertility. In his dream or tobacco-induced ecstatic trance, he travels to the House of Tobacco Smoke in the eastern part of the universe. The celestial bridge of tobacco smoke, which he frequents and maintains between his community and the abode of the Bird-Spirit of the East, is a channel of energy that guarantees health and abundance of life on earth. Protected by a light shaman, no harm can befall the people, even if someone were to be "shot" by the sickness projectile of a hostile shaman. A shaman who feeds his tutelary spirits properly with tobacco smoke can count on their assistance in curing such magically induced disease. When he places his hand on the affected body part of his patient, the spirit helpers diagnose the nature of the arrow of sickness. The healer then sucks it out, inhales great quantities of tobacco smoke, and lets the magic arrow travel through his arm and through an exit hole into his hand, where it is "born" for the patient and all his kin to see.

Dark shamans, on the other hand, reverse the life-conferring energy of the light shaman's blowing of tobacco smoke, for they blow to debilitate and to kill. For example, the dark shaman of the Warao lights a cigar which contains his spirit "sons." While smoking, he chants his destructive song, and with this the ends of a snare of tobacco smoke that he carries wound up in his breast slowly begin to emerge from the corners of his mouth. When these ends arrive at their intended destination, the shaman pulls heavily on his cigar, turns it around and, holding the burning end in his closed mouth, blows into it. Out come ribbons of smoke, and these then transport the magic projectile to the victim. The instant the arrow enters the body, the snare of tobacco smoke closes and the magic projectile travels to the heart to kill (Plate 6, Plate 7).

Not only the shaman but also the ordinary individual can count on the power of the smoke when it comes from his own mouth. I was often told by my Warao friends that I should not smoke on the river or in the forest if I wanted to avoid attracting the spirits. Guyana Caribs, such as the Akawaio, use tobacco in ritual shamanic and personal blowing "because it has an exceptionally strong and powerful spirit"; hence they resort to smoke blowing especially to protect themselves on their way through the forest (Butt 1956). With great piety the Tukano direct private invocations to some animal spirit by uttering a spell and combining it with tobacco smoke. "In all invocations tobacco smoke is the principal medium because the request (or threat, as the case may be) is directly transmitted through the smoke. . . . Invocation, combined with the use of tobacco is probably the ritual attitude that is most frequently observed by the individual" (Reichel-Dolmatoff 1971:153, 155).

Within the ideational framework of many indigenous cultures in South America, the concept of life-giving energy associated with tobacco smoke, and with tobacco in general, can be taken quite literally. In the religious symbolism of the Tukano, for example, tobacco has seminal characteristics:

In the act of smoking there is a complex symbolism in which the act of nursing is combined with a phallic symbol, the cigar, and a uterine symbol, burning, and

Plate 6.   Tupinamba shamans wearing leather cloaks, smoking a cigar, and carrying rattles (After Métraux, 1928)

O fumador de tabaco e a fabricação do fogo (Thevet).

Plate 7.   Woodcut published by André Thevet in *Les sigularitez de la France antartique* . . . Paris 1557, showing Tupinamba Indians smoking a cigar and making fire

ashes, the latter being the "residue." On the other hand, smoke is *bogá*, an element of fertilizing energy that rises from below in an upward direction to unite the Milky Way with the great universal *bogá*. The tiny seeds of the tobacco plant also have seminal meaning. When the forked cigar holder is used, the sexual symbolism is clear: sticking it into the earth like a world axis, the phallic union between the various planes of above and below is achieved (Reichel-Dolmatoff 1971:152).

Indeed, the most pervasive connotation of tobacco is the concept of fertility in the broadest sense of the word. Fertility is the objective pursued by man through this medium of communication between himself and the supernatural sphere, be it by means of a simple invocation, a curing séance, initiation ceremony, vision quest, or ecstatic trance. The question arises, of course, how tobacco in its various forms came to acquire such a pervasive role. A purely pharmacological explanation would probably be easier than a religious one. However, despite the general paucity of ethnographic data on the metaphysical meaning of tobacco, some general observations are possible.

CONCLUDING REMARKS

It has become obvious that whatever the form in which it is taken, tobacco plays a central role in South American shamanism and religion. Like the sacred mushrooms, peyote, morning glories, *Datura, ayahuasca*, the various psychotomimetic snuffs, and a whole series of other New World hallucinogens, tobacco was and is employed by Indians to achieve shamanic trance states, in purification, and in supernatural curing. The chewing of tobacco appears to be the least potent mode of tobacco consumption to achieve these aims, while drinking and snuffing are clearly more effective. Smoking, however, outranks them all, in distribution as well as physiological and metaphysical functions. This may have several reasons. As a vaporous carrier of the nicotine alkaloid, smoke was easily assimilated into preexistent beliefs about the exhalatory powers of the shaman. Smoke makes his breath visible, and with it the benevolent, or, as the case may be, malevolent, charges that emanate from the shaman. In addition, tobacco smoke, corresponding to the merging of air and fire, acquired the rich antithetical symbolic complex of incense as a medium between earth and heaven through fire.

The nonmaterial smoke is the ideal and most appropriate food of spirits. Taken in liquid form, as, for example, among the Jivaro, Conibo, and Guyana Caribs, tobacco enables one to propitiate and visit the world of spirits and induce it to bestow blessings upon man. Tobacco in smoke form, however, once discovered, was quickly recognized as a most immediate and direct way to the spirits and hence became the preferred sacrificial gift to the supernaturals in many parts of the New World. The gods and spirits, it is widely held, crave tobacco smoke so intensely that they are unable to resist it. Since there is no tobacco smoke other than that produced by man through fire, the supernaturals in a very real sense depend on him for their favorite food and sustenance. What seems to have occurred here is the attribution to the gods and other supernaturals of the same near addiction to tobacco that is characteristic of many shamans. Just as the tobacco shaman of the Warao requires tobacco smoke with tremendous physiological and psychological urgency, and is literally sick without it, so the gods await their gift of tobacco smoke with the craving of the addict, and will enter into mutually beneficial relationships with man so long as he is able to provide the drug. Foodstuffs like mead, beer, manioc gruel, moriche flour, etc., are simply not adequate substitutes.

This projection onto the supernaturals of the shaman's tobacco habit in no sense represents a profanization of the gods, however. On the contrary, the essential shamanic quality of the supernaturals (e.g., their craving for tobacco) lies precisely in their origin; the gods and other denizens of the metaphysical sphere are themselves shamans of former times who upon death became transformed into pure spirit.

If tobacco is a life-giving essence for man in the indirect sense by allowing him access to the protective powers of the spirit world, it serves the same life-assuring purpose for the gods themselves in a direct way. Because it is their food and sustenance, they are forced into a dependency relationship with man as their chief provider. In the Mundurucú tobacco myth, even the Mother of Tobacco, who created tobacco smoke *sui generis* and carried it in a calabash from which she periodically sucked her vital sustenance, died as soon as she ran out of the life-giving smoke (Kruse 1951–1952:918).

This relationship of man as provider of nourishment for the spirits has been documented for many tribes in South America, from Brazil to the Caribbean, and from the Atlantic coast to the montaña. The spirits of the Guyana Indians are said to be "crazy" for smoke, and the shamans control and manipulate them through offerings and regular feedings of tobacco. This is true, above all, of smoke, but it applies as well to its other forms, particularly as a liquid and as snuff, which seem to have preceded the discovery of smoking. The supernatural Tobacco Woman of the Akawaio, for example, is persuaded by a shaman to offer "a drink of tobacco juice . . . to *Imawali*, representing the chief order of nature spirits," for the purpose of dissuading other supernaturals of the forest and of vegetation from causing sickness to a fellow tribesman (Butt 1956–1957:170). The Waiwai shaman feeds tobacco smoke to a magic stone as a means of summoning his own helping spirits, whose sustenance is tobacco (Fock 1963:126). And again, much of the Warao Indian's life is spent in propitiating a number of Supreme Spirits, referred to as Grandfathers, and a female spirit called Mother of the Forest, who together inhabit the world mountains at the cardinal and intercardinal points of the universe and who require nourishment from the people in the form of tobacco smoke. Like the Balam gods of the four directions in the Maya universe, the Warao gods consume enormous cigars and are well disposed toward mankind so long as men propitiate them with tobacco, moriche flour, honey, fish, and crabs. But the spirits keep only the tobacco for themselves, for tobacco is their appropriate food. If neglected in this vital aspect, they spread sickness and death among the people by means of their magic projectiles (i.e., behave like dark shamans of an especially powerful kind).

The shaman-priest of the Warao carries out the feeding of the gods by holding the long cigar vertically and pointing it in the direction of the Supreme Spirits, all the while deeply inhaling with hyperventilation and swallowing the smoke (Plate 8). Smoking offerings are also made to the

Plate 8.   Priest-Shaman carrying out the feeding of the gods by holding the long cigar vertically and pointing it in the direction of the Supreme Spirits (Photograph by Johannes Wilbert)

sacred rattle, as the spirit stones within it require tobacco smoke as well. As in the case of the Tupinambá of Brazil, the Warao rattle is a head-spirit that can be consulted in the fashion of an oracle. However, instead of blowing tobacco smoke into the rattle as do the Warao, the Tupinambá burn tobacco leaves inside the rattle and hold communion with their spirit by inhaling the smoke that emerges through the head-spirit's various orifices (Métraux 1928:67; Wilbert 1972).

A related idea seems to be that of the Mundurucú, whose shaman inhales clouds of tobacco smoke blown on him by fellow practitioners through reversed cigars. In the resulting trance the shaman feeds the Mother of Game Animals with sweet manioc gruel (Murphy 1958:40). In a similar context of hunting magic many other Brazilian tribes propitiate their Master (or "Owner") of Animals (Barbosa Rodrígues 1890:9, 12).

I have previously referred to the Campa of the Peruvian montaña whose shaman must feed the sacred rock a daily diet of tobacco syrup. Harner (1972:163) reports that among the Jivaro the shaman seeks to reassure himself, by means of periodic tobacco feedings, of the benevolence of his spirit helpers who appear to him under the influence of *Banisteriopsis* (*ayahuasca*) in "a variety of zoomorphic forms hovering over him, perching on his shoulders, sticking out of his skin, and helping to suck the patient's body." Every four hours he drinks tobacco water in order to keep these spirits fed, so that they may remain his willing helpers and not desert him.

To sum up, on the basis of such widespread evidence we can assume that tobacco was generally considered the proper nourishment of the supernaturals among the South American Indians. The supernaturals need man to provide this food for them and hence are anxious to establish and maintain a good reciprocal relationship with him. For his part, man is needful of supernatural protection for his life, his health, and his goods, and only the supernaturals are capable of providing for these needs. Both sides are therefore anxious that, as the Guaraní put it, it "comes to an understanding" (Cadogan 1965:212), and they avail themselves of the services of the shaman to accomplish their respective but interdependent ends. It is in this light that tobacco can clearly be seen in its role as medium between the natural and supernatural worlds. On the one hand, tobacco transports man into the realm of the spirits, where he can learn how "to see" things that are beyond his physical field of vision. He can participate in a life of bliss, devoid of the suffering, starvation, and death of his own world. On the other hand, the spirits and their sphere are attracted through tobacco to the physical earth, where some of the transcendent blessings of their metaphysical world are conferred upon man. No wonder that the Indians considered themselves fortunate, in their humble position as mortals, nevertheless to be able to offer something of value to the immortals! No wonder that in the indigenous world tobacco was considered too sacred for secular or purely hedonistic use.

In South America, then, tobacco served as the bond of communion between the natural and supernatural worlds, functioning, as it were, as the actualizing principle between the two. Without the shaman and his tobacco ceremonies mankind and the spirit world remain separated from each other and may perish. Today, in many tribes, under the varied pressures of acculturation and the disintegration of traditional values, the Indians have increasingly stopped providing tobacco for their supernaturals, and the spirits have indeed faded away. One day, predicted a Cubeo woman, the Indians too will die of hunger and starvation and then "only tobacco would remain" (Goldman 1940:243).

It is this pervasive metaphysical dimension of tobacco that the early European explorers, locked into their own narrow field of vision, were bound to miss and that, sad to say, has largely continued to elude us ever since.

REFERENCES

Listed in these references are only works that have been quoted in the text. However, in preparing to write this paper, the author, together with a group of UCLA students, consulted approximately 600 works on South American Indians and on the subject of tobacco in general. I feel greatly indebted to these men and women for their enthusiastic assistance. The library research was coordinated by Diane Olsen.

BARBOSA RODRÍGUES, JOÃO
  1890   *Poranduba amazonense.* Rio de Janeiro.
BENZONI, GIROLAMO
  1565   *Historia del mondo nuouo.* Venice: F. Rampazetto.
BERNAL VILLA, SEGUNDO
  1954   Medicina y magia entre los Paeces. *Revista Colombiana de Antropología* 2 (2):219–264. Bogotá.
BIOCCA, ETTORE
  1970   *Yanoáma: the narrative of a white girl kidnapped by Amazonian Indians.* New York: E. P. Dutton.
BROOKS, JEROME E.
  1937   *Tobacco: its history illustrated by the books, manuscripts and engravings in the library of George Arents, Jr. (1507–1615),* volume one. New York: Rosenbach.
BUTT, AUDREY
  1956   Ritual blowing: *taling* as a causation and cure of illness: among the Akawaio. *Timehri* 35:37–52. Georgetown, British Guiana (Guyana).
  1956–1957   The shaman's legal role. *Revista do Museu Paulista* 16:151–186. São Paulo.
CADOGAN, LEÓN
  1965   A search for the origin of Ojeo, Ye-jharú or Tupichúa. *Anthropos* 60:207–219.

1958   The eternal pindó palm and other plants in Mbyá-Guaraní myth and legend. *Miscellanea Paul Rivet Octogenario Dicata* 2:87–96. Mexico City.

CASPAR, FRANZ
1952   Die Tupari, ihre Chicha-Braumethode und ihre Gemeinschaftsarbeit. *Zeitschrift für Ethnologie* 77 (2):254–260.
1953   "Ein Kulturareal im Hinterland der Flüsse Guaporé und Machado (Westbrazilien)." Dissertation, University of Hamburg.

COOPER, JOHN M.
1949   "Stimulants and narcotics," in *Handbook of South American Indians*, volume five, 525–558. Bureau of American Ethnology Bulletin 143. Washington, D.C.: Smithsonian Institution.

DE LÉRY, JEAN
1592   *Americae tertia pars.* Frankfurt.

ELICK, JOHN W.
1969   "An ethnography of the Pichis Valley Campa of eastern Peru." Dissertation, University of California, Los Angeles.

FOCK, NIELS
1963   Waiwai: religion and society of an Amazonian tribe. *Nationalmuseets Skrifter, Etnografisk Raekke* 8. Copenhagen.

GABRIEL, PADRE
1944   Los indios Kaimito (Familia Witoto). *Amazonia: Colombiana Americanista* 2 (4–8):56–58.

GOLDMAN, IRVING
1940   Cosmological thoughts of the Cubeo Indians. *Journal of American Folklore* 53 (210):242–247.

GOODSPEED, THOMAS HARPER
1942   "The South American genetic groups of the genus *Nicotiana* and their distribution," in *Proceedings of the Eighth American Scientific Congress*, volume three. Washington, D.C.: Pan American Scientific Congress.

HARNER, MICHAEL J.
1972   *The Jivaro: people of the sacred waterfalls.* Garden City, New York: Doubleday.

HISSINK, KARIN, ALBERT HAHN
1961   *Die Tacana; Ergebnisse der Frobenius-Expedition nach Bolivien 1952 bis 1954*, volume one: *Erzählungsgut.* Stuttgart: Kohlhammer.

KAMEN-KAYE, DOROTHY
1971   Chimó: an unusual form of tobacco in Venezuela. *Botanical Museum Leaflets* 23(4). Cambridge, Massachusetts: Harvard University.

KARSTEN, RAFAEL
1920   Beiträge zur Sittengeschichte der südamerikanischen Indianer. *Acta Academiae Aboensis: Humaniora* 1(4). Turku.
1935   The headhunters of the western Amazonas: the life and culture of the Jivaro Indians of eastern Ecuador and Peru. *Societas Scientiarum Fennica. Commentationes Humanarum Litterarum* 29 (1). Helsinki.

KOCH-GRÜNBERG, THEODOR
1923   *Zwei Jahre bei den Indianern Nordwest-Brasiliens.* Stuttgart: Strecker und Schröder.

KRUSE, ALBERT
1951–1952   Karusakaybë, der Vater der Munduruku. *Anthropos* 46:915–932; 47:992–1,018.

MÉTRAUX, ALFRED
1928 *La civilisation matérielle des Tribus Tupi-Guarani.* Paris.
MURPHY, ROBERT F.
1958 *Mundurucú religion.* University of California Publications in American Archeology and Ethnology 49. Berkeley: University of California Press.
NIMUENDAJÚ, CURT
1948 "The Tucuna" in *Handbook of South American Indians,* volume three, 713–727. Bureau of American Ethnology Bulletin 143. Washington, D.C.: Smithsonian Institution.
1952 *The Tucuna.* University of California Publications in American Archeology and Ethnology 45. Berkeley: University of California Press.
OVIEDO Y BAÑOS, J. DE
1940 *Historia de la conquista y población de la provincia de Venezuela.* New York. (Originally published 1526.)
PURCHAS, S.
1626 *His pilgrimage,* volume five. London: H. Fetherstone.
PUTNAM, HERBERT
1938 *Books, manuscripts, and drawings relating to tobacco from the collection of George Arents, Jr.* Washington, D.C.: Library of Congress.
REICHEL-DOLMATOFF, GERARDO
1971 *Amazonian cosmos: the sexual and religious symbolism of the Tukano Indians.* Chicago: University of Chicago Press.
SAUER, CARL
1950 "Cultivated plants of South America and Central America," in *Handbook of South American Indians,* volume six, 487–543. Bureau of American Ethnology Bulletin 143. Washington, D.C.: Smithsonian Institution.
1969 *Agricultural origins and dispersals: the domestication of animals and foodstuffs.* Cambridge: Massachusetts Institute of Technology Press.
SCHULTES, RICHARD EVANS
1967 "The botanical origin of South American snuffs," in *Ethnopharmacological search for psychoactive drugs.* Edited by D. Efron, 291–306. United States Public Health Service Publication 1645. Washington, D.C.: United States Government Printing Office.
1972 "An overview of hallucinogens in the western hemisphere," in *Flesh of the gods: the ritual use of hallucinogens.* Edited by Peter T. Furst, 3–54. New York: Praeger.
VON SCHLOEZER, AUGUST L.
1775–1781 *Briefwechsel meist statitischen Inhalts.* Göttingen: Dieterich.
WALDSEEMÜLLER, MARTIN
1507 *Cosmographiae introductio.* St. Dié, France: Gualterus Lud.
WAVELL, STEWARD, AUDREY BUTT, NINA EPTON
1966 *Trances.* London: George Allen and Unwin.
WHIFFEN, THOMAS W.
1915 *The north-west Amazonas: notes on some months spent among cannibal tribes.* London: Constable.
WILBERT, JOHANNES
1972 "Tobacco and shamanistic ecstasy among the Warao Indians of Venezuela," in *Flesh of the gods: the ritual use of hallucinogens.* Edited by Peter T. Furst, 55–83. New York: Praeger.

ZERRIES, OTTO
1964   *Waika*. Munich: Klaus Renner.
1969   "Primitive South America and the West Indies," in *Pre-Columbian American religions*. By Walter Krickeberg, Herman Trimborn, Werner Müller, and Otto Zerries. Translated by Stanley Davis, 230–358. History of Religions. New York: Holt, Rinehart and Winston.

Coca and Popular Medicine in Peru: An Historical Analysis of Attitudes

JOSEPH A. GAGLIANO

The cultivation and consumption of coca in Peru have aroused controversy since almost the very beginnings of the Spanish conquest. Many of the earliest coca opponents urged its destruction because they claimed that its prevalent use in Inca religious practices impeded the Christianization of the Indians. Over the centuries, subsequent critics often asserted that coca contributed to Indian crime and racial degeneration. Others affirmed that coca chewing has militated against the assimilation of the Indian into the Hispanicized culture of coastal Peru. More recent adversaries have focused their attention on the possible narcotic effects of the coca habit. Despite their polemics, these opponents historically have failed in their efforts to eradicate the shrub from the Andes because of their inability to refute the prevalent opinion that coca is a beneficial stimulant and an invaluable medicinal plant which has been essential in preserving the well-being of the highland Indians.

Preceding the Spanish conquest of Peru by at least a generation, the earliest observations relating the medicinal use of coca among the natives of the New World were those of colonists on the Caribbean islands. Ramón Pané, a missionary on the island of Hispaniola during the closing decade of the fifteenth century, was the first to comment on the shrub and the curative virtues of its leaves (Pané 1932:61). He wrote that the Indians on the island "ate" a leaf resembling Mediterranean basil, which they referred to as *guayo*. They employed large quantities of this basillike leaf not only in their elaborate funeral rites but as a common medicinal herb to treat assorted minor ailments.[1]

The substantial commentary regarding coca which followed the Span-

---

[1] There are several early-sixteenth-century descriptions of the general use of coca in the Caribbean region. Of these, see especially de las Casas (1951: vol. 2, p. 514); d'Anghera (1912: vol. 2, p. 369); Vespucci (1825–1837:252–253).

ish conquest of Peru initially ignored its significance as a medicinal plant among the Andean natives. Giving the coca folklore, which has grown over the centuries, a European dimension, the first observers either described its seemingly miraculous stimulative virtues or expounded its value as a barter item. In his 1539 letter to the Spanish Crown, Vicente Valverde, the Bishop of Cuzco, claimed that the natives, sustained only by this refreshing leaf, could walk and labor all day in the sun without ever feeling its heat (Valverde 1864–1884:98). Pedro de Cieza de León, one of the soldier-chroniclers of the Spanish conquest, emphasized both the stimulative and anoretic properties of coca in his mid-sixteenth-century narrative (de Cieza de León 1959:259–260). The Indians informed him that they chewed coca because it provided them with vigor and strength while repressing their hunger. Scornful of what he termed a disgusting habit fit only for Indians, he nevertheless believed that it aided them in performing their hard work. Similarly, Agustín de Zárate, the Royal Accountant, who was assigned to Peru during the initial years of Spanish colonization, related that the natives learned from experience "that he who holds this leaf in his mouth feels neither hunger nor thirst" (de Zárate 1555:15). He appeared far more impressed, however, when witnessing their eagerness to exchange gold and silver for coca leaves. Expressing astonishment, he indicated that the Indians not only bartered precious metals to obtain leaves from the Spaniards but volunteered to work in the mines if provided with coca rations.

Detailed descriptions of the common use of coca as a medicinal plant among the sierra and altiplano Indians began appearing in historical literature during the second half of the sixteenth century as the shrub became the subject of controversy in Peru. Appalled by the enormous number of Indian lives lost in the cultivation of the shrub in the disease-infested montaña region east of Cuzco and convinced that the availability of the leaf (which had been frequently employed in Inca religious rites) obstructed the Christianization of the natives, for it constantly reminded them of their pagan past, many missionaries petitioned the Spanish crown to direct the destruction of the coca plantations. These prohibitionist demands were challenged by other missionaries and viceregal officials who contended that coca served the undernourished Indians as a beneficial stimulant and nutritive supplement. Recommending protective labor legislation to reduce the death toll among plantation workers, the defenders of the leaf usually emphasized its economic significance, informing the crown that the Indians would refuse to work in the mines unless given daily coca rations.[2]

As the coca controversy became more heated, apologists for the coca habit focused increasing attention on the reputed miraculous healing

[2]   For a discussion and summary of conflicting colonial opinions regarding coca and the laws which were established to protect the coca workers, see Gagliano (1963:43–63).

powers of the leaf. Juan de Matienzo, a judge in the Audiencia of Charcas and perhaps the most articulate spolesman for the coca interests during the sixteenth century, asserted that acceding to the demands of the prohibitionists would lead to the extinction of the Andean Indians. Among the many arguments supporting the coca habit that he presented to Philip II was that it served to preserve the teeth of the Indians. If they were deprived of the leaf they would quickly lose their teeth and, unable to chew and eat their food, they would all starve (de Matienzo 1910:89–90).

Other coca defenders cataloged its prevalence as a remedy in various illnesses among the highland Indians. The most common mixture consisted of coca leaves and quinoa ashes, which the sierra Indians regarded as a panacea for a host of minor sicknesses. Applications of steamed seeds were used frequently to arrest such hemorrhages as nosebleeds. Cooked leaves, combined with several sierra herbs and honey, were prescribed to alleviate stomach disorders and nausea. Mixed with egg whites and salt, ground leaves were applied in a plaster to hasten the knitting of fractured bones. This same concoction, prepared in a poultice, was administered to dry and heal skin ulcerations.[3] Perhaps ironically, contemporary references do not indicate whether this common sierra remedy was used on the coca plantations to treat the disfiguring skin ulcerations caused by the fatal *mal de los Andes* [leishmaniasis]. Presumably, only the common mercury chloride preparation known as *solimán* was used (de Toledo 1921–1926:29–30).

Confronted with the conflicting polemics of the prohibitionists and defenders, Philip II chose to accept the claim that coca was in fact a necessary stimulant which afforded the Indians "a mitigation" for their hard work. While sanctioning official tolerance of the coca habit among the Andean Indians in a law dated October 18, 1569, Philip II addressed himself to the prohibitionist charge that the presence of coca impeded the Christianization of the natives. He urged the churchmen of the viceroyalty to maintain "a constant vigilance" to prevent its use in superstitious practices and witchcraft (*Recopilación* 1943: vol. 2, p. 306).

The prohibitionists regarded the crown's admonition as a justification for continuing their efforts to discredit the use of coca. Antonio Zúñiga, a missionary who had spent eighteen years among the Andean Indians, informed the crown in 1579 that the shamans employed coca more often than not for evil purposes and that the shrub was assuredly the creation of the devil, who used it to ensnare Indian souls (Zúñiga 1842–1895:90, 93, 94). His assertions reflected the claim among many prohibitionists that no actual distinction existed between the use of coca as a remedy in the

[3] Many sixteenth- and seventeenth-century chronicles describe the medical applications of coca among the sierra Indians. Of these, see especially Cobo (1890–1895: I, 351, 476–477); Valera (1945:131–132); de Acosta (1894: I, 381).

popular medicine of the highland Indians and its employment as a fetish in their *costumbre* rituals. Likewise, these critics insisted that no distinction existed between the highland *curandero* [folk healer] and the *brujo* [sorcerer]. They chose to identify the shaman who used coca in treating the sick as a practitioner of black magic, pointing out that his ministrations were preceded by elaborate superstitious rituals.[4] Adding to the contention that the healing virtues of coca represented a diabolical illusion, an account circulating in Peru near the mid-seventeenth century described what was termed "a very subtle idolatry" which had emerged among the Christianized Indians. *Curanderos*, who were in reality secret pagan shamans, often informed the persons they were summoned to treat that their illness arose from their collaboration with the Spaniards and their submission to Christianity. The shamans then made a traditional offering of coca leaves to propitiate the gods for the ideological sins of these patients (de Vega Bazán 1655:2–3).

Blas Valera, the Jesuit missionary and chronicler of the late sixteenth century from whom Garcilaso de la Vega, *El Inca*, borrowed generously in preparing his royal commentaries, criticized the prohibitionists who denied the curative virtues of coca and clamored for its eradication because it was associated with idolatry. He indicated that long before the arrival of the Spaniards, the Andean Indians had known the efficacy of coca in treating illness. The Spaniards became aware of its obvious benefits when they observed that the natives who habitually chewed coca were stronger and better disposed to strenuous labor than those who abstained from the leaves. This was to be expected, he concluded, for if coca had proved so beneficial as an external application in curing, its powers as a tonic were even greater when its juices were taken internally. Questioning the affirmations of the prohibitionists, he argued that if coca were the only Andean plant used by the shamans in their secret rites, its extirpation would be justified. It was, however, one among the many things of nature which the Indians idolized. The task of the missionary, he admonished, was to teach the neophytes to use coca in a Christian manner, with moderation and only for good purposes (Valera 1945:131).

Writing in the seventeenth century, Bernabé Cobo, another Jesuit chronicler, whose understanding of the Indian mentality surpassed that of his contemporaries, demonstrated greater restraint than Blas Valera in analyzing the imprecise powers attributed to coca. From his own observations and personal experience, he realized that the shrub was a valuable medicinal plant. He concluded, however, that the Indians never completely separated its curative virtues from its avowed preternatural powers. When summoned to treat a sick person, the shaman might employ the coca he carried either as a remedy or as a fetish. If he

[4]   Emphatic sixteenth-century statements expressing this sentiment are seen in de Atienza (1583: chapter 42) and de Vega (1600: folios 126, 147).

diagnosed the affliction as arising from a neglect of worship, he instructed the person to mollify the angry deities with various offerings, including coca leaves. While the shaman watched, his patient blew some leaves toward the sun, imploring the offended gods to restore his health (Cobo 1890–1895: vol. 4, p. 139; for similar observations, see de Acosta 1894: vol. 1, p. 381).

The growing distinction between the medical applications of coca and its role in *costumbre* practices was evident in the witchcraft cases brought before the Inquisition tribunal in Lima during the seventeenth century. Those accused of sorcery were invariably asked whether they used coca solely in curing or also for evil purposes, such as the conjuring of the devil.[5] This distinction was also suggested in a manual prepared to guide missionaries in the highlands and published in 1631. Although admonishing the priests to remain vigilant in preventing the superstitious use of such commodities as chili peppers and *chicha*, a beer made from fermented maize, in healing, it made no mention of coca (Pérez Bocanegra 1631: item 43). By the eighteenth century, the leaf had come to be generally regarded as an essential herb in the paraphernalia of the highland *curandero*. Acknowledging its acceptance in popular medicine, an *informatión* [report] submitted to the Inquisition in Lima in 1739 told of an aged shaman in Vilcabamba, known as Juan Alonso, who used a seashell filled with coca leaves both in divination and in treating the sick (Archivo Arzobispal de Lima 1739: folio 7). According to the report, the clergy in Vilcabamba made no serious effort to dissuade Juan Alonso from such practices because they regarded him primarily as a *curandero* rather than as a sorcerer.

In describing the prevalent use of coca in highland folk medicine, Ricardo Palma, the nineteenth-century Peruvian litterateur who wrote extensively on Indian customs, affirmed that the creoles became tolerant of the *curandero's* practices once he incorporated Christian traditions into his diagnostic rituals (Palma 1937:68). The *curandero* added to his chant, which had probably been sung since before the time of the Incas, an invocation of Christ and various saints. After scattering coca leaves over a poncho or shirt of his patient and again soliciting the aid of the Christian saints, he blew vigorously on the leaves. He determined the cause of illness according to the direction in which most of the leaves accumulated.

Ricardo Palma's analysis, which reflects his interest in the quaint in the process of acculturation in Andean society, ignored creole tolerance

---

[5]   An investigation of Inquisition cases in the archbishop's archives of Lima demonstrates that the question appeared in virtually every witchcraft trial of the seventeenth century. For examples see Archivo Arzobispal de Lima 1657, folios 4, 5, 10, 22; 1681; 1689; folios 52, 148). The question was also asked in eighteenth-century cases (Archivo Arzobispal de Lima 1723: folios 6, 10).

which was based on the increased acceptance of coca as a medicament among Peru's white population. Initially the creoles were reluctant to experiment with the leaf because the prohibitionists insisted that it was a satanic creation and its healing powers were actually a diabolical illusion (de Atienza 1583: ch. 16). In addition, many prominent sixteenth-century Spanish commentators shared de Cieza de León's contempt for coca, regarding its use as being appropriate only for the Indians. Nicolás Monardes, the respected Seville physician, was scornful and suspicious in describing the shrub in his 1574 treatise on the medicinal plants and stones of the New World (Monardes 1574:115). Although including coca among the important medicinal plants of Peru, he particularly empha-sized its possible euphoric effects and suggested its apparent use for ritualistic intoxication. When the Indians wished to become intoxicated or "to be out of their senses," he wrote, they chewed a mixture of coca and tobacco leaves. Monardes related that this combination caused the chewers to fall into a drunken stupor which filled them with great con-tentment.

The persuasive arguments of the coca apologists such as Blas Valera and Bernabé Cobo encouraged the creoles to begin using the leaf as a medicament. By the end of the sixteenth century, white colonists in the sierra and altiplano settlements had adopted a host of native coca remedies, including its use in the treatment of skin ulcerations and the common cold.[6] Relating his own experience, Bernabé Cobo indicated that coca had come to be regarded as an effective cure for toothaches among the white population of the highlands (Cobo 1890–1895: vol. 1, p. 476). He asked a barber to extract a painful molar. Advising against its removal because the tooth appeared healthy, the barber suggested that he chew large quantities of coca leaves for several days to relieve the pain. This remedy proved even more successful than Cobo had hoped, for the pain not only disappeared, never to recur, but the tooth was soon as strong and sound as the rest.

The esteem for coca as a valuable medicinal plant became evident even in Lima, the hub of Hispanic culture in Peru. While those creoles who became habituated to coca were often disowned by their disgraced families (Mantegazza 1859:477),[7] the Limeños employed it without question in the medications their physicians prescribed. Coca prepara-tions were recommended to treat maladies as disparate as upset stomach and rheumatism. The Limeño physicians attempted to duplicate the

[6] For descriptions of the prevalent medicinal use of coca among white colonists in the highland communities, see Valera (1945:131–132); Garcilaso de la Vega, *El Inca* (1941–1946: vol. 3, pp. 56–57); Cobo (1890–1895: vol. 1, p. 476; Unanue (1914:114); and Julián (1787:31).
[7] For other comments demonstrating the social stigma attached to coca habituation among non-Indians, see especially Garcilaso de la Vega (1941–1946: vol. 3, p. 59); Haënke (1901: 108); von Tschudi (1849:315–316), and von Poeppig (1835–1836: vol. 2, p. 252).

elaborate coca poultice, which they were informed the sierra *curandero* administered successfully in treating patients suffering rheumatic pain.[8] In simple remedies, the leaves were usually taken as infusions in a tea. This preparation was frequently prescribed as a placebo for hypochondriacs and dyspeptics (Unanue 1821:398). Ordinarily, the coca tea was taken with varying quantities of sugar to make it more palatable to white tastes. In addition, reflecting their disdain for coca chewing, the creoles believed that only those identified with Indian culture could tolerate using the limestone alkaloid or quinoa ashes the natives employed to form their plugs (Unanue 1914:110; von Tschudi 1849:315).

The only significant exception to the widespread use of coca among Andean medical practitioners was in the presidency of Quito, whose jurisdiction encompassed much of modern-day Ecuador. Intense prohibitionist sentiment, as well as the production of a food supply more adequate than elsewhere in the viceroyalty of Peru, contributed to the virtual disappearance of coca cultivation and consumption in the region by the beginning of the eighteenth century (León 1952:23; Unanue 1914:107). Several prominent Quitans protested the complete exclusion of coca from the presidency near the end of the seventeenth century. Praising its remarkable curative virtues, which they indicated were recognized throughout the viceroyalty, they petitioned the civil officials and the Bishop of Quito for permission to introduce coca into the presidency solely for use in medicinal preparations. Their appeal was denied. Although acknowledging its medicinal value and wide applications elsewhere, the church spokesmen asserted that even a limited relaxation of the coca ban to serve the worthy purpose of curing the sick represented a danger to the Christian neophytes, for the secret shamans would seize upon such an opportunity to acquire leaves for their pagan rites. The Quitan clergy regarded violation of the coca prohibition as so serious that offenders were subject to excommunication, even though they claimed to have obtained the leaves only for medicinal purposes (de la Peña Montenegro 1754:570–571).

Increased attention was given to the importance of coca as a medicinal plant beginning in the eighteenth century with the development of significant botanical studies in Europe. Many European naturalists, who were attracted to the Andean region during the 1700's, commented on the extensive use of coca as a panacea among all classes of Peruvian society. Few of these observers, however, suggested that the shrub might serve as an equally beneficial medicament if introduced into Europe. Joseph de Jussieu, the French botanist responsible for introducing the first coca

---

[8]   Unanue (1914:97–114). A Spanish witness testifying before the Inquisition tribunal in Lima in 1681 informed the judges that the Indians throughout Peru employed coca leaves mixed with *aguardiente* as a remedy for several pains. Even the Spaniards in Lima, he claimed, used the concoction for medicinal purposes. See Archivo Arzobispal de Lima (1681b: folio 3).

plants into Europe, and an original participant in the scientific expedition of Charles de Condamine to the viceroyalty of Peru in the 1730's, seemed far more impressed with the medicinal properties of quinine than with those of coca, having seen both used as remedies among Indians in the Andean region (de la Condamine 1751:75, 186, 217–218). Jorge Juan y Santacilla and Antonio de Ulloa, the Spanish naturalists dispatched to the New World to survey conditions for the crown in the 1740's, made only passing references to the use of coca in their *Noticias secretas*. They did not even include it with the other medicinal plants which they listed as among the important riches and valuable crops of Peru.[9] Hipólito Ruíz, whose *Relación* was intended not only to inform Europeans concerning the flora of the New World but also to identify economic plants for the Spanish crown, noted the prevalent use of coca in Andean folk medicine (Ruíz 1931:294) and even sent two shrubs to Spain in 1786. He observed that the sierra Indians used various coca preparations to treat disorders ranging from headaches to gout. Hot coca infusions served as an effective diuretic. Despite the obvious medical significance of coca in Peru, Ruíz did not recommend that Spain attempt to develop a European market for it as a medicinal plant.

Eighteenth-century Andean naturalists demonstrated far more enthusiasm than their European counterparts in expounding the medicinal value of coca and speculating on its potential as a major Peruvian export. One of the foremost propagandists was Hipólito Unanue, whose 1793 dissertation on coca was intended in part to promote its use in Europe and North America as a stimulant and a medication. His descriptions demonstrated that no stigma was attached to its medical applications, for even in Lima it was commonly regarded as a panacea. Attempting to arouse greater European curiosity concerning its virtues, he stated that since the time of the Incas, the Indians had employed coca as an incomparable tonic for the aged. He suggested that it might prove effective in geriatrics, serving to rejuvenate the aged in Europe as it had prolonged the lives of the Andean Indians (Unanue 1914:97). Although less precise than Unanue in his analysis of coca's medicinal properties, Antonio Julián, a former Jesuit who served the Spanish crown following the suppression of his order, was equally enthusiastic. During his long residence in New Granada, he became aware of the vigor and robust health of the Guagiro Indians who were inveterate coca chewers. Advising Charles III to consider coca as an important economic plant, as well as an invaluable medicament, he urged its exploitation so that Spain might profit, while providing European workers with a tonic which would improve their health and even prolong their lives (Julián 1787:24–25, 31–33).

[9]   Juan y Santacilla and de Ulloa (1918: vol. 2, part 2, ch. 9). Although not recommending its medicinal use in Europe, they observed in their joint work that the sierra Indians regarded coca as a panacea (vol. 1, p. 469).

Laudatory world opinion regarding the stimulative and curative virtues of coca grew rapidly during the nineteenth century when numerous foreign travelers wrote of their experiences in the newly independent Andean nations. While these visitors suffered from the debilitating effects of climatic aggression when they ventured into the highlands, the undernourished, coca-chewing Indian porters and guides whom they engaged performed prodigious feats of strength and endurance. In their often exaggerated narratives, these observers seemed awed by the healing powers of coca, which some viewed as almost miraculous (Gagliano 1965:167–169). Recounting its wide use in popular medicine as a remedy for ailments ranging from stomach disorders to colds, several nineteenth-century coca commentators called particular attention to its employment as a cure and preventive for veneral diseases among the sierra Indians (Enock 1908:205; Fuentes 1866:13; Freud 1884:505). In their treatment of syphilis, the highland *curanderos* applied a poultice similar to that used in the healing of skin ulcerations.

Unquestionably Paolo Mantegazza, an Italian physician who had practiced medicine in Peru for several years, was the most exuberant coca propagandist of the nineteenth century. After returning to Italy, he wrote a lengthy article in 1859 urging European scientists to investigate the medical potentialities of Peruvian coca. Referring to the shrub as the true treasure of the New World, he extolled its efficacy in various remedies. For example, he recommended that European dentists adopt it in their practice, for it was an excellent dentifrice and tooth preservative widely used among all elements of Peruvian society (Mantegazza 1859:497). He further claimed that the sierra Indians had long been successful in treating hysteria with coca preparations. Suggesting that European physicians might consider experimentation with coca in cases involving mental disorders, he speculated that it would prove more effective and far less dangerous than opium, the prevailing drug used in the treatment of melancholia (1859:498, 501). To emphasize how harmless coca was, he told of its efficacy in ending caffeine addiction. Persons in Peru and Argentina who wished to cure themselves of the caffeine habit added coca infusions to their beverage. Without indicating whether the caffeine habit was replaced by a craving for coca, Mantegazza asserted that within a short time, those following this regimen lost their desire for coffee. Terming it the "stimulant par excellence," he advised European physicians to have their patients replace their coffee and tea with coca decoctions (1859:498–499). Much like the earlier efforts of Unanue to enhance interest in this potent Andean shrub, his works stressed its possible applications in geriatrics. Since the time of the Incas, he wrote, the sierra Indians had known of coca's rejuvenating and aphrodisiac virtues (1859:503).

Despite the plaudits of Mantegazza and other propagandists, some adverse commentaries appeared, questioning the value of coca as a medicinal plant. Among the nineteenth-century travelers, Eduard von Poeppig, the German naturalist who visited Peru shortly after its achievement of independence and frequently observed the ubiquitous coca chewers, was the most critical of the habit. Writing in 1836, he warned against the medical application of coca in Europe, regarding it as not only dangerous but also capable of producing effects similar to opium addiction (von Poeppig 1835–1836: vol. 2, pp. 252, 257). Several subsequent observers, including Mantegazza, recommended cautious and exhaustive experimentation to determine whether it might have harmful effects as a medicament. Although cocaine was employed successfully as a local anesthetic after its isolation from coca in 1860, misgivings concerning its wider medical applications spread rapidly through Europe and the United States following Sigmund Freud's unsuccessful experiments with the drug in treating opium and morphine addicts.[10]

New apologists for the shrub attempted to refute the warnings that coca and cocaine were potentially dangerous. W. Golden Mortimer, a United States physician and surgeon, tried to enhance confidence in the therapeutic values of cocaine among his colleagues. Writing an encyclopedic defense of the shrub in 1901, he referred to coca as the "divine plant" of the Incas. He emphasized that medical practitioners among the Andean Indians had used its leaves effectively since long before the time of the Incas. Often assuming a polemical tone in his attempts to reassure his colleagues, Mortimer insisted that cocaine was "not only harmless, but usually phenomenally beneficial when properly administered" (Mortimer 1901:xiii).

While controversy regarding the possible harmful effects of cocaine was evident in Europe and the United States, many prominent nineteenth-century Peruvian scientists appeared convinced that the coca shrub indigenous to their nation was perhaps the most beneficial medicinal plant known to man. Although aware of the possible hazards of cocaine, they generally denied that coca could produce drug addiction among the Indian chewers. Alfredo Bignón, a chemist, concluded from his experiments that the Indians ingested too small a quantity of cocaine to make their habit harmful. He furthermore speculated that because the Indians began chewing coca when still boys, they gradually developed a tolerance for the cocaine they ingested and could not possibly become addicted (Bignón 1885:245–246; for similar observations written earlier in the nineteenth century, see Raimondi 1868:125). In the 1880's, the Peruvian government appointed a scientific commission, under the leadership of José Casimiro Ulloa, the dean of Peruvian physicians, to recommend new uses for coca which would increase its export. The

[10] The nineteenth-century scientific controversy concerning the possible harmful effects of coca and cocaine is analyzed in Gagliano (1965:171–174).

commission's report, published in 1889, emphasized that coca should be promoted as an unparalleled stimulant which, if utilized in Europe and the United States, would enable miners, farmers, and factory workers to derive the same invigorating benefits as the Andean Indians gained from the leaf (Ulloa, Colunga, and de los Ríos 1889:29, 31).

The growth of the Indianist Movement in twentieth-century Peru, which concerned itself with social reform and the assimilation of the hinterland Indians into the Hispanicized culture of the coast, as well as increasing international concern that coca-chewing represented a form of narcotic addiction, led to renewed criticism of the shrub's medicinal value. Hermilio Valdizán (1885–1929), a psychiatrist who became intensely active in Indianist reform projects, contended in his polemics that the use of coca was the gravest sociomedical problem of the Andes. The coca habit not only enhanced the cultural isolation of the highland Indians, preventing their assimilation into national life, but also led to racial degeneration, he insisted. He urged governmental action as rapidly as possible to prohibit the cultivation and consumption of coca (Valdizán 1913:264, 267, 274–275).[11]

Supporting most of these affirmations, subsequent colleagues in the medical profession, who shared Valdizán's concern for Indianist reforms, proposed legislation to curtail the coca habit. In general, they recommended the establishment of a governmental monopoly that would restrict the cultivation and distribution of coca leaves, as well as the production of crude cocaine, to those levels needed for solely medical purposes (Ricketts 1936:7, 9–14, 33–35, *passim*; Paz Soldán 1929:598–599, 601; 1939:19; Sáenz 1938:220–221, *passim*). The efforts of these modern coca critics, which contributed to Peru's increased cooperation with the Economic and Social Council of the United Nations in seeking methods to control the manufacture of crude cocaine, culminated in the creation of a national coca monopoly in 1949 (*El Peruano* 1949:1; United Nations 1950:79). An agency of the ministry of finance, the monopoly had among its major objectives the elimination of coca cultivation within twenty-five years.

The gradual commitment of Peru to restrict and eventually end coca cultivation and consumption in the twentieth century aroused both skepticism and controversy in scientific circles. Many sociologists and anthropologists theorized that the use of coca had become so institutionalized in the amenities, *costumbre* practices, and popular medicine of the higland Indians that its eradication or even reduced consumption seemed unlikely. Even Valdizán had conceded its prevalent medical application among the highland Indians in a joint study on Peruvian folk medicine (Valdizán and Maldonado 1922: vol. 1, pp. 79,

---

[11] For early criticism of the Valdizán contention that coca-chewing caused degeneration among the Indians, see especially Graña y Reyes (1940:31); Sáenz (1938:165).

99, 129, 167–169, 178–179; vol. 2, p. 219; *passim*). Writing in the 1930's, Estanislao López Gutiérrez, a noted sociologist, questioned the wisdom of attempting to curb the use of the leaf, whose healing and stimulative virtues were traditionally esteemed in the sierra. He speculated that creating the governmental control agency which the Indianist reformers demanded might lead to the sort of gangsterism and bootlegging that attended the Volstead act in the United States (López Gutiérrez 1938:139, 141; a similar pessimism expressed earlier, albeit less imaginatively, is found in Castro Pozo 1924:204–206). In his 1950 study of the role of coca in Andean folklore, Sergio Quijada Jara cataloged the extensive modern use of the leaf by the highland *curanderos*. Although speculating that an intensive and prolonged educational program of social hygiene might diminish coca chewing, he doubted whether the sierra Indians would ever alter their opinion regarding the leaf's curative powers (Quijada Jara 1950:59–60, 73). In addition, proponents of the "Andean man theory" (which affirms that the dwellers in the high Andes represent a different biological type), with their insistence that coca chewing contributes to the environmental adaptation of the sierra Indians, have stimulated an outpouring of polemics (Monge 1946; Gutiérrez-Noriega 1948; Domínguez 1930). These recent and continuing controversies demonstrate the persistent divided opinion concerning the use of coca as a stimulant and a medicament which has been evident in Andean literature since the sixteenth century.

REFERENCES

ARCHIVO ARZOBISPAL DE LIMA
   1657 "Causa de idolatría: los indias y indias hechiceros . . . del pueblo de
          S. Juan de Macachaca." Expedientes, Sección Idolatrías y Hechicerías,
          Archivo Arzobispal de Lima. Seventeenth and eighteenth centuries
          (1606–1700), file 4.
   1681a "Información dada por . . . María de la Cruz . . . en la causa criminal."
          Expedientes, Sección Idolatrías y Hechicerías, Archivo Arzobispal de
          Lima. Seventeenth and eighteenth centuries (1604–1697), file 2. April.
   1681b "Causa criminal: testigo . . . Juan Deochoa Aranda." Expedientes,
          Sección Idolatrías y Hechicerías, Archivo Arzobispal de Lima. Seven-
          teenth and eighteenth centuries (1604–1697), file 2.
   1689 "Causas criminales contra María de la Cruz y Agustín González."
          Expedientes, Sección Idolatrías y Hechicerías, Archivo Arzobispal de
          Lima. Seventeenth and eighteenth centuries (1660–1700), file 1.
   1723 "Causa criminal contra Juan de Rojas, su mujer y otros indios."
          Expedientes, Sección Idolatrías y Hechicerías, Archivo Arzobispal de
          Lima. Seventeenth, eighteenth, and nineteenth centuries (1660–1850),
          file 3.
   1739 "Información de brujo: pueblo de Vilcabamba." Expedientes, Sección
          Idolatrías y Hechicerías, Archivo Arzobispal de Lima. Seventeenth,
          eighteenth, and nineteenth centuries (1660–1850), file 3.

BIGNÓN, ALFREDO
1885   Propriedades de la coca y de la cocaína. *El Monitor Médico* 1:245–246.
CASTRO POZO, HILDEBRANDO
1924   *Nuestra comunidad indígena*. Lima.
COBO, BERNABÉ
1890–1895   *Historia del nuevo mundo . . .*, four volumes. Edited by Marcos Jiménez de la Espada. Seville: E. Rasco.
D'ANGHERA, PETER MARTYR
1912   *De orbe novo, the eight decades . . .* two volumes. Edited and translated by Francis Augustus MacNutt. New York: G. P. Putnam's Sons.
DE ACOSTA, JOSEPH
1894   *Historia natural y moral de las Indias*, two volumes. Madrid.
DE ATIENZA, LOPE
1583   "Compendio historial del estado de los indios del Perú, con muchos doctrinas i cosas notables de ritos costumbres e inclinaciones que tienen." Transcript from the original manuscript in Madrid made for E. G. Squier. Rich Collection, Division of Manuscripts, New York Public Library.
DE CIEZA DE LEÓN, PEDRO
1959   *The Incas of Pedro de Cieza de León*. Translated by Harriet de Onis. Edited by Victor Wolfgang von Hagen. Norman: University of Oklahoma Press.
DE LA CONDAMINE, M.
1751   *Journal du voyage fait par ordre du Roi . . . servant d'un introduction historique à la mesure de trois premières degrés du méridien*. Paris.
DE LA PEÑA MONTENEGRO, DON ALONSO
1754   *Itinerarios para parochos de Indios, en que se tratan las materias más particulares tocantes a ellos para su buena administración* (new edition). Amberes.
DE LAS CASAS, BARTOLOMÉ
1951   *Historia de las Indias*, three volumes. Edited by Augustín Millares and with a preliminary study by Lewis Hanke. Mexico City.
DE MATIENZO, JUAN
1910   *Gobierno del Perú: obra escrita en el siglo XVI*. Buenos Aires.
DE TOLEDO, FRANCISCO
1921–1926   "Ordenanzas . . . relativos al cultivo de la coca, tabajo de los indios en él y obligaciones de los encomenderos; enfermedades de indios . . . Cuzco, 3 de octubre de 1572," in *Gobernantes del Perú: cartas y papeles, siglo XVI, documentos del Archivo de Indias*, volume eight. Edited by Roberto Levillier, 14–33. Madrid.
DE VEGA, ANTONIO
1600   "Historia . . . de las cosas succedidas en este colegio del Cuzco . . . de estos reynos del Perú, desde su fundación hasta hoy . . . año de 1600." Division of Manuscripts, Library of Congress, Washington, D.C.
DE VEGA BAZÁN, ESTANISLAO
1655   *Testimonio auténtica de una idolatría muy sutil que el demonio avia introducido entre los indios . . . hizo por comisión y particulares instruciones que le dió Pedro de Villagomes, Arzobispo de Lima, 19 de octubre de 1655*. Lima.
DE ZÁRATE, AGUSTÍN
1555   *Historia del descubrimiento y conquista del Perú*. Antwerp.
DOMÍNGUEZ, JUAN A.
1930   La coca como factor dinamogénico de uso habitual en el altiplano

argentino-chileno-boliviano. *Trabajo del Instituto de Botánica y Farmacología* 47:3–16.

EL PERUANO
1949 Establecase el Estanco de la Coca, Decreto Ley 11046. *El Peruano: Diario Oficial.* July 22.

ENOCK, C. REGINALD
1908 *Peru: its former and present civilization, history and existing conditions.* South American Series. London: T. Fisher Unwin.

FREUD, S.
1884 Coca. (Translated by S. Pollak.) *Saint Louis Medical and Surgical Journal* 47:502–505.

FUENTES, MANUEL A.
1866 *Mémoire sur la coca du Pérou.* . . . Paris.

GAGLIANO, JOSEPH A.
1963 The coca debate in colonial Peru. *The Americas* 20:43–63.
1965 The popularization of Peruvian coca. *Revista de Historia de América* 59:164–179.

GARCILASO DE LA VEGA, EL INCA
1941–1946 *Los comentarios reales de los Incas*, six volumes (second edition). Edited by Horacio H. Urteaga. Lima.

GRAÑA Y REYES, FRANCISCO
1940 *La población del Perú a través de la historia* (third edition). Lima.

GUTIÉRREZ-NORIEGA, CARLOS
1948 Errores sobre la interpretación del cocaísmo en las grandes alturas. *Revista de Farmacología y Medicina Experimental* 1:100–123.

HAËNKE, TADEO
1901 *Descripción del Perú.* Lima.

JUAN Y SANTACILLA, JORGE, ANTONIO DE ULLOA
1748 *Relación histórica del viaje a la América meridonial hecha de ordenes de S. Mag* . . . , four volumes. Madrid.
1918 *Noticias secretas de América* . . . , two volumes. Biblioteca Ayacucho, Madrid.

JULIÁN, ANTONIO
1787 *La perla de la América, observada y expuesta en discursos históricos.* Madrid.

LEÓN, LUIS A.
1952 The disappearance of cocaism in Ecuador. *Bulletin on Narcotics* 4:21–25.

LÓPEZ GUTIÉRREZ, ESTANISLAO
1938 *El alma de la comunidad, bosquejo sobre la génesis y el desenvolvimiento de los aborígenes peruanos.* Lima.

MANTEGAZZA, PAOLO
1859 Sulle virtù igieniche e medicinali della coca e sugli alimenti nervosi in generale. *Annali Universali de Medicina* 167:449–519.

MONARDES, NICOLÁS
1574 *Primera y segunda y tercera partes de la historia medicinal de las Cosas que se traen de nuestras Indias Occidentales, que sirven en medicina.* Seville: Alonso Escriuano.

MONGE, CARLOS
1946 El problema de la coca en el Perú. *Anales de la Facultad de Medicina* 29:311–315.

MORTIMER, W. GOLDEN
1901   *Peru: History of coca, the "divine plant" of the Incas* . . . . New York: J. H. Vail.
PALMA, RICARDO
1937   *Anales de la Inquisición de Lima.* Buenos Aires.
PANÉ, RAMÓN
1932   "Relación . . . acerca de las antiguedades de los indios por mandato del almirante," in *Historia del almirante Don Cristóbal Colón por su hijo*, volume two. By Hernando Colón, 35–99. Madrid.
PAZ SOLDÁN, CARLOS
1929   El problema médico-social de la coca en el Perú. *Mercurio Peruano: Revista Mensual de Ciencias Sociales y Letras* 19:584–603.
1939   Luchemos contra la esclavitud del cocaísmo indígena: sugestiones para una acción nacional. *La Reforma Médica* 25:19, 21, 24.
PÉREZ BOCANEGRA, JUAN
1631   *Ritual formulario e institución de curas para administrar a los naturales de este reyno los santos sacramentos . . . con advertencias muy necesarias.* Lima.
QUIJADA JARA, SERGIO
1950   *La coca en las costumbres indígenas.* Huancayo, Peru.
RAIMONDI, ANTONIO
1868   Elementos de botánica applicada a la medicina e industria. *Gaceta Médica de Lima* 12:125–128.
Recopilación
1943   *Recopilación de leyes de los reunos de las Indias*, three volumes (revised edition). Madrid.
RICKETTS, CARLOS A.
1936   *Ensayos de legislación pro-indígena.* Arequipa, Peru.
RUÍZ, HIPÓLITO
1931   *Relación del viaje hecho a los reynos del Perú y Chile por los botánicos . . . extractado de los diarios por el orden que llevó en estos su autor.* Madrid.
SÁENZ, LUÍS N.
1938   *La coca: estudio médico-social de la gran toxicomanía peruana.* Lima.
SÁENZ, MOISES
1933   *Sobre el indio peruano y su incorporación al medio nacional.* Mexico City: Secretaría de Educación Pública.
ULLOA, JOSÉ CASIMIRO, MIGUEL F. COLUNGA, JOSÉ A. DE LOS RÍOS
1889   Informe sobre la coca. *La Crónica Médica* 6:27–31.
UNANUE, J. HIPÓLITO
1821   Abstract from a communication . . . to Samuel L. Mitchell, dated at Lima, first February, 1821. *American Journal of Sciences and Arts* 3:397–399.
1914   "Disertación sobre el cultivo, comercio y las virtudes de la famosa planta del Peru nombrada coca," in *Obras científicas y literarias*, volume two, 90–125. Barcelona.
UNITED NATIONS
1950   *Report of the commission of enquiry on the coca leaf.* New York: United Nations, Economic and Social Council.
VALDIZÁN, HERMILIO
1913   El cocaínismo y la raza indígena. *La Crónica Médica* 30:263–275.

VALDIZÁN, HERMILIO, ÁNGEL MALDONADO
1922   *La medicina popular peruana,* three volumes. Lima.
VALERA, BLAS
1945   *Las costumbres antiguas del Perú y la historia de los Incas.* Edited by Francisco A. Loayza. Lima.
VALVERDE, VICENTE
1864–1884   "Carta del Obispo del Cuzco al Emperador sobre asuntos de su iglesia y otros de la gobernación de aquel país, Cuzo, 20 de marzo de 1539," in *Colección de documentos inéditos relativos al . . . antiguas posesiones españoles de América,* volume three (first series). Edited by J. F. Pacheco, 92–136. Madrid.
VESPUCCI, AMERIGO
1825–1837   "Las cuatro navigaciones . . . carta al Ilustrismo Renato, Rey de Jerusalen y de Sicilia . . . [1504]," in *Colección de los viajes y descubrimientos que hicierón por mar los españoles desde fines del siglo XV, con varios documentos inéditos,* volume three. Edited by Martin Fernández de Navarrete, 191–290. Madrid.
VON POEPPIG, EDUARD
1835–1836   *Reise in Chile, Peru und auf dem Amazonenströme, während der Jahre 1827–1832,* two volumes. Leipzig.
VON TSCHUDI, J. J.
1849   *Travels in Peru during the years 1838–1842. . . .* Translated by Thomasina Ross. New York.
ZÚÑIGA, FRAY ANTONIO
1842–1895   "Carta . . . al Rey Don Felipe II, Peru, 15 de juilo de 1579," in *Colección de documentos inéditos para la historia de España,* volume twenty-six. Edited by Martín Fernández de Navarrete et al., 87–121. Madrid.

Was Espingo (Ispincu) of Psychotropic and Intoxicating Importance for the Shamans in Peru?

S. HENRY WASSÉN

When the early Spanish chroniclers in South America wrote about *hechiceros* and their use of certain drugs, etc., we cannot always identify them with shamans or medicine men. The best translation seems to be "sorcerer." Among the Inca:

> . . . the sorcerers (*omo*) claimed to speak directly with the spirits. They usually dressed differently from ordinary people, and wore their hair long or cut in some special way. They were usually consulted to find lost or stolen articles or to learn what was happening at a distance. They talked to the spirits in the dark, and theirs and the spirits' voices could be heard but not understood (Rowe 1946:302).

Other words for *hechicero* are "diviner" and "witch doctor." Rowe continues his text by saying that "some diviners summoned the spirits by saying a spell and drawing lines on the ground, others drank themselves into insensibility and gave their answers when they recovered" (Rowe 1946:302). He also refers to Cobo's statement that the latter "put the juice of the *wil'ka*, a berry also used as a purge, into their *chicha* to give it

I am deeply grateful to my Swedish friends, Dr. Victor Hasselblad, Gothenburg, and Dr. Herbert Tigerschiöld, Stockholm, who, with their liberal view of the importance of international scientific cooperation, have given their financial support so that I might accept the invitation of the President of the Organizing Committee of the IXth International Congress of Anthropological and Ethnological Sciences.

I have friends both in Sweden and in the United States who have taken a keen interest in this paper and participated scientifically. My sincere thanks to all of them: in Stockholm, Dr. Wolmar E. Bondeson, Professor Bo Holmstedt, M.D., Dr. Eskil Hultin, Dr. Jan-Erik Lindgren, and Dr. Benkt Sparre; in Gothenburg, Professor Gunnar Harling; and, in the United States, Professor José Cuatrecasas, Washington, D.C., and Professor Richard Evans Schultes, Cambridge, Massachusetts.

Mrs. Sharlie Otterström, an American living in Gothenburg, has very kindly helped with translation and text correction, and Miss Maj-Britt Berglund, of the Gothenburg Ethnographic Museum, has typed the manuscript. To both of them my best thanks.

more strength." This has been treated in more detail by Siri von Reis Altschul (1967:307) in her paper, "Vilca and its use":

Around 1571, Polo de Ondegardo reported that the witch doctors of the Incas foretold the future by speaking with the devil in some dark place by means of various ceremonies, for which office they intoxicated themselves with an herb called *Vilca*, pouring its juice into *chicha* or taking it another way. The reporter stated that, although only old women were reputed to practice this craft, in fact its use was widespread but concealed among men and boys, as well.

The same author has also mentioned several other sources in which we find references to *vilca* as a purgative, as a stimulant, etc. During her herbarium search at Harvard University, two specimens labeled *Vilca* were found. Both belonged to *Anadenanthera colubrina*, one was from southern Peru, the other from east of La Paz. "These data indicate that *A. colubrina* indeed is identifiable with *Vilca*, but they do not insure that *Vilca* is referable exclusively to this plant" (von Reis Altschul 1967:308).

I have quoted this passage especially for the fact that in the old literature we find another plant product used by sorcerers as an admixture to *chicha* which no one seems to have taken interest in until now. What I am thinking of is *espingo*, seeds, that obviously were used in old Peru in the same way as the abovementioned *vilca*, namely, as an added ingredient to *chicha*, with effects the chroniclers described as in part purely medicinal, and in part quite drastic, plainly with psychotropic effects. "They became crazy from it" is a common phrase. I therefore consider that learning about *espingo* can add to our knowledge of the different means used by South America's medicine men.

With respect to pursuing my research on *espingo*, I wish to acknowledge my gratitude to an Argentine-born friend and colleague, Dr. Ana María Mariscotti de Görlitz, now of Marburg, Germany. It was she who, in connection with a scientific correspondence between us on the burning of *khoa* or *khoba* (*Mentha pulegium*, of the family *Labiatae*) during the so-called *señaladas* or traditionally old offering ceremonies to Pachamama (see Wassén 1967:276–277), insisted that I should not lose track of *espingo*. She kindly gave me some references to the literature — e.g. to de Arriaga's *Extirpación*, where we find the following report:

Espingo is a little, dry fruit with round kernels (*al modo de unas almendras redondillas*), with a very intense smell, although not particularly good. One gets it from the Chachapoyas,[1] and it is said to be very medicinal [to be used] for stomach pains, stool bleedings (*cámaras de sangre*) and other sicknesses, and that it is taken in powder form and is expensive to buy. It was usually sold for these

[1]   Chachapoya would seem here to be one of the tribes from "deep in the Andean valleys of the upper Marañón River in North Central Perú," and who "apparently had diverse languages and Tropical Forest cultures" (Steward and Métraux 1948:614–615).

purposes. In Jaén de Bracamoros[2] not too many years ago, the Indians paid their tribute with *espingo*. The previous archbishop forbade, on risk of excommunication, that it be sold to the Indians, since he knew it was a question of an extraordinary offer to *huacas*,[3] especially in the flatlands, where there is no one who does not have *espingo*, since all who have been visited there have *conopas*[4] (de Arriaga 1920:46).

A similar but shorter piece of information appears in the work *Exortaciones* written by the sixth archbishop of Lima, Pedro de Villagomes (1585–1671). He says, concerning what the Indians offer, only the following: *"Espingo, es una frutilla seca, al modo de unas almendras redondillas de muy vehemente olor, aunque no muy bueno, y no hay quien no tenga espingo teniendo conopa"* [*Espingo*, is a small dried fruit, similar to a round almond, with a strong odor, although not a good one, and anyone who has *conopa* will certainly also have espingo] (de Villagomes 1919:165–166). He continues, as de Arriaga did, to tell of *aut*, another little, dry fruit, not dissimilar to *espingo*. He himself has explained that he' had de Arriaga as a source as well as other chroniclers (see Urteaga's preface to the edition used here of de Arriaga's *Extirpación* [1920:xiv]).

I return to the beginning of de Arriaga's fourth chapter, where he declares those who used *espingo* to be sorcerers, and describes some of its effects. His reports are in translation: "On the plains from Chancay and downwards, the *chicha* that was presented to the *huacas* was called *yale*.[5] It is made of *zora*[6] mixed with chewed corn and powder of *espingo* is put into it. It [the *yale*] is made very strong and thick and then one gives of it what one considers suitable to the *huaca*; the sorcerers drink the rest and they are driven crazy (de Arriaga 1920:42).[7]

De Arriaga has also reported on nocturnal sessions of *"hechiceros, chupadores de sangre"*: "During these sessions the devil appears, sometimes in the figure of a lion, other times as a tiger, and as he sits down very

---

[2]   Jaén de Bracamoros was a "city" founded by Diego Palomino (in 1549?) near the junction of the Chinchipe and Marañón rivers (see Steward and Métraux 1948:616).
[3]   *Huaca*, sacred shrine.
[4]   *Conopa*, sacred image.
[5]   *Yale*, possibly from the Chancay language, "once spoken on the Chancay river, department of Lima" (Loukotka 1968:272).
[6]   *Zora, sora*, or *jora*. According to Friederici (1947:570), "malted Indian corn used for preparing a very strong *chicha*, the use of which, according to Garcilaso, was forbidden by the Incas." In Garcilaso de la Vega's original text (1943:177, *libro octavo*, 9): "Algunos indios más apassionados de la embriaguez que la demás comunidad echan la cara en remojo, y la tienen assí hasta que echa sus raízes; entonces la muelen toda como está y la cuezen en la misma agua con otras cosas, y, colada, la guardan hasta que se sazona; házese un brevaje fortíssimo, que embriaga repentinamente: llámanle *uiñapu*, y en otro lenguaje *sora*. Los Incas lo prohibieron, por ser tan violento para la embriaguez; después acá, me dizen, se ha buelto a usar por algunos viciosos."
[7]   In Spanish: "En los lianos desde Chancay a baxo la chicha que ofrecen a las Huacas se llama Yale, y se haze de Zora mezclada con maís mascado, y la hechan polvo de Espingo, hazen la muy fuerte y espesa, y después de aver hechado sobra la Huaca lo que les parace, beven la demás los Hechiceros, y les buelve como locos."

ferociously, resting on his forelimbs, they worship him" (de Arriaga 1920:40–41).[8] This reference to the mighty felines (puma and jaguar) in the sphere of conjuring Indian sorcerers or shamans is evidently of great interest, especially if we think of the nearly pan-American distribution of jaguar figures in combination with the *alter ego* motif.[9]

Cobo is another chronicler who mentions *espingo*. According to him:

> ... the gentle Indians of the Andean provinces in Peru used to get from the peoples of their frontier some small capsules [Cobo uses the word *vainillas*] as *algarrobas*, of a dark, tawny color, the curdled substance of which is like *Sangre de Drago* (*Pterocarpus draco*), however brilliant with a shade of black, and of a mild and intense smell. These *"vainillas"* are produced by a tree called *Espingo*, found in those regions. The rude Indians bring forth these capsules as a precious thing to barter them for knives, scissors and other trifles which they highly value; and this they obtain easily from the Spaniards as these capsules are held to be very medicinal.

Cobo continues to tell how the powder, taken in different ways, cures various forms of serious bleeding (1891:95–96).

There are some more references to espingo in various sources. De Murúa (1946:306) says that it was the *trébol* (Latin *Trifolium*) which was called *espinco*, and that the Indians connected this plant with various superstitions. The same information, but without mention of *trébol*, is found in Antonio Ricardo's Quechua vocabulary from 1586, where it is said that *Yspincu* is a certain plant and fruit which is fragrant and used for various bewitchments (1951:93).[10]

Lastres (1951:305) also gives *espingo* (*ispunku*) as botanically *trébol*. According to the Peruvian Quechua Indian, Dr. Salvador Palomino Flores (who, at this writing, is at the University of Copenhagen), the correct spelling should be *ispunku*; *espingo* could, however, be a phonetic variation of the word in the Quechua of Bolivia (letter of January 30, 1973). As meaning *trébol*, Lastres (1951:305) also quotes the names *chullku* and *cchikmu*. *Trébol*, however, cannot be the source for the samples treated here, and we must draw the conclusion that the Indian word has been used for several plants, or seeds from several plants. Thus we do not know which *espingo* Lastres (1951:250) is referring to when he, without any indication of his source, reports that *chicha*, prepared from Indian corn and *espingo*, was used as an offering to the *huacas* during the great Inca ceremonial feasts Raimi, Citua, and Aymoray. The

---

[8]   In Spanish: "En estas juntas se les aparece el Demonio, unas vezes en figura de León, otras vezes en figura de Tigre, y poniéndose asentado, y estrivando sobre los braços muy furioso, le adoran."
[9]   Dr. Ana María Mariscotti de Görlitz observing this wrote to the author: "Allí tiene su alter ego!"
[10]   The original text: "*Y spincu*, cierta yerua y fruto oloroso con que se hazen muchos hechizos."

same is the case when he mentions (1951:291) a medicinal use of *espingo* powder.

What we have determined thus far, from the testimony of the original written sources, is that *espingo* is used as an admixture with *chicha*; it is said to have medicinal uses, and was even used for certain purposes by the shamans. It soon became clear that knowledge of *espingo* was minimal, and really, from a scientific point of view, nonexistent. Neither La Barre (1938) nor Hartmann (1958), writing about alcoholic beverages among the natives of South America, named the *espingo* additive to *chicha* in old Peru. On the other hand, the Bolivian ethnobotanical specialist, Enrique Oblitas Poblete (1969) listed *asango-espingo* together, explaining that the *callahuayas* receive these remedies from Cajamarca, Peru; that they are used in cases of neuralgia and muscular pains; and, taken with *agua de llantén*[11] and wine, also are used for curing *cámaras de sangre* (Oblitas Poblete 1969:80). If the information presented by Oblitas Poblete was received from modern *callahuayas*, it would mean that the traditions about the use of *espingo* for certain bleedings, etc., has been carried on from the time of its discovery.

As I wanted to find out what *espingo* really was, I started a correspondence with Dr. Oblitas Poblete, and one reason for going to La Paz in the summer of 1970 was the *espingo* problem. When we met in La Paz, Dr. Oblitas Poblete gave me two seeds of *asango* (possibly from the family *Rubiaceae*), and two quite different seeds, about one centimeter long and half a centimeter wide, of *espingo*, without, however, knowing anything about the botanical names for the plants producing these seeds. We also went to the Bolivian capital's historical museum, Casa de Murillo, with its collection of medicinal plants, seeds, etc., and among the specimens on exhibit were some *espingo* seeds of exactly the same appearance as those I had received that day. When Oblitas Poblete gave me the two samples, he also left a little note saying (in translation): "Seeds of a small tropical plant from the department of Loreto, Peru. It is used antiseptically (against stomach disorders) and it is taken pulverized or it has to be chewed."[12] The *espingo* samples had and still have a fragrant smell, as stated in the old sources. This curious odor has been referred to as being similar to that of fenugreek, typical for all species of *Quararibea*.[13]

On my way back to Sweden, the samples were left in the hands of Dr. Richard Evans Schultes, director of the Botanical Museum at Harvard University. Dr. José Cuatrecasas of the Smithsonian Institution also

[11]   *Llantén, Plantago* species.
[12]   Original text: "Semilla de una planta pequeña de zona tropical, departamento Loreto, Perú. Aplicación antiseptical (para desarreglos estomacales). Se toma pulverizado o se masca."
[13]   Letter from Dr. Richard Evans Schultes, Cambridge, Massachusetts, March 14, 1973.

inspected the *espingo* samples and suggested they might originate from the family *Lauraceae*. When Schultes was in Gothenburg in September 1971, he, however, considered the *espingo* samples to represent a *Quararibea*, in this case of the family *Bombacaceae*. This determination was confirmed in 1973 by Dr. Benkt Sparre of the Botanical Section of the Natural History Museum, Stockholm, and by Professor Gunnar Harling, Gothenburg University's Institution for Systematic Botany, Sweden.

Two small samples (one of the seeds weighing 0.4470 gram) constitute too limited a supply for a real investigation of the chemical compounds found in the *espingo* seeds (Collection 71.35.2a-b in the Gothenburg Ethnographic Museum), but I have submitted the material anyway to Professor Bo Holmstedt for chemical research and to Dr. E. Bondeson for a pharmacognostical examination (see Wassén 1973: appendix).

As Cajamarca in Peru was referred to in connection with *espingo*, I got in touch with Dr. Luís Ibérico Mas of the Universidad Técnica de Cajamarca. He kindly sent a considerable quantity of a Peruvian plant called *ishpingo* (Collection 71.36 in the Gothenburg Ethnographic Museum). Samples were forwarded to Dr. José Cuatrecasas in Washington, D.C., via Dr. R. E. Schultes, and according to a written statement of August 30, 1971, Dr. Cuatrecasas has determined the *ishpingo* material (leaves and stalks, no seeds) to be *Gnaphalium dysodes* Spreng. This plant, however, has nothing to do with the plant *espingo* of a *Quararibea* species.

Valdizán and Maldonado (1922:397) have included *ishpingo* in a list of popular names for plants used medicinally, but botanically unknown. The reference seems to be from the region of Madre de Dios, and they present this *ishpingo* as a tree with very fragrant seeds, useful for curing dysentery and other diseases.

As has already been pointed out, both American and Swedish botanical experts have reached agreement on a *Quararibea* as the mother plant to the *espingo* seeds. My collaborator, Wolmar Bondeson, Stockholm, has therefore been able to send me a list of not fewer than twelve species, that according to MacBride (1951–1956) are known from the department of Loreto. Furthermore, the list names four additional Peruvian *Quararibea* species (Bondeson, personal communication, March 7, 1973).

We must now go on to further botanical clarity, and above all, through chemical-pharmacological research, to find out if the old sources spoke the truth when they described the psychotropic effect of *espingo*. Dr. Eskil Hultin of Stockholm, in a letter written January 9, 1973, considered some form of folk-etymological idea association: "*à la absinthe* with the fragrant scented addition of *Artemisia.*" Perhaps the Indians' intoxication on strong beer, with the addition of *espingo*, was what the Spaniards disliked?

Lévi-Strauss (1950:483; 1948:368) has mentioned "the rosin of certain *Bombacaceae* as a magical poison," with references to the *Nambicuara* (the rosin of the barrigudo tree). We do not know, however, if this last idea could have a direct connection with the use of *espingo* as an added ingredient to beer and a means of magic in ancient Peru.[14]

REFERENCES

COBO, BERNABÉ
1891 *Historia del nuevo mundo*, volume two. Seville: E. Rasco.
DE ARRIAGA, PABLO JOSEPH
1920 *La extirpación de la idolatría en el Perú*. Collección de Libros y Documentos Referentes a la Historia del Perú 1, second series. Lima.
DE MURÚA, MARTÍN
1946 *Historia del origen y genealogía real de los reyes incas del Perú*. Madrid: Consejo Superior de Investigaciones Científios.
DE VILLAGOMES, PEDRO
1919 *Exortaciones e instrucción acerca de las idolatrías: del arzobispado de Lima*. Collección de Libros y Documentos Referentes a la Historia del Perú 12. Lima.
FRIEDERICI, GEORG
1947 *Amerikanistisches Wörterbuch*. Hamburg: Cram, de Gruyter.
GARCILASO DE LA VEGA, EL INCA
1943 *Commentarios reales de los Incas*, volume two. Buenos Aires: Emecé.
HARTMANN, GUNTHER
1958 *Alkoholische Getränke bei den Naturvölkern Südamerikas*. Berlin.
LA BARRE, WESTON
1938 Native American beers. *American Anthropologist*, n.s. 40:224–234.
1972 "Hallucinogens and the shamanic origins of religion," in *Flesh of the gods: the ritual use of hallucinogens*. Edited by Peter T. Furst, 261–278. New York: Praeger.
LASTRES, JUAN B.
1951 *Historia de la medicina peruana*, volume five: *La medicina incaica*. Lima.
LÉVI-STRAUSS, CLAUDE
1948 "The Nambicuara," in *Handbook of South America Indians*, volume three, 361–370. Bureau of American Ethnology Bulletin 143. Washington, D.C.: Smithsonian Institution.
1950 "The use of wild plants in tropical South America," in *Handbook of South American Indians*, volume six, 465–466. Bureau of American Ethnology Bulletin 143. Washington, D.C.: Smithsonian Institution.
LOUKOTKA, ČESTMÍR
1968 *Classification of South American Indian languages*. Edited by Johannes

---

[14] To quote La Barre (1972:277): "Whether shaman alone, or shaman and communicants, or communicants alone imbibe or ingest *Ilex* drinks, *Datura* infusions, tobacco in whatever form, native beers and wines, peyote cactus, ololiuqui or morning-glory seeds, mushrooms, narcotic mint leaves or coca, the ayahuasca "vine of the dead spirits" (*Banisteriopsis caapi*) or any of the vast array of Amerindian psychotropic plants, the ethnographic principle is the same. *These plants contain spirit power.*"

Wilbert. Los Angeles: University of California, Latin American Center.

MACBRIDE, J. FRANCIS
1951–1956   *Flora of Peru*. Chicago: Field Museum of Natural History.

OBLITAS POBLETE, ENRIQUE
1969   *Plantas medicinales de Bolivia.* Cochabamba, Bolivia.

RICARDO, ANTONIO
1951   *Vocabulario y phrasis en la lengua general de los indios del Perú, llamada Quichua.* Edited by Guillermo Escobar Risco. Lima: Instituto de Historia de la Facultad de Letras.

ROWE, JOHN HOWLAND
1946   "Inca culture at the time of the Spanish conquest," in *Handbook of South American Indians*, volume two, 183–330. Bureau of American Ethnology Bulletin 143. Washington, D.C.: Smithsonian Institution.

STEWARD, JULIAN H.
1948   "Tribes of the montaña: an introduction," in *Handbook of South American Indians*, volume three, 507–533. Bureau of American Ethnology Bulletin 143. Washington, D.C.: Smithsonian Institution.

STEWARD, JULIAN H., ALFRED MÉTRAUX
1948   "Tribes of the Peruvian Ecuadorian montaña," in *Handbook of South American Indians*, volume three, 535–636. Bureau of American Ethnology Bulletin 143. Washington, D.C.: Smithsonian Institution.

VALDIZÁN, HERMILIO, ÁNGEL MALDONADO
1922   *La medicina popular peruana*, volume two. Lima.

VON REIS ALTSCHUL, SIRI
1967   "Vilca and its use," in *Ethnopharmacologic search for psychoactive drugs*. Edited by D. Efron, 307–314. United States Public Health Service Publication 1645. Washington, D.C.

WASSÉN, S. HENRY
1967   "Anthropological survey of the use of South American snuffs," in *Ethnopharmacologic search for psychoactive drugs*, 233–289. Washington, D.C.
1973   "Ethnobotanical follow-up of Bolivian Tiahuanacoid tomb material, and of Peruvian shamanism, psychotropic plant constituents, and *espingo* seeds," in *Göteborgs Etnografiska Museum årstryck 1972* [Gothenburg Ethnographic Museum yearbook 1972], 35–52. Gothenburg. (With an appendix by Wolmar E. Bondeson: "Anatomical notes on *espingo* and seeds of *Quararibea*.")

Yagé *Among the Siona:*
Cultural Patterns in Visions

E. JEAN LANGDON

Investigations and literature concerning the use of hallucinogens among indigenous groups in the Amazon basin have been increasing at a rapid rate.[1] One aspect of the use of hallucinogens that needs further investigation is the role of cultural variables in the altered states of consciousness induced by drugs. Although Wallace (1959) drew attention to the problem some years ago, only a few studies have addressed themselves directly to it.[2] The purpose of this paper is to present a brief description of the use of *yagé* (*Banisteriopsis*) among the Siona Indians of the northwest Amazon basin with reference to the cultural influences on the *yagé* experience.[3] Two Siona texts will be presented to illustrate the nature of "culturally influenced" visions.[4]

The data upon which this work is based were gathered during eighteen months of fieldwork in Colombia between 1970 and 1972. The study was supported in part by the Tulane University International Center for Medical Research grant AI–10050 from NIAID, NIH, United States Public Health Service.
[1] Some of the recent sources include Bristol (1966); der Marderosian et al. (1968, 1970); Dobkin de Ríos (1970a, 1970b, 1971, 1972, 1973); Harner (1962, 1968, 1972, 1973); Katz and Dobkin de Ríos (1971); Pinkley (1969); Reichel-Dolmatoff (1970, 1971); Robinson (1972); Schultes (1957, 1960, 1963, 1967, 1970); and Seijas (1969a, 1969b).
[2] See Dobkin de Ríos (1974) for an overview; also Dobkin de Rios and Katz (n.d) and Siskind (1973).
[3] *Yagé* is the term most widely used in Colombia for species of *Banisteriopsis*. In Peru and Ecuador it is known as *ayahuasca*, "vine of the souls," as *caapi* in Brazil, and as *kahi* and *pinde* in other parts of Colombia.
[4] The term "culturally influenced" visions is similar to Dobkin de Ríos's use of the term "stereotypic visions" (1974:15). I have chosen "culturally influenced" visions to emphasize the role of cultural variables in the visionary experience.

HISTORY AND SETTING

Traveling down the Putumayo river in southern Colombia, one is un-
aware of passing through an Indian community unless an elder in traditional dress appears along the river bank. The Siona, once a large group
that ruled the upper Putumayo, have been reduced to approximately 250
individuals. About half are located in the communities of Buena Vista,
Granada, and Piñuña Blanca below Puerto Asis in the Intendencía of the
Putumayo. The rest are further downstream scattered along the river
mixed among the white and black colonist population. Many traditional
beliefs and practices have been abandoned, and they are rapidly
assimilating into the mestizo culture. The indigenous political and religious organization based on the role of the shaman and the use of *yagé* has
completely broken down. Previously subsistence activities were divided
evenly between hunting, gathering, and horticulture, but cash crops have
altered the organization of labor and resources. Western dress and food
have been adopted by most Siona, and the younger generations deliber-
ately speak Spanish as a first language and avoid addressing their children
in Siona (a Western Tukanoan affiliate). Only the elders maintain the old
traditions and language.

YAGÉ AMONG THE SIONA

Prior to the 1950's, the indigenous political and religious organization
centered on the shaman and his ability to influence all aspects of life
through his power gained from *yagé*. He played the key role in the
ingestion of *yagé* and the maintenance of cultural practices surrounding
it. Due principally to missionary activities, but also to the growing colonist population during the first half of this century, only a handful of Siona
have pursued the career of shaman during the last forty years, and those
that did failed in their endeavors to achieve the level of full competence,
that of the master shaman. When the last shaman died in the 1960's, no
elder felt competent to take his place as leader. Several survivors had
sufficient knowledge and curing powers to cure minor illnesses stemming
from supernatural causes. Moreover, they possessed extensive knowledge about the supernatural world that is reached through *yagé*. However, all of them had been through repetitive bad experiences with *yagé*
and were fearful of assuming the full responsibility of shaman. The belief
system and use of *yagé* described here has not yet disappeared among the
Siona. Among the elders it is acknowledged in its most complete form.
Even the younger generations hold to the general principles outlined,
although their knowledge of the details and full complexity of the system
is severely limited. *Yagé* still occupies a role of fundamental importance

in the indigenous religious and curing beliefs of the Siona. The problem they face today is a renewal and reaffirmation of those beliefs through performance of the rituals surrounding *yagé*, since no Siona feels competent to lead the community in the ceremony. Thus, the Siona now resort to shamans of neighboring tribes to lead them in the *yagé* ceremony. Naturally, the frequency of ingestion has been severely reduced, and moreover, the goals now sought in such ceremonies are limited primarily to the curing of serious illnesses and no longer include the other goals sought in the past, such as the securing of game, good weather, or prophecy of the future.

The use of *yagé* among the Siona is very similar to that of other tribes in the Amazon basin. It is ingested to know the ultimate reasons or causes for past, present, or future events, as well as to influence events, such as changing the weather, curing, or sorcery. In Siona cosmology, the events in this world are affected by hundreds of spirits that lie behind each plant, tree, rock, or animal; by spirits that populate the rivers; by those in the underworld; by those in the three heaven levels of the universe; and by those in the "ending place" at the edge of the world. Everything that happens in the world has its ultimate cause in the supernatural. This includes the normal rhythm of life, such as the change of seasons, the appearance of game or fish, and the maintenance of good health. Equally, all disruptions of this rhythm, particularly misfortunes, illness, and death, have their ultimate causes in the actions of the spirits. Contact with the supernatural beings is necessary, therefore, to assure that life proceeds normally and to defend oneself if misfortune occurs. *Yagé* provides the major means of this contact. Although many other additives are employed in the tealike brew, and other vision-producing stimulants are also taken separately, *yagé* sets the pattern for their use.

The Siona term for *yagé* is *?iko*, which signifies "remedy" in the language. All other remedies, whether used for attacking the physical symptoms of an illness or the supernatural causes, are designated as a subclass of *?iko*. The concept of *yagé* as "remedy" has a much wider application among the Siona than in Western society. For the Siona, "well-being" involves more than the physical health of an individual; it also implies the well-being of society — that all is proceeding normally, that there is food, that people and animals are performing their roles, and that there is no sickness in the Western sense. When they speak of the state of well-being, they use the term *wahi*, which signifies being alive, being in a state of fatness, greenness in the sense of ripeness as well as color, freshness, and rawness. The term *wahi* represents the growing force of life. It contrasts with the destructive force represented by the term *hū?i* "to be dying" or by *dau*, which implies sickness, thinness, blackness, darkness, and rottenness. Thus, for the individual or society there are two forces operating, one of growing life force and one of destructive force of death and rottenness. Through *yagé* one can influence these forces.

The Siona do not have two separate terms to distinguish between hallucinogenic "remedies" aimed at supernatural causes and those which cure nonsupernaturally caused symptoms, such as Kensinger (1973:13) has described for the Cashinahua. It is apparent, however, that the distinction between the two kinds of remedies is understood covertly within the culture. Often the Siona will state that a certain remedy does not work because the cause is a supernatural agent and that *yagé* must first be taken by a shaman before the patient can "receive" the other remedies. This distinction has allowed easy acceptance of white man's remedies as those which work well upon naturally caused symptoms, while *yagé* still must be employed for the supernaturally caused illnesses. Those which are suspected of having a supernatural cause are generally the more serious and uncommon diseases.[5] In this respect, *yagé* is the central part of the Siona religious and cosmological system. It deals with the meaning of life; it provides answers to the question of the ultimate "why" of events, as well as offering protection, provision of food, and curing powers.

The shaman, the specialist in *yagé*, is singularly important in this system. Through many years of apprenticeship and training, he builds up power and knowledge so he can interpret and influence events by contacting spirits. On most occasions, the spirits are neutral powers, with potential for good and evil. The shaman acts as a mediator, attempting to influence the supernatural beings. He bargains with them in a manner similar to that of the Desana shamans, described by Reichel-Dolmatoff (1971:125). The power of the shaman to deal with the spirits enables him to influence all aspects of Siona life. He drinks *yagé* to contact the spirit parents of the game or fish so that the animals will come out of their houses under the ground to be hunted. He drinks to influence the seasons to favor agriculture, hunting, and fishing. He drinks to find individuals lost in the jungle, and to cure people of serious illnesses and behavioral disorders. He occasionally will also use his powers to cure animals, particularly the hunting dogs. It must also be mentioned that a shaman can cause harm when he wishes, and much illness and misfortune within the tribe are blamed on sorcery.

When there were living shamans among the Siona, the *yagé* experience was a communal experience. Under the guidance of a master shaman, the adult men of the community and a few women not in a state of contamination due to pregnancy or menstruation gathered weekly to drink *yagé*.

---

[5] See Seijas (1969b) for a complete explanation of this distinction. Although she is describing the distinction as it operates among a different group, it applies in a manner similar to the Siona. Also, Langdon and MacLennan (n.d) address themselves to this distinction and to the adoption of Western medical practices.

They also united on special occasions when the necessity to take *yagé* was urgent. It appears that much of the Siona ceremony was influenced by early missionaries of the seventeenth and eighteenth centuries. The ritual paralleled the Catholic mass in many ways. The Siona drank *yagé* in a separate shelter located in an isolated part of the jungle. The shaman sat at one end of the shelter, with the others around the sides. The implements of the ceremony were placed on a small bench in front of the shaman. Their organization resembled that of an altar, and the *yagé* implements included a chalice for holding the *yagé* while the shaman blessed it. In recalling the ceremony, Siona informants emphasize how the shaman's role in administering the ceremony is similar to that of the priest during mass, and say it is because God authorized the shaman to be his representative among the Indians.[6]

No *yagé* ceremony can be conducted without the presence of a shaman, and for this reason they now rarely occur in Siona communities. The shaman's role is one of guiding the people through the other realities that are visited during the night of drinking *yagé*. There are two aspects of this guidance. The first is to set the theme of the visions by telling the people what they are seeing. Before they drink *yagé*, he "arranges" the *yagé* by singing of the spirits and places that he wishes to contact and chases away malevolent spirits. Then, when under the affects of *yagé* he sings of what he is seeing; he sings of the spirits who are coming and describes their clothing, faces, houses, and furniture. All the spirits have designs on their bodies and belongings, and the shaman sings of the motifs of the designs by naming the motifs and their colors. These different motifs are already known to the Siona, for they occur on the painted faces of the elders, on the decorated pots and other artifacts, and in times past on their clothing. Moreover, much of Siona oral literature includes the descriptions of the spirits and journeys to see them. Siona dress has been a conscious attempt to emulate the elegantly dressed spirit people with their beads and necklaces, sweet-smelling plants, and feather crowns. Thus, that which is supposed to be seen by the participants in the *yagé* visions is already familiar to them. Choosing from these elements, the shaman guides the visions of his people, helping them to experience other realms and spirits of the universe.

The second aspect of the shaman's role is that of protection on these journeys. There is constant danger of bad experiences due to the presence of evil spirits or contaminating agents that may arouse the "jealousy" of the *yagé*. A bad experience on *yagé* is not seeing and hearing what is

---

[6]   The format and description of the Siona ceremony closely parallels that of the Campa, as described by Weiss (1973). However, review of the historical sources indicate that at least in the case of the Siona, the priestly elements of the shaman's role were a definite result of early missionary influence (Langdon 1974:24–45, 110–116) rather than elements reflecting an evolutionary transition from shaman to priest as suggested by Weiss for the Campa.

expected. Instead, the individual is plunged into blackness and silence or hears the shrill zing of insects singing in the darkness. Menacing black spirits may come and attempt to tie one up. If a guiding shaman is not there to return the individual to normal consciousness by chants and beatings with nettles, it is feared the individual will die.

THE TRAINING OF SHAMANS

As already pointed out, the shaman has the knowledge and experience to contact and influence the spirits and to lead others in the visions. This "knowledge" is gained through prolonged training with an experienced or "master" shaman. When a young man decides to undergo apprenticeship, he first spends a month or more in isolation, purging his body of the substances that would otherwise obstruct his learning and cause bad visions. Then he begins prolonged periods of ingesting *yagé*, such as drinking for three nights in a row, resting one, and resuming again. This continues for periods ranging from two weeks to two months at a time. Throughout these sessions, the apprentice attempts to pass through a set of "culturally influenced" visions. It is recognized that all men must pass through the same experiences and visions if they are to accumulate knowledge.

The knowledge gained by *yagé* is not a limited concept, nor is it conceived as a single stage of enlightenment. If the comparison can be made, it is more like our educational system with a series of subjects in which one may master and specialize. All the spirits have their "design" as well as their songs which the novice learns when he "arrives" at their place. He first must pass through the visions necessary for all who wish to leave their bodies and travel. Then he is shown the visions that his teacher shaman has acquired. As the novice enlarges his repertoire of visions and songs, he increases his power with the spirits he knows and can deal with. Once well established in his knowledge, he may visit other shamans and learn their specialities. He may find that he has a facility for certain specialities, i.e. drinking to see specific spirits, for hunting, or for curing. Once he is sufficiently trained to lead his own *yagé* sessions, he may show others what he knows, but the road to knowledge never ends, for a shaman constantly strives to contact more and more spirits and see their visions.

The initial part of the *yagé* training is particularly influenced by culturally expected visions whose nature and content are common knowledge to all Siona. The following text is an account of one informant's first experiences with *yagé*. Similar accounts with the same basic elements were collected from all the other informants who began shamanistic training as young men. The text not only represents an account of what all

Siona novices expect to see when they begin training, but also illustrates the stages of knowledge that must be achieved if one is to eventually master the *yagé* experience.[7]

When I First Left My Body and Arrived

When we lived in San Antonio, my father gave me *?ɨo yagé* (1) for the first time and I drank. At the time when the sun had reached the tops of the trees, it dawned a good day. At this hour I shouted and fell from the hammock to the ground (2). I lay there unconscious, and my older brother tied my feet. Then I saw (3).

First a big screaming fire came burning the whole world (4). In this way came *yagé* the first time, and I remembered nothing of this world. The fire came, and then the Jaguar Mother (5) appeared and said to me, "You are going to die forever, grandson. Why did you drink the *yagé*? You are to blame and will die forever. You will not see your mother, your older sisters and older brothers. What kind of a person are you, poor child, for drinking the *yagé* and dying?" Then she began to cry (6).

To the side of her I saw my casket placed and arranged. There was my twisted *chambira* fiber for making hammocks, the clothing I wear, and all my things. All of my things were put there.

"These things of yours you are going to leave. Why did you drink the *yagé*, for you will die?" she said to me screaming and crying (7).

Then a big machine burning with fire came to me. As it came toward me, it was grinding up everything in sight (8). She gathered me in her arms and said to me, "Ah, poor little grandson, you will die" (9). Then she put me on her knee and wrapped me in a long piece of cloth. The cloth was full of designs (10). Then she threw me out to the side as the cloth wrapped around me unwound.

Thus the elders have said that one must do in order to be able to see in *yagé* (11). When she throws you out, on this side one is seen as falling from the hammock, lying on the ground and turning over and over (12).

Again she came and gave me her breast to suck. "Suck this, child, the breast of the Jaguar Mother," she said to me. So I sucked her breast. "Now, good, grandson, you have sucked my breasts," she said (13).

Then seeing, I turned and when leaving (14) [my body] I saw the *yagé* people all pretty and gold. They are like people, like us (15).

They came to me singing. The youths came down singing their songs, "To you little parrot (16) the visions have been ugly, and you have suffered and cried. But now you have left and now you will cry no more, for when you drink *yagé*, you will see us here. When you arrive to us, you will no longer think of crying. Here we are,

[7] Mallol de Recasens (1963) also presents examples of the culturally expected visions.

the living *yagé* people. We are coming to you. And you personally have come to know us; thus there will be no bad visions."

They spoke, and I saw them. Then the reed flutes came down hanging in the air. It was not yet the time for me to play them, so I just looked at them (17).

"If you had arrived, you would have played these flutes," they said to me. "But you still have not arrived to play them. Drinking another house of *yagé*, you will play them" they said to me (18). I watched as they spoke.

Thus I saw what my father gave me to see (19). When I saw, "Good," I thought, and I was very happy. Later I woke up on this side. I came back to this side and the visions were over (20). "Now it is good; I saw the visions," I thought.

The informant said that he was about twelve years old when he had this experience. The following analysis clarifies some of the elements in the text:

Prior to this experience, the informant had prepared himself for drinking *yagé* by isolating himself in the jungle and taking a series of emetics under the supervision of a shaman. The Siona relied principally on the leaves of the *yagé* vine to purge themselves till they reached a state of dizziness and momentary visions. Once the visions begin to occur, the student is then ready to begin actually drinking *yagé*. In the early stage of training, *?ɨo yagé*(1), a class named for its burnt and thick consistency, is administered.

The first stage of drinking *yagé* is a period of plain dizziness, or "only drunkenness" (*do gwebeyɨ*), as expressed by the Siona. No visions accompany the dizziness but the stage must be passed through if one is to see the visions later. It is said that the dizziness and sometimes resulting "craziness" cannot be avoided, for the pleiad people left it as a necessary stage when they walked on the earth and established the customs surrounding the ingestion of *yagé*. A Siona myth tells of how the Pleiades' youngest brother, playing the role of trickster, screamed, shouted, defecated, and urinated on himself before he saw the visions. In this text the narrator refers to this period when he fell from his hammock (2) and his brother bound his feet to prevent kicking (3).

After passing through the stage of drunkenness, the narrator begins to see his first set of visions (3), which are marked by an intense fear of death (4, 8), and his first acquaintance with the Jaguar Mother (5). Facing the idea of death (4, 8) is a very important aspect of drinking *yagé*. It is said by all Siona that a man must be very strong to drink *yagé* and become a shaman. Thus, facing an intense fear of death is a test he must pass through to prove he has the strength. Throughout his entire career in *yagé* he is constantly threatened by death from spirits and other shamans. Only the strongest are able to continue living and drinking it; the weak must give it up or perhaps even die. It could be suggested that, in this respect, only the men of strong egos or personalities became master shamans, for the weaker characters perhaps coud not withstand the constant ingestion of *yagé* that is necessary for a shaman.

The Jaguar Mother (5), also known as the *Yagé* Mother, is a principal figure in the *yagé* system, for she is also the mother of the shamans, who are jaguars in their transformed state. Before she accepts the novice as her son (10), she also tests him as to his strength and fearlessness by reinforcing the fear of death. She cries and tells him that he will die (6, 7, 9). As his "grandmother" she sings the Siona mourning chants as she points to his coffin and personal effects (7). According to Siona myth, the mourning chants practiced by the Siona were originally learned from her.

When the novice sucks her breasts (13), we can see another aspect that is necessary to gain knowledge. Not only does the novice have to be strong, but the mystical death also symbolizes a return to a state of innocence and dependence upon the Jaguar Mother. Shamans transform into jaguars when they drink *yagé*, and the Jaguar Mother becomes their mother when they become shamans. Thus, this vision is a symbol of mystical death in which the apprentice leaves this world through death and is reborn as a child of the Jaguar Mother. His dependency and infant status are symbolized by drinking from her breasts.

Once the stage of fear is completed, the informant "turns" from his fear and begins to experience the visions that will give him knowledge and power (14). These visions are pleasant and beautiful to see. In them one meets the spirit companions, the *yagé* people, who accompany the Siona shamans and instruct them as to what they are seeing. The informant tells us that they look like the Siona, not only in their physical features, but also in their dress and adornments (15). The Siona say that their own manner of dress has come from copying the clothing and markings of the beautiful people in the visions.

The *yagé* people address him as *ho?ya Kíyi* [domesticated parrotlet] (16). The term *ho?ya* means "domesticated" and refers to a fundamental social order perceived by the Siona. Man's domain is the domesticated domain, and all his animals and plants are his "domesticates," implying his role as master and protector of them. In the same sense, the *yagé* people become the spirit allies of the novices and have the role of protecting him. The relation between the shaman and his people is expressed in the same way. The people are the *ho?ya* of the shaman. In the spirit world, the wild animals are the "domesticates" of their spirit parent.

The term "parrotlet" (*kíyi*) refers to a small parrot that is regarded as a representation of the novice's soul. Very often in dreams and *yagé* visions, the soul of the Siona appears in the form of a bird. The shaman's soul appears as a scarlet macaw; an adult's soul as a species of oriole; and that of children and youths as the parrotlet.

As mentioned, the spirits all have their songs, and the learning of their songs and other music is an important aspect of acquiring knowledge. All shamans play small reed flutes bound in red or white thread. The Siona say that these flutes fall from the sky where the *yagé* people live. In this case, the informant sees the flutes, but cannot reach them yet in order to play them (17). The *yagé* people inform him that he must drink another night (house) of *yagé* to do so (18). This demonstrates the cumulative nature of the visions. Each night of drinking the novice sees and learns a little more of what he is desiring and expecting to see.

The informant tells us that he is happy to have seen what his father intended for him to see (19). His father conveyed this when he "arranged" the *yagé*, singing about the visions that would occur, and when he sang during the time that they were both under the effects of *yagé*. Earlier in the text, we have already been told that he was prepared by the elders to expect the stage of fear (11). Moreover, the motif content of the geometric designs (10) are part of common knowledge, since in the past the Siona decorated their faces, clothing, pottery, and other implements with designs inspired by *yagé*.

In three parts of the text the narrator reminds us that the experience is one of double reality (12, 14, 20). In the first he contrasts the two sides by pointing out that the spinning thrust from the Jaguar Mother is seen on "this side" as one falling from the hammock and turning over on the ground (12). When he passes from the stage of fear to that of visions of knowledge, he then leaves his body and travels in the other side (14). Finally, when the travels are over, he returns to "this side" of reality (20).

The informant continued to drink *yagé*. He "arrived" to play the flutes and continued to build up his knowledge. The accumulation of this knowledge is marked by the growth of a substance called *dau* within the body. The substance *dau* is both a symbol of the shaman's knowledge and his power that results from that knowledge. When one learns from another shaman, he receives part of the teacher's *dau*. The Siona concept of *dau* is very similar to the Jivaro *tsentsak* as described by Harner (1973:17), although it is not possible to verify if an actual object was passed from the master shaman to the novice in the same manner. When it is in the shaman's body, it is an intangible substance dispersed throughout the body, but when it is taken out to pass to the novice or to cause illness, it appears as a physical object. The common forms are a spine, a rock, or a lump of rottenness. At times it may appear as a shield around the shaman which is used for protection when other shamans are throwing their *dau* at him.

LOSS OF KNOWLEDGE

Dau has a double-edged meaning. As it grows and gives more power to the man, it also makes him more susceptible to its damage. The Siona say it makes the shaman "delicate." This means that he can be affected by the contamination of menstruating or pregnant women and their spouses. This contamination will harm the *dau*, causing bad bodily feeling and bad visions when drinking *yagé*. *Dau* may also be damaged through the conscious effort of another shaman to destroy the power of a rival. This may be done by the shaman who gives the *yagé* to the other to drink. He can "think evil" as he arranges the *yagé*, and thus the victim will suffer a bad trip. The bad visions generally result in sickness afterward, and it is said by the Siona that the cure involves removing all the damaged *dau* from his body. In other words, it causes a great setback in one's progress, for it means that one loses part or all of one's knowledge and power. The other manner in which *dau* can be damaged is through sorcery in which the aggressor sends a spirit to cause illness to the other, so that the *dau* must be removed to cure him. When an individual's *dau* is damaged, it is very difficult for him to continue his work with *yagé*. Instead of seeing the expected visions that the master shaman is preparing for him, the victim is plagued by frightening and evil visions. As is shown in the following text, these visions are not without their cultural content. They are full of cultural symbols that represent sickness, sorcery, and death to the Siona. The symbols take on frightening and realistic visual forms that force the victim once again to face death. In the first test, the narrator was expecting the frightening experience; however, in the following text, the fear of death is unexpected and the surprise element inspires in the victim the thought of never returning to this side of reality.

How I Lost my Knowledge

When I was about fifteen I went to the jungle with my brother-in-law. "Let's go kill a tapir," said Dūtu Wati. We went into the jungle a long way. As we walked, the dogs made a wild turkey fly, and my brother-in-law went after it. "Stand here and wait," he said.

"Okay," I said and stood and waited. I was standing by the root of a *chonta* palm (1), and suddenly there was a *tūūūūūūh* sound from the ground (2). "What did I hear?" I thought, listening.

Then from the ground came the sound like a newborn baby. "Ūmmu Ūmmmm," growled the earth. Then like a child crying, "Ūmmee ūmmee umnn ūnnnee ūnneeh," the spirit growled. It cried, and I listened.

"Who cried?" I thought. Then my brother-in-law whistled, but I could not shout at all. My mouth was paralyzed. I couldn't walk and was completely stunned. "Who is doing that speaking?" I thought, listening. Again my brother-in-law shouted, and I didn't answer at all. Then again he shouted, and I took hold of myself and went to him.

"Why didn't you answer?" he said.

"No," I said, "Someone spoke to me like a child crying from inside the roots of the *chonta* palm" (3).

"A spirit wants to eat you, and for this he cried," he said (4).

"What cried as a small child?" I said.

"Perhaps the spirit has eaten you," he said.

"I don't know," I said.

He had found the tracks of a tapir, and we followed and killed a small tapir. "Let's return now, for we can't walk in the jungle if you are bad," he said. We returned. "How does your body feel?" he asked me.

We arrived at the house, and it became dark. I went to the river to bathe and returned. Very rapidly the sickness came (5). A very strong fever came to me. "Are you dying, child?" said my father (6).

"Yes, I am dying," I said. Then I had diarrhea, and I felt very bad as my whole stomach churned. The diarrhea was a black liquid (7) with rotten leaves (8). I told my father, "Father, black leaves are coming out."

"If that is so, a spirit has eaten you, child," he said (9). I began to vomit a lot. I vomited green leaves (10). "Someone has thought evil and for this the spirit has eaten you," my father said. Then he sang a chant of the spirits over a remedy (11). He said nothing as he gave me the remedy to drink. Then he went to the jungle to look for jungle remedies. He came back and chanted over the remedy and said, "Vomit this child. Don't be afraid."

So I drank it and threw up. I threw up only black liquid. Then again I drank and vomited. Finally clear liquid (12), only the remedy came out. So I told my father, "Father, I threw up well."

"How did you vomit?" he said.

"First only black liquid I vomited. Then afterwards. water liquid I vomited."

"Thus being, perhaps the spirit did not eat you but only frightened you," he said (13). Then he blew over me (14), and saw a bad dream (15). "Ignacio has thought evil of you. Since you were beginning to see the *yagé* visions, he thought evil so that the spirit would scare you in order that the visions that he gave you would be lost," he said (16). "Thus being, he did that, and the spirit didn't eat you. He only frightened you to clean you of the visions that he had given you." I listened to him without speaking.

Then they cooked *yagé*, and my older brother carried me to the *yagé* house. My father blew *dáu* (17). He cured all the spirit *dau* that had been sent to me when I was frightened. He sang *yagé* songs and seeing all that the spirit had given me, he cured me (18). I got better and became well.

Time passed and they cooked another house of *yagé*. They cooked, and I thought that I would drink *yagé*. My father sang many *yagé* songs (19). He sang, and then he cured me (20), and I asked him to give me *yagé* to drink.

"You want to drink?" he said.

"Yes, I want to drink," I said. He began to cure the *yagé*. He arranged it, finished, and then blew (21). "Drink one mouthful, child, and you will see," he said (22).

So I drank one mouthful, and the *yagé* came to me. When it came, the *yagé* showed only black insects. Then I saw black men and their land (23). Thus the *yagé* came to me. Then the drunkenness spirit people came, the *yagé* drunkenness spirits (24). They arrived and tried to tie me up (25). They tried to do so, but I defended myself. I worked to defend myself, and then the drunkenness people pulled out their tongues and came screaming at me. I was not remembering anything of this side. I was dying (26). My father had gone to the jungle singing (27). When he returned, I was not remembering anything of this world.

"Oh! Little brother is dying," said my older brother coming over to me.

"Singing parrot," he said (28). I wasn't thinking anything. Then he sang a chant of the spirit. I couldn't swallow, so he got a knife and pried open my teeth and poured some water in my mouth. The water flowed in smoothly. Then he blew *dau*. I saw then the heaven people, *yagé* people; like us they are (29). They came as if arriving personally and came down on a big mirror. With this mirror my father was seeing and curing me. He blew and saw the place of drunkenness. Much *yagé* language he spoke, also spirit language. He blew, and I was seeing what he did and thus came back to this side. I turned, and all the *yagé* people seemed to be coming down to the place of my father. Thus, my father showed me the visions. Thus he cured me from dying, and rapidly I came turning to this side. When I came back, I was well (30).

In the text presented here, the narrator tells of a frightening experience in the forest which led to his loss of power. The experience related is a common means of sorcery among the Siona. A shaman enlists the collaboration of a spirit to take his victim by surprise, and the frightening encounter results in sickness. In recounting the experience, the narrator includes several culturally significant elements that indicate evidence of sorcery and supernatural elements in the events. The first is the sound *tūūūh* that is heard in the quiet of the jungle (2). The sound is that of a door in the ground opening. It is said by the Siona that when the spirits of the earth leave the "house," the opening and closing of their door can be heard. Another element, mentioned twice, is that of the *chonta* palm (1, 3). This palm has spines covering its trunk. When describing *dau* in the form of a witchcraft substance, the Siona often say that it resembles the spine of this particular palm. Mention of it twice helps to set the scene for sorcery.

Following the frightening experiences, the narrator becomes ill. The manner of onset of the illness also indicates supernatural causation (5). It comes quickly and severely after a bath in the river. Many supernaturally caused illnesses begin in the same way. After a strange experience or dream, the victim bathes in the river and becomes ill immediately. A possible interpretation of this is that the initial fright resulting from the spirit encounter created a weakened state in the victim so that he was vulnerable to a river spirit during his bath.

When describing the illness, its symptoms, and the process of the disease, certain fundamental concepts regarding the dichotomy between "well-being" and dying are expressed. True sickness is referred to by the Siona as *dau*. It is distinguished from minor ailments which are referred to by describing the symptoms, i.e. "it hurts," "it itches," "it burns." However, when an ailment persists, it becomes a true sickness, *dau*. Here the double meaning of *dau* comes into play. Not only does it mean that the patient is truly ill, but also that the *dau* within him may consist of a substance of sorcery that a shaman has sent. If so, the *dau* must be removed by a shaman before the patient can become well, regardless of the progression of his physical symptoms. In this use, *dau* also signifies the destructive forces in life that operate against the positive forces of growth. Synonyms for having *dau* as an illness include terms that mean the person is thin or dying (6), or has rottenness (8) or blackness (7). Synonyms which are associated with living *wahɨ* include being fat, being green (in the sense of color and of growth), or being well. In the text we can see how these symbolic concepts operate on a concrete level. Very early after the fright, the brother-in-law speculates that a spirit wishes to "eat" the victim (4, 9), thus causing thinness and emaciation that is associated with death. The victim tells his father that he is dying (6), and he vomits black and rotten leaves (7, 8). Luckily, the black liquid is followed by green leaves (10), indicating that he is not totally rotten nor dying inside. When administered the emetic, he eventually purges himself of all the rottenness and vomits only water and the remedy (12).

Sorcery is immediately suspected (4, 9, 13), because of the fright and rapid onset of serious symptoms (5). The narrator's father, a shaman, performs a minor curing rite of "blowing" (14). This ceremony helps the shaman to dream (15). Like visions, dreams also help to interpret events. In this case, the dream not only confirms the suspicions, but also indicates the aggressor to be another shaman, Ignacio. Ignacio, who once had shown his visions to the victim, was jealous and fearful of the victim's potential as a shaman and thus sent the spirit to destroy the victim's knowledge (16).

The process of curing is not complete. The narrator has been administered herbal emetics (11) for purging the rottenness within him. These emetics help to cure the physical symptoms, but the witchcraft substance *dau* still remains within him and requires a ritual curing ceremony. It is partially begun in a "blowing" rite, and is completed by the full ritual in which *yagé* is ingested and full explanation of the event is known (17, 18). The Siona often speak of this dual nature of curing by remarking that without the *yagé* ceremony, any disease resulting from sorcery cannot be cured, regardless of the curing of the physical symptoms.

Once well, time having passed, the narrator wishes to resume drinking and learning from *yagé*. His father prepared it by cleansing it and singing of the visions that would be seen once it was ingested (19, 21). He cleansed his son in order to remove any possible evil substance or spirit that might be about to cause bad visions (20). Once fully cleansed and knowing what visions his father intended to show him, the informant testingly drinks a small amount of *yagé* to see if the effects will be as expected (22).

Instead of seeing the beautiful visions, he is plunged into a world of blackness. As discussed, this blackness is associated with the dying forces of life (23). The black men are standardized conceptions of the spirits that also appear in nightmares. Seeing blackness and feeling nauseated (24), the informant faces the possibility of death as the black men try to tie him up to prevent him from returning to this side of reality (25), of which the informant is slowly losing consciousness (26).

Once his father returns from his journeys to the jungle spirits (27), he calls to his son using his *yagé* name (28). He performs a curing ceremony to show his son the spirit allies, the *yagé* people, so that they will defend him from the black men (29). He also goes to the place of darkness and, with his knowledge of songs, he brings his son back to this side of reality (30).

Although the informant was cleansed again after this experience by prolonged periods of ingesting emetics, when he resumed the study of *yagé*, he had more bad visions as well as spirit encounters that never let him progress far enough to become a shaman who can lead the ceremonies. His knowledge is sufficient to do so, for he has had extensive experience with *yagé*, but he cannot resolve the problem of bad visions.

CONCLUSIONS

This informant's inability to continue the *yagé* study to its full culmination resulting in the status of shaman is an example of a frequent occurrence. All the Siona elders in the community of Buena Vista claim that similar incidents destroyed their knowledge so they could not lead the ceremonies by themselves. All Siona men attempted to go as far as possible in the study of *yagé*. It was expected of men as part of their role as protector, provider, and master of the family. Once a man became a shaman, he performed a similar role for the community. However, few of the men who attempted to become shamans actually achieved the status, and among those who did, many often lost the status due to bad visions. These bad visions are always blamed on sorcery rather than on incompetence.

Given the high incidence of bad visions, one can see the importance of the cultural determinants therein. The culturally expected visions are intimately related to a psychic equilibrium which enables a Siona who is constantly ingesting the hallucinogen to retain some sense of normal reality. The *yagé* experience is treated with great respect. It is taken only under certain conditions when a master shaman is present to lead the visions and help those who may encounter trouble. Moreover, the constant ingestion of *yagé* that is necessary when serving as an apprentice is influenced very heavily by cultural elements. The novice strives to see culturally expected visions. The Siona have known through oral literature and experiences related by their fathers what they should expect when they drink *yagé*. Moreover, the shaman sings of the visions before they drink and also during the period of inebriation so that his songs play a role in guiding the visions the novice is seeing. These cultural determinants function to help the individual organize his hallucinogenic experience. When he becomes experienced with *yagé*, he then may do his own guiding. However, by the time this stage is reached, it can be inferred that he has sufficient experience and confidence to handle the unknown without the support of a master shaman. Those who do not have the psychic stability within them to withstand prolonged periods of ingesting *yagé* experience bad visions and tend to reduce their use of it. Bad visions occur when the individual loses the direction that is being given to him, and he is plunged into darkness filled with the symbolism of death and destruction. They are unexpected visions filled with symbolic elements that frighten them and cause the experience to be unpleasant. The culture, however, provides an explanation for the man who cannot follow the career of shaman. There is no shame in saying that a shaman with greater knowledge has destroyed your own and that you cannot continue to fulfill the masculine duty of becoming a shaman.

REFERENCES

BRISTOL, MELVIN
  1966   The psychotropic *Banisteriopsis* among the Sibundoy of Colombia. *Botanical Museum Leaflets, Harvard University* 21:113–140.
DER MARDEROSIAN, A. H., *et al.*
  1968   Native use and occurrence of N-N-dimethyltryptamine in the leaves of *Banisteriopsis rusbyana*. *American Journal of Pharmacy* 140(5):137–147.
  1970   The use and hallucinatory principles of a psychoactive beverage of the Cashinahua tribe (Amazon Basin). *Drug Dependence* 5:7–15.
DOBKIN DE RÍOS, MARLENE
  1970a   A note on the use of *Ayahuasca* among urban mestizo populations in the Peruvian Amazon. *American Anthropologist* 72(6):1419–1422.
  1970b   *Banisteriopsis* in witchcraft and healing activities in Iquitos, Peru. *Economic Botany* 24(3):296–300.
  1971   *Ayahuasca*, the healing vine. *International Journal of Social Psychiatry* 17(4):256–269.
  1972   *Visionary vine: psychedelic healing in the Peruvian Amazon*. San Francisco: Chandler.
  1973   "Peruvian hallucinogenic folk healing: an overview," in *Psychiatry: proceedings of the fifth World Congress of Psychiatry*, volume two. Edited by Ramon de la Fuente and Maxwell Weisman. Amsterdam: Excerpta Medica.
  1974   "Cultural persona in drug-induced altered states of consciousness," in *Social and cultural identity*. Edited by Thomas K. Fitzgerald. Southern Anthropological Society Proceedings 8. Athens: University of Georgia Press.

DOBKIN DE RÍOS, MARLENE, FRED KATZ
n.d.   "Hallucinogens, music, and the jungle gym in consciousness." *Ethos*. In press.
HARNER, MICHAEL J.
1962   Jivaro souls. *American Anthropologist* 64:258–272.
1968   The sound of rushing water. *Natural History* 77(6):28–33, 60–61.
1972   *The Jivaro: people of the sacred waterfalls*. Garden City, New York: Doubleday.
HARNER, MICHAEL J., *editor*
1973   *Hallucinogens and shamanism*. New York: Oxford University Press.
KATZ, FRED, MARLENE DOBKIN DE RÍOS
1971   Hallucinogenic music: an analysis of the role of whistling in Peruvian *Ayahuasca* healing sessions. *Journal of American Folklore* 84(333):320–327.
KENSINGER, KENNETH
1973   "Banisteriopsis usage among the Peruvian Cashinahua," in *Hallucinogens and shamanism*. Edited by Michael J. Harner. New York: Oxford University Press.
LANGDON, E. JEAN
1974   "The Siona medical system: beliefs and behavior." Unpublished doctoral dissertation, Tulane University, New Orleans.
LANGDON, E. JEAN, ROBERT A. MAC LENNAN
n.d.   "Conceptos etiológicos de los Sibundoy y la medicina occidental. *Revista Colombiana de Antropología*. In press. Bogotà.
MALLOL DE RECASENS, M. R.
1963   Cuatro representaciones de los imagenes alucinatorias originadas por la toma del *yagé*. *Revista Colombiana de Folclor*, second series 3(8):59–79. Bogotà.
MALLOL DE RECASENS, M. R., T. JOSÉ DE RECASENS
1964–1965   Contribución al conocimiento del casique curaca entre los Sions. *Revista Colombiana de Antropología* 13:91–145. Bogotà.
PINKLEY, HOMER
1969   Plant admixtures to *Ayahuasca*, the South American hallucinogenic drink. *Lloydia* 32(3):305–314.
REICHEL-DOLMATOFF, GERARDO
1970   Notes on the cultural extent of the use of *yagé* (*Banisteriopsis Caapi*) among the Indians of the Vaupés, Colombia. *Economic Botany* 24(1):32–34.
1971   *Amazonian cosmos: the sexual and religious symbolism of the Tukano Indians*. Chicago: University of Chicago Press.
ROBINSON, SCOTT
1972   "Shamanism entre los Kofanes," in *Actas y memorias del XXXIX Congreso Internacional de Americanistas, 1970*. Lima: Instituto de Estudios Peruanos.
SCHULTES, RICHARD
1957   The identity of the malpighiaceous narcotics of South America. *Botanical Museum Leaflets, Harvard University* 18:1–56.
1960   Pharmacognosy. *The Pharmaceutical Sciences* (third lecture series) 1965:138–185.
1963   Botanical sources of the New World narcotics. *Psychedelic Review* 1(2):145–166.
1967   "The place of ethnobotany in the ethnopharmacologic search for

psychotomimetic drugs," in *Ethnopharmacologic search for psychoactive drugs*. Edited by D. Efron, 33–57. Public Health Service Publication 1645. Washington, D.C.

1970   The plant kingdom and hallucinogens (part III). *Bulletin of Narcotics* 22(1):24–52.

SEIJAS, HAYDEÉ

1969a   Algunos aspectos de la etnomedicina de los Indios Sibundoy de Colombia. *Boletín del Departamento de Antropología IVIC* 6:5–16. Caracas.

1969b   "Medical system of Sibundoy Indians." Unpublished doctoral dissertation, Tulane University, New Orleans.

SISKIND, JANET

1973   "Visions and cures among the Sharanahua," in *Hallucinogens and shamanism*. Edited by Michael J. Harner. New York: Oxford University Press.

WALLACE, ANTHONY

1959   Cultural determinants of response to hallucinatory experience. *American Medical Association Archives of General Psychiatry* 1:58–69.

WEISS, GERALD

1973   "Shamanism and priesthood in light of the Campa *Ayahuasca* ceremony," in *Hallucinogens and shamanism*. Edited by Michael J. Harner. New York: Oxford University Press.

PART TWO

Medical Anthropology

Introduction

DAVID L. BROWMAN and RONALD A. SCHWARZ

Medical anthropology is perhaps the most rapidly expanding of all sub-divisions of anthropology to emerge in the past two decades. It is mislead-ing, however, to view the perspectives and concerns of medical an-thropologists as a radically new development in the scientific study of man. A more accurate view is that the multidisciplinary character of the field is a return to the traditional roots of anthropology which are deeply buried in the biological and medical sciences. Physical anthropologists, for example, have a long history as faculty members within medical schools.

Research in medical anthropology draws theoretically and methodologically from many disciplines including population genetics, human biology, demography, ecology, nutrition, pharmacology, epidemiology, psychiatry, nursing, and health services administration. Today, cultural anthropologists are teaching behavioral science in medi-cal schools and are involved in a wide range of research and training activities in medicine, nursing, dentistry, population control, public health, and health care delivery. While the scope of the field and its rapid evolution make it difficult to delineate boundaries for medical anthro-pology, such ambiguity appears to have a healthy function.

The papers in this section reflect the efforts of a variety of profession-als. Some contributors are anthropologists, while others are physicians, biologists, psychiatrists, and one is a native folk healer. They provide a small but diverse sample of medical anthropological research on the continent of South America.

In the first article, Rubim de Pinho draws on a wide range of source material for his description and analysis of the sociocultural and medical dimensions of marihuana use in coastal Brazil. He covers some historical aspects of cannabis, including its use among several groups and the effects of legal strategies to prohibit it. He also presents information from recent Brazilian studies on the psychological effects of smoking marihuana.

Bartolomé provides a brief ethnographic sketch of the Avá-Chiripá tribe of Paraguay and a detailed analysis of the shaman's role. He describes the changes that have occurred in the society and the effect of recent government policy on the shaman's role. His analysis of multiple functions of shamanism in contemporary Avá-Chiripá society reveals the continuing importance of these individuals for the maintenance of social cohesion and cultural persistence.

Quintanilla, a Peruvian physician, analyzes the medical problems of highland Indians who have migrated to the urban center where he conducts his medical practice. He presents a brief description of the indigenous beliefs about health and illness, and shows why an understanding of the native system is essential for physicians treating patients whose cultural background is different from their own.

Singer (an anthropologist), Araneta (a psychiatrist), and Naidoo (an indigenous healer-informant) discuss the results of their collaborative efforts at mutual education and support in the area of mental health. The authors present the traditional approach to healing among practitioners of the Kali cult of Guyana, and contrast these with the therapeutic modalities of psychiatric services at the mental hospital and clinics. They present case material illustrating the details of working together and educating one another as patients are being treated.

The study by McDaniel, Harris, and Katz describes and integrates sociocultural, ecological, and biological factors influencing parasitic disease in a Peruvian community. They combine census and sociocultural data obtained through survey methods and participant observation, with epidemiological findings on the incidence of several types of parasites. They show that even in a community which one would normally describe as homogeneous, there exist systematic variations in preventive practices which affect health status. Their work is an excellent example of collaborative research in medical anthropology and demonstrates the utility of interdisciplinary efforts in suggesting solutions to public health problems.

Social and Medical Aspects
of the Use of Cannabis in Brazil

ALVARO RUBIM DE PINHO

It is not certain if cannabis already existed in Brazil when the first Portuguese discoverers arrived. It is certain, however, that by the first half of the fifteenth century, cannabis seeds were brought by African slaves. The planting of sugar cane was localized in the northeast, the same region in which, through the centuries, the largest cannibis plantation and the greatest number of smokers in the rural areas were concentrated.

The majority of the slaves imported at this time came from Angola and nearly all the traditional synonyms for marihuana in Brazil (*maconha, diamba, liamba, moconha*) had their origin in the Angolan language. Another name, seldom used now, is very significant as to origin: *fumo d'Angola* [smoke of Angola].

Describing the habits of the population in the sugar plantations in the northeast during the colonial period, Freyre (1937) noted that the owners allowed the slaves to plant cannabis amidst the sugar cane. And, while the whites smoked cigars and tobacco, the Negroes smoked marihuana, and in it found dreams and stupefaction. Freyre affirms that during the periodic intervals of activity on the plantations, such a pastime avoided the risks of slave laziness, thus contributing to the stability of the workers.

The opposite occurred on the coffee plantations in the southeast, where the slave work load was heavier and the discipline more intense. In this area, it appears that the use of cannabis was uncommon and, moreover, was not tolerated. A popular saying remains in the region: *Maconha em pito faz negro sem-vergonha* [Marihuana cigarettes make a shameless Negro].

There are indications that smoking marihuana was observed among the Indians during the colonial period, although we do not know whether it already was present or introduced during the contact period. In the north, including the Amazon, whose rural population developed with less participation of Negroes, marihuana smokers are also found in certain communities.

There are records of the utilization of cannabis in popular religious rites in the interior zone of the northeast. The predominant sect there is the Catimbó, of Indian origin, with private and public ceremonies, in which spirits are received and sick people cured. Religious syncretism in Catimbó includes the cult of African deities and the use of plants presumed to be of value for medical treatment and magical practices. Among them, marihuana is judged capable of inducing divination, revelation of secrets, and mystic hallucinations. Such influences came directly from the Angolan groups, who formed the *candomblé de caboclo*, on the northeast coast, *macumba* in Rio de Janeiro, and *umbandismo* in the southern region. In these cults, alcohol use is frequent and marihuana does not fail to appear. This does not occur in the *candomblé nagô*, in Bahia. In this sect, derived from the Sudanese Negroes, there is less receptivity to syncretism — alcohol and marihuana do not appear in the rituals and are, in general, considered undesirable and condemned as vices.

Proclamations from the nineteenth century on impeded the use of marihuana in urban centers, including Rio de Janeiro, capital of the empire, where imprisonment was the penalty for offenders. The prohibitions of the nation's capital, however, did not reach the planters and smokers of the provinces and were not accompanied by police vigilance.

The most extensive plantations were always maintained in the northeast, particularly in the state of Alagoas, and the cannabis was sold in the capital cities of the region and in the south. Some smokers in the rural zone had small plots of cultivation next to their own houses, exclusively for personal use, a fact that is still not uncommon.

According to the observations made in 1915 (Doria 1958) some preconceptions and superstitions were tied to the cultivation of the plant. When it began to branch, the terminal bud was cut to foster the development of the plant. This process was called *capacão*, a popular synonym for castration. It was not to be done by women, especially during menstruation, under the sanction of acquiring masculine qualities. While cutting the bud, whistling and speaking obscenities were to be avoided (habitual practices among agricultural workers in the region). Harvesting was done by the men and the women's participation in this activity restricted.

Preparations of cannabis in teas and brews were always exceptional in Brazil. It is reported that they were prescribed, in the rural milieu, for therapeutic purposes: for toothache and menstrual colic. It is possible that, in such cases, there is some anodyne effect.

Smoking in clay pipes, known as *maricas*, seems to have been the preference of the slaves. This has continued in some places, of evident Angolan influence, especially among the inhabitants along the banks of the São Francisco river.

Descriptions of the past century and the beginning of this one emphasize the northeastern custom of group meetings for the *queima da herva* [burning of the grass]. On Saturday nights and on holidays, the smokers got together, generally in the house of the oldest member, and, seated around a table, passed the *maricas* from one to another. Similarly, *jangadeiros* [raft fishermen] and canoemen in the same boat at sea or on the São Francisco river, adopted an identical system of "assemblies." It is doubtful that these traditional meetings for collective smoking still occur in such populations; at least, it can be affirmed that they are no longer frequent. Smoking in the form of cigarettes became, in this century, the dominant form of marihuana use among peasants and probably the only form seen in the urban populations.

In the period from 1915 to 1930, several doctors from the northeast related their observations on the use of marihuana, which was no longer restricted to rural areas. While it was a traditional habit in the country encompassing population groups from certain localities, the use of cannabis took another form in the coastal cities. Still another name was added to the extensive terminology — "opium of the poor" — faithfully expressing the economic level of the smokers. The greatest frequency of use was among fishermen, longshoremen, and agricultural workers, but the use was also spread among prostitutes and vagabonds. The presence of the vice reached a significant level in the penitentiaries and in some military barracks.

For the same period and subsequent years, there are newspaper articles revealing the clandestine trade that was established, transporting marihuana from the northeast by sea to the large capitals of the south. Rio de Janeiro became the largest importer, but cargoes for distribution in São Paulo were also unloaded in the port of Santos. The correlation between cannabis and social marginality was established in all these cities. To the newspaper articles were added pronouncements by doctors, warning against the criminal effects of marihuana. During the war, information from the health and police authorities (Farias 1958) expressed a concern about the migration of dealers to Bahia, where North American sailors were seen as buyers capable of paying high prices. It was referred to as a secret fact that some foreigners of an elevated economic level in Brazil were also consumers of marihuana, in sharp contrast to the sociocultural level of the great majority of the users.

In the decade of the 1950's, it was noted that some eccentric writers and artists were secretly habitual smokers of marihuana. In 1957 and 1958 (Pires da Veiga and de Pinho 1962), we examined the subjective symptoms of acute intoxication. Although we had the declared support of the police authorities for the research, and we assured the subjects of confidentiality, it was not possible for us, in Bahia, to obtain the collaboration of any of the intellectuals who were supposed users. This was probably a consequence of their respect for social pressures. The investigation was made partly in the prisons and partly in our private clinic, interviewing only known criminals or marihuana users without criminal records but who were adopting irregular family and professional lifestyles very like the *marginais* [people who are in a marginal state with regard to the rest of the society].

In a prison of 321 convicts (de Pinho 1962) all, without exception, had already tried marihuana, although there were only 36 habitual smokers. The proportion of cannabis users among criminals who had committed crimes against property was twice as high as that of criminals who had committed crimes against persons. Such findings were discovered when we sought to correlate alcoholism with the type of criminal offense. This fact confirmed findings among nonprosecuted offenders: the incidence of marihuana use was high among the thieves of the city. Nearly always, there were corresponding childhood antecedents of family disorganization and moral abandonment besides poverty and dependence on other intoxicants.

Comparison of the age of first use of marihuana between smokers never prosecuted and those in prison is interesting. Among those in prison, the habit began much later, while among the former it began, generally, during childhood or adolescence. Reevaluation of the material permitted us to conclude that for those who had been prosecuted, the prison frequently functioned as an environment conducive to the habit.

A study (Pires da Veiga and de Pinho 1962) of 50 marihuana users at this time revealed that the effects of intoxication were conditioned by multiple factors: the authenticity of the cannabis (much is adulterated by the dealers) and its varieties; the age of the plant; the method of smoking; the rhythm of consuming cigarettes; and the personality and nutritional condition of the user. Also, tranquility, comfort, and liberty appeared as very important factors, proportionate to the noisier euphoric stimulations. There were individual preferences with regard to the surroundings, and in general, the beaches appear to be the preferred setting. Collective smoking in small groups was preferred by nearly everyone.

In 1969 and 1970, the habit was appreciably diffused, at least in the regions of greatest population density. The commercial trade of marihuana multiplied in the large cities and along the highways. In Bahia, we observed its increased incidence in a well-defined group — that of professional drivers. They were almost all men of the lower middle class with stable families, consuming one to three cigarettes a night. They smoked alone, at home, without the tumult of intoxication. The influence of this habit was not evident in their work or ethical conduct.

During this period an increase in very diverse social aspects occurred with regard to the use of cannabis in Brazil. In the larger population centers there was a great diffusion of fortuitous or habitual use among middle- and upper-class adolescents. This started merely with recognizably maladjusted youth, assimilated more or less transitionally to the hippie communities. Later, it appeared in clubs, bars, public festivals, and even in dances at private residences.

In spite of legal prohibitions, the trade is easily carried on. Vendors of cigarettes, tobacco, and ice-cream, cashiers at restaurants and bars, and employees of the schools are frequently middlemen for the sale of marihuana. Low-class brothels, patronized by *marginais*, continue to permit the storage and sale of marihuana. But, in the larger cities, the plazas and the beaches of the residential neighborhoods — the most elegant and those of the middle class — also have their special places for this trade. The majority of buyers are young, at the preuniversity level. In the universities, appreciable differences are noted according to the course of study. Diverse observers concur that the students of the arts, communications, and human sciences seem to adopt the habit more than the candidates in medicine, engineering, and other technical professions. Nearly always, the attitude of older people is that of rejection of the use of marihuana, and at times even terror of its use. But young people, even those who do not adhere to the habit, take a relatively permissive position with regard to its use.

In one of the studies carried out in the decade of the 1950's (de Pinho 1962), on the basis of material from the *marginais* and prisoners, our attention was drawn to the frequency with which dependency on other intoxicants was recorded in the histories of chronic marihuana users. This fact gained significance in comparison with the backgrounds of alcoholics who in general are dependent only on alcohol. What is observed at present among young Brazilians who become habitual cannabis users is that once the continual use of marihuana is established, there follow in progression experiences with other intoxicants, established simultaneously or successively, and other dependencies, especially upon amphetamines. According to the police authorities, the chronic user of only marihuana is rare or, if they exist in great numbers, they do not become known or arrested. The offenders in prison, including the adolescents, are, nearly always, multidependents.

With regard to the comparison with alcoholism, it is worthwhile to record two interrelated facts. Contrary to tradition, the present adolescents of the upper and middle classes reveal an appreciable disinterest in alcoholic beverages. On the other hand, parents do not show the anxiety formerly observed with regard to the possibility of alcoholism among their children. This contrasts with their accentuated fear in relation to marihuana and other intoxicants.

It is important to appreciate the problem as it refers to medical aspects. Clinical and laboratory examinations in 1969 (de Pinho 1969) of 15 heavy smokers did not reveal any bodily disturbance related to chronic intoxications. There was even some coincidence, in several of our observations, with an excellent state of nutrition, perhaps comprehensible, if one takes into account the appetite that acute intoxication customarily provokes.

Brazilian psychiatrists are divided with regard to the means of evaluating the mental consequences of chronic use of cannabis, reaching radically opposed positions: those that underestimate and those that exaggerate the possibility of the occurrence of mental consequences. Such a debate is not relevant to the frequent theme of ethical decadence, which ought not to be attributed to the pharmacological action of the intoxicant, but to a set of social and economic conditions habitually associated with the situation. The divergence grows in importance in the relationship between the chronic use of marihuana and psychoses. This difference of attitudes cancels out an appreciation of the statistical data, since the acute psychopathological pictures occurring in chronic marihuana users are diagnosed by some as toxic psychoses and by others as schizophrenias. And the etiopathogenic role of cannabis becomes even more difficult to delimit in view of the constant coincidence with other pharmacodependencies.

In 1957 (de Pinho 1962), we made an inquiry at the public psychiatric hospital of Bahia, obtaining responses from 728 patients that we deem reliable. Among this group, there were 327 schizophrenics and 44 patients diagnosed as psychopathic personalities. Of the total, there were eight individuals with backgrounds of marihuana use. Among these eight, only four had been admitted in psychosis: one with the Korsakoff syndrome, one with general paralysis, and two with well-defined schizophrenia. We concluded that the role of marihuana in these cases was not significant.

Keeping in mind the dissemination of marihuana in recent years, especially among young people, it is understandable that, at the present time, a much larger number of the patients hospitalized reveal a background of marihuana use. It is, however, worth noting that the psychoses observed in marihuana users without a history of other dependencies have, in common, a schizophreniform physiognomy, never presented in our casuistry, and other traditionally known syndromes of exogenous reaction.

Our personal observation conforms fully to the taxonomy proposed by Lucena (1961) on relating the psychoses of cannabis users at least as they are presented in our milieu: (1) precipitation of a previously unapparent schizophrenic process; (2) intensification of the symptomatology already characterized before, especially, proportionate to the exacerbation of delirious production; (3) rise of symptomatic schizophrenic complexes, with benign evolution.

In each of these possibilities, it is evident that there should be supposed the participation of an endogenous factor (the constitution) and an exogenous factor (the intoxicant). In all the cases, it is necessary to recognize the essentiality of predisposition, but there is no reason to deny the additional performance of cannabis.

Analyzing the etiopathogenic complex in a wider multidimensional perspective, we think that psychogenic factors can be included, whether they contribute toward the precipitation of psychosis, or whether they provide the content for psychopathological production. It is important to bear in mind, also, the change of life plans and the loss of social roles.

Between 1968 and 1971, political modifications were reflected in youth movements, interrupting certain social programs, avoiding collective manifestations, and impeding the exercise of some leadership roles. Our cases at the time included acute schizophrenic psychoses occurring in some of these young people who were known to have used marihuana more or less continuously. Complete and rapid remission of the psychoses was demonstrated. Such cases behaved thus like "psychogenic reactions in an altered sphere," in the sense of Kurt Schneider. A predisposed constitution and the intoxication to precipitate the traumatic events repeat themselves, meanwhile, in all the characteristics of the symptomatic schizophreniform model.

In 1971, an antitoxicant law was passed in Brazil which prohibits the private planting, cultivation, harvesting, and exploitation of all varieties of toxic plants. In spite of the formal enforcement of this law and the strongly repressive measures that it prescribes, it does not appear to have caused until now any appreciable change in the system of marihuana trade, in its diffusion or in its medical repercussions. Police activity seems more oriented toward the dealers and users of lower social levels who, in general, present a social behavior and reactions of various types. Families of the middle and upper classes are anxious about conflicts between children and parents, and marihuana is frequently the theme of these conflicts. Among parents, there is a tendency to attribute to cannabis the slowness of young people in assuming their identities and responsibilities. The younger generation, while it includes many individuals with deviant behavior, including dependence on drugs, has a much greater proportion of those who harmoniously overcome the problems of age and launch themselves in the adequate fulfillment of their social roles. Many among these have had an occasional marihuana experience; they do not seem to have any biases against it, but are pessimistic with regard to the productivity of those who use it continually.

In Brazil, there are those who think that the juvenile vogue of smoking marihuana is beginning to decline. There are those who judge that there is less talk of the subject in certain areas, because acceptance by the communities is consolidating. It is too early to confirm or deny either of these two possibilities, as well as the consequences that will result from one or the other.

SUMMARY

In Brazil, where the use of cannabis has existed since the colonial period, it was first a habit of the slaves. Its use was later consolidated in certain population groups in the rural zones. In this century, it spread to the small cities of the coast and, later, to the metropolises. In the urban areas it has lasted for decades, particularly among the criminals and *marginais* which has led, always, to the image of asociality and danger attributed to the users.

In recent times, occasional or habitual use appeared extremely common among middle- and upper-class youth in the urban nuclei. The young people who established the habit followed it by other intoxicants, especially amphetamines. Upper-class adults transferred to marihuana the fears they formerly had about alcohol, while the young people, even the nonusers of marihuana, appear to have a permissive attitude with regard to cannabis.

In recent years our attention has turned to the relationship between chronic use of marihuana and psychosis. It is beyond doubt that marihuana exacerbates the delirious production of the schizophrenics. But we have also observed benign schizophrenic syndromes in cannabis users. The analysis of such cases in a multidimensional perspective suggests the interrelationship of the constitutional and the toxic factors, but also of psychogenic factors, including the relationships with social situations.

REFERENCES

DE PINHO, ALVARO RUBIM
  1962 Problemas sociopsicológicas do maconhismo. *Neurobiologia* 25:9–19.
  1969 Paper read at the *IX Congresso da Sociedade de Neurologia, Psiquiatria e Higiene Mental do Brasil*. Rio de Janeiro.
DORIA, RODRIGUES
  1958 "Os fumadores de maconha: efeitos e males do vicio," in *Maconha*, 1–14. Rio de Janeiro: Ministério de Saúde. (Memoria presented to the second Pan American Scientific Congress, Washington D.C., December 27, 1915.)
FARIAS, ROBERVAL C.
  1958 "Relatorio apresentade aos Srs. Membros da Comissão Nacional de

Fiscalizacão de Entorpecentes. Inspecão realizada de 7 a 19 de Novem-
bro de 1943 nos Estados do Bahia, Sergipe e Alagoas, visando o
problema do comérico e uso da maconha," in *Maconha*, 105–113. Rio
de Janeiro: Ministério da Saúde.

FREYRE, GILBERTO
1937 *Nordeste*. Rio de Janeiro: Jose Olimpio.

LUCENA, JOSÉ
1961 "La symptomatologia du cannabisme," in *The Third World Congress of
Psychiatry*, volume one, 401–406. Toronto: University of Toronto
Press.

PIRES DA VEIGA, E., ALVARO RUBIM DE PINHO
1962 Contribuicão ao estudo do maconhismo na Bahia. *Neurobiologia*
25:38–68.

Shamanism Among the Avá-Chiripá

MIGUEL ALBERTO BARTOLOMÉ

> To *she ru angá* Avá-Nembiará in the hope
> that I shall never betray his trust.

In the course of these pages, I shall attempt to portray the institution of
shamanism as it exists, at the present time, among the Avá-Chiripá. The
feature of shamanism around which I have focused my observations is the
dream, a process which enables them to receive supernatural revelations
and by means of which the shaman continues to safeguard the relations of
the people in an increasingly difficult environment. I shall describe the
process of initiation into shamanism and shall show how this institution
plays an active role in the daily life of the community. Hence, I shall refer,
as briefly as possible, to the social and cultural context in which the
shamans operate, in order to demonstrate that the changes which have
taken place in shamanism reflect wider social and cultural modifications.
That is to say that the functions of the shaman have increased in proportion to the changes taking place in the environment in which he
performs his activities and that he has adapted to a new role: that of
intercultural agent.

On the other hand, we shall see how the shaman, in his capacity as a
social leader and representative of the tribal religion, is the axis around
which cultural identity revolves, while his role as interpreter of religious
law maintains and guarantees cultural continuity.

In order to do this, I shall give a general outline of the most important
aspects of the cosmology of the Avá-Chiripá, and the place of shamanism

This work is the result of field studies carried out in the northeastern region of Paraguay.
The first study was carried out from January to May, 1968 and the second from January to
May, 1969, the latter made possible by a grant from the Argentinian National Council for
Scientific and Technical Research.

in it, thus establishing the following hypothesis: that tribal religion, continuously reinforced by shamanism, is the key factor in the preservation of ethnic identity among the Chiripá.

There will be no attempt to apply the results of this research more widely than to this subgroup of the Guarani, the Chiripá, especially those living in the settlement of Colonia Fortuna in Paraguay. It has to be borne in mind that each Guarani group faces a special situation as regards both its internal social structure and its relations with the regional society. Nevertheless my research among Guarani subgroups, in Argentina, Brazil, and Paraguay, suggests that the phenomenon of shamanism among the Guarani possesses greater coherence and integration than is generally attributed to it.

THE AVÁ-CHIRIPÁ

In the forested eastern region of Paraguay, there are, at present, three large Guarani subgroups, namely, the Mbya, the Paí Cayuá, and the Avá-Chiripá. It is possible to include with these the Guayakí, related to the Guarani either by origin or by assimilation, the nature of their affiliation still being the subject of much discussion.

The Avá-Chiripá — they call themselves the Avá-Katú-Eté, meaning "the true men" — possess ancestral lands which extend to the south of the River Jejuí Guazú, in the department of Alto Paraná and to the south of the Yguazu. Today they move around in the areas bordering the Paraguayan localities of Laurel, Curuguaty, Yvyrarobaná, Ytakyry, Hernandarias, Yerbal, Santa Teresa, Ygatimi, San Estanislao, Yhú, and so on (Map 1). From the point of view of the present political division of the eastern region, the Chiripá occupy the northern section of the tenth department, Caaguazú. But this present location has only recently taken place, thanks to the removal of some of the northern groups of the Mbya. There are also groups of Chiripá in Brazil, living mostly in the areas round Bananal, Arariba, Ytariri, Dourados and Jacareí. The Apapokuvá studied by Curt Nimuendajú (1944) can be considered as one of the migrant, messianic bands of the Chiripá, established in the south of Mato Grosso since the end of the last century.

The origins of the present-day Chiripá have been traced by Cádogan (1959:8), who sees them as survivors of the destruction experienced at the time of the Tarumá pacifications. Cádogan arrived at these conclusions by studying the history of the Chiripá, not only as recorded by the chroniclers, but also in the form of oral traditions gleaned from the groups themselves, drawing attention to the fact that the two versions, the historical and the legendary, do not contradict each other. The legend that Cádogan found among the Mbya, as well as the Paí and the Chiripá,

Map 1. Paraguay showing Avá-Chiripá communities (after Chase-Sardi 1972:306)

tells of the great chiefs, Paraguá and Guairá. The first of these had allied himself with the Spaniards and permitted the subjection and Christianization of his people, thereby reducing Guairá's band to the status of rebels. Guairá's men, not wanting to be subjugated, fled into the depths of the forest, thus gaining for themselves the epithet of *ka'aguayguá* [wild men]. This description in its abbreviated form (*ka'inguá*) came to be applied to numerous Guarani groups. The Guarani of the southern missions (Paraguá's men) mustered to pacify Guairá's partisans, returned to their forest life when the Jesuits were expelled (1768), fearing to fall into the hands of the private landowners whose reputation were justifiably sinister. The descendants of these natives are the present-day Chiripá, among whom I have often heard told the story of the struggles of Guairá and Paraguá, thus confirming Cádogan's version.

  We believe, therefore, that the Avá-Chiripá are Guarani who returned to their forest habitat after having lived for 150 years under the tutelage of the priests of the Society of Jesus. At the present time, they are, relatively speaking, the most acculturated Guarani group of eastern Paraguay. Some of them have even acquired economic positions similar to those of the peasantry, possessing horses and grazing animals. In most of their groups this situation is quite common. But if some individuals are behaving like rural laborers, there are still many (the majority) who maintain the structure of a tribal life centered around the *nande'rú* [our fathers], shaman leaders of great prestige. Even those who work for the Creoles often return to their traditional life-styles — so strong are the bonds of tribal solidarity which unite them. The numbers of the Avá-Chiripá fluctuate between three and four thousand (Chase-Sardi 1972:245), although these figures are extremely tentative, given the difficulty of counting a population with a very high level of mobility.

COLONIA FORTUNA

I shall now give a short, descriptive outline of the chief characteristics of the Colonia Fortuna community. The only object of this outline is to give the reader a picture of the real situation in which the present-day Avá-Chiripá find themselves. It is not my intention to give a detailed evaluation of the fundamental aspects of Guarani cultural life.

Habitat

Colonia Fortuna is situated six-and-a-half kilometers from the Creole settlement of Curuguaty, in the department of Caaguazú (eastern Paraguay). Access to the community from Curuguaty is by means of an "improved" forest track which is sometimes impassable during the rainy season. It is a Fiscal Reservation with a total area of 1,600 hectares, set aside by the Directory for Indian Affairs (DAI). Physically it is an undulating terrain of gentle hills and valleys. The climate is subtropical with some frost occurring in June, July, and August. The average annual rainfall varies from 1,400 to 1,600 mm. This heavy precipitation results in the erosion of organic matter (humus) from the slopes. Deposited in the valleys, it makes them suitable for cultivation. Within the reservation there are three natural sources of drinking water: the Curuguaty river and the arroyos of Paí-y and Yukyry, with most of the population concentrated near the arroyos. The fauna of the area is very important for the group, since, together with gathering, hunting provides a significant complement to the agricultural economy. Some of the animals most frequently hunted for food are deer (*guazú'ti*), agoutis (*acutí*), wild pigs (*cure'i*), smaller, "Indian" pigs (*apere'a*), armadillos (*tatú-aí*), wild boars (*tayasú ca'ti*), partridges (*ynambú guazú*), wood pigeons (*pycasú*), and so on. The flora is represented by the typical, damp, subtropical woodland with thick undergrowth of shrubs, predominantly ferns. Hardwoods are abundant, especially quebracho, cedar, and lapacho.

Population

The principal cluster of dwellings is situated in a large clearing opened artificially in the forest. There are, in fact, two centers, separated by a swampy ravine through which flows the Yukyry arroyo. Although the population is divided fairly equally between the two centers, there are numerous huts scattered around the surrounding forest, linked to the centers by narrow but well-used paths. Colonia was established in 1966 by individuals from Avá-Chiripá bands. One of the bands was led by the shaman chief, Canuto Sales (Avá-Nembiará) and the other by the chief Adriano Portillo (Avá-Tapé). The two original groups must have been joined later by several families attracted by the reputation of Sales and by the possibility of obtaining land and supplies (from the DAI). A DAI census of 1966 gives a total of 54 families comprising 114 persons. These have been increased up to a total of 200 individuals at the present time (1969). Although the group is basically Chiripá, they have living with them two native Apyteré (Mbya) and two Creoles married to Guarani women.

The population maintains political allegiance to the paramount chief of the Chiripá, Juan Pablo Vera, who, from the locality of Paso Cadena, where he lives, exercises real authority over his scattered people. As proof of the above, I have known people walk more than sixty kilometers through the forest to lay before Vera problems which local chiefs had not been able to solve. On the other hand, emissaries from him often visit the different groups. More than once I had the opportunity of witnessing the arrival of these envoys and can testify to the respect with which they are received. The themes of these visits frequently concern problems of a religious nature, demonstrating the need to continue their traditional cult practices in spite of the pressures exerted by Catholic and Protestant missionaries.

The language of the group is Chiripá-Guarani (Cádogan 1959:12), which constitutes an intermediate form between the general mestizo Guarani of Paraguay, Yopará, and the much more archaic Guarani spoken by the Mbya. Only two persons out of the whole community express themselves moderately well in Spanish; one is the son of Chief Portillo and the other the grandson of Chief Sales. But all the others speak Yopará perfectly, a language common to all the Creole peasants of the region, many of whom speak no Spanish themselves, and which is spoken throughout Paraguay. Because of this, and because Paraguayan Guarani has an officially recognized written form, I shall not resort to phonetic symbols in this work, using only the letter *y* to represent the sixth gutteral vowel.

Settlement

The pattern of settlement among the ancient Guarani was based on the *teko'a guazú* [large agricultural community] headed by military, religious, and agrarian chiefs and sometimes by individuals who combined in themselves the qualities of all three categories. These *teko'a guazú* were defined in terms of a kinship pattern, or *ñandeva* [all of us (inclusive)], and consisted of a variable number of *ty'y* [extended families] organized in a system of lineages (Susnik 1969:103). The *ty'y* represented an economic, political, and kinship unit under the leadership of a *ty'y rú* [common father], who generally possessed shamanistic attributes and therefore acted as the "spiritual head" of his lineage. The *ty'y* conformed to an *oreva* [all of us (exclusive)] pattern and the unity of the *teko'a* inhabitants depended on the combinations and associations between the varios *ty'y*. Each *ty'y*, traditionally occupying a common house, had jurisdiction over a piece of land which was worked in conjunction with all the members of the extended family. The *ty'y* based their growth and continuity on exogamy with the other *ty'y* and the circulation of women from one *ty'y* to another put into operation the social mechanism of the *tovaya* [brother-in-law]. This meant in practice that a woman's brothers were obliged, by the bonds of reciprocity, to work on the land belonging to the *ty'y* of their sister's husband (Susnik 1969:106). Following the conquest and the arrival of the missionaries, the large units of settlement (the *teko'a*) dissolved into their constituent nuclei (*ty'y*). These have been able to remain intact up until the present day thanks to their unity in terms of kinship, economy, and magico-religious practices, under the direction of the shaman, acting as overall leader.

Colonia Fortuna represents therefore the union of various exogamous *ty'y*, each of these endowed with its portion of arable land subdivided among the nuclear families comprising it. Each *ty'y* is led by a *ty'y rú*. The *ty'y rú* jointly respect the authority of the shaman carrying most prestige in the community, Avá-Nembiará. As the aftermath and continuation of Jesuit rule, every community similar to Fortuna has a formal leadership system comprising a captain, a sergeant, and a corporal, appointed by the regional military authorities. Their function is to mediate between the group and the authorities. But, as we shall see, their authority is merely nominal compared to the leadership exercised by the shamans. In spite of this conflicts often arise and I shall refer to these later.

The old, communal houses no longer exist in Colonia Fortuna. These have been replaced by individual huts for each nuclear family, but their position in relation to each other is in accordance with *ty'y* membership. Generally the houses are of two types:

1.   Quadrangular groundplan, roof of two sloping sides held up by supports of hardwood, with ridge, rafters, and "cock's foot" (the beam

which forms the junction between the roof and the end of the wall) in palm wood (*pin'do — Arecastrum romanzoffianum*). The roof is made of straw tied into bundles with fibers of *wembe'pi* (*Phylodendron sellum*), this fiber being a substitute for the fine, galvanized wire used by the Creole peasants. The frame is made of reeds (*tak'ua*). The houses have large gable ends and lack walls. At one end is the fireplace and, at the other, the hammocks and bunks (shelves) on which they sleep.

2. Similar but with an internal recess, screened off in one corner. The recess is made of pieces of wood driven into the ground and tied together with strips of deer hide (*guazú'ti*) or plant fibers. This construction takes up a third of the interior of the dwelling and recalls the family compartments which existed in the traditional communal houses of the Guarani. In a few cases, the buildings are walled on four sides by rows of planks and reeds.

Traditions and Culture

In terms of material objects not much of their inherited culture survives. Their dress as well as their articles of daily use (machetes, axes, and so on) are similar to those of the Creole peasants of the area. Their own traditional pottery has disappeared and has been replaced by Paraguayan earthenware pitchers (*kambu'chi*) and by three-legged metal pots. They still retain the calabash receptacles, placed in a net of plant fiber to make them easier to carry, in which they fetch and store water. Also, they make bows (*wira'pa*) from palm wood (*guayá ywi — Patagonula americana*) cut into sections along a convex plane, or from *wirá-pe'pe* (*Holocalyx balancea*). Their arrows (*ju'y*) have reed shafts and points (smooth and sharp, blunt for stunning, or serrated) of *wirá-pe'pe* wood. Bows and arrows are gradually being replaced by shotguns, but all the young people and adult men are still adept at their construction and use. The women, for their part, make hammocks of cotton and other vegetable fibers, weaving them on vertical looms.

In fact, the traditional artifacts which have remained most in evidence are those connected with religious ceremonial. Extremely common are the *mbaraká* [dance rattles], the *kuruzú* [feathered crosses], the *takuapú* [rhythm sticks], used by the women, and the feather ornaments which symbolize the separate shamanistic grades and ranks.

As far as painting the body is concerned, it is possible, at any time, to see the older women with their cheeks and extremities painted red with the *urukú* (*Bixa orellana*), and on some occasions the young ones as well. It is interesting to note that, though not in habitual use, the designs for painting the face and those for other parts of the body are known to all the women. This lack of conservatism with respect to their material culture is the reason why numerous authors (Métraux 1948; Susnik 1969:179; Cádogan 1959:8) consider the Chiripá the most acculturated of all Guarani groups, notwithstanding that this acculturation is more apparent than real since it does not extend to the most profound aspects of their culture.

Economy

The Chiripá practice subsistence farming complemented by hunting, gathering, and, to a lesser degree, fishing. For cultivation they use the slash-and-burn method. The felling takes place during the dry part of the winter, the bigger trees being cut down with axes in such a way that they all fall in the same direction, crushing the smaller ones as they do so. They are then left to dry and are burnt before the rains come. Planting is done at the beginning of the rainy season in the ash-covered soil and between the carbonized trunks. Both the felling and the burning are done collectively, but afterward the land is divided among the families who have taken part in the work of clearing. For sowing they use a digging stick in the form of a plank sharpened at one end and hardened by fire (*ywra jha'cua*). The principal crops are maize (*avatí*), which regulates all their agriculture and their calendar since there is a definite cycle of ceremonies corresponding to each stage of its cultivation — before the trunks are burnt, before planting, when the plants are half a meter high, when the grain has formed, when the green maize can be picked, and when the first chicha (*ka'gu'y*) is made; manioc (*mandi'o*), which is their staple diet; pumpkins (*kuara pe'pe*); beans (*kumondá*); tobacco (*pe'ty*); potatoes (*ye'ty*); sugarcane (*taua're'e*); and so on.

They raise a small number of chickens, pigs, and ducks, but almost all the meat they eat comes from hunting. For this they mostly use traps — with nets (*ñu'ha*), as well as weights (*mon'de*) — each family owning a number. They also hunt with dogs and machetes and with bows and arrows or shotguns. Fishing is another important, albeit less frequent activity. They use hooks, traps, and vegetable poison from a toxic liana plant called *ysypó tim'bo* (*Serjania paullina*), which stuns the fish and so facilitates their capture.

There is not much storing of grain. Their only granaries consist of the crops which they do not themselves grow. As far as gathering is concerned, apart from the occasional discovery of fruit, edible larvae, heart of palm, and other forest foods, this is mainly concerned with vegetable species, as for example the almost daily search for the wild herb, *Ilex paraguayensis*, which is found in natural herb beds or "patches" in the forest around Fortuna. The other main item gathered is the large number of wild oranges which yield an abundant annual harvest.

Much sought after as well is the honey of bees whose hives are to be found in the hollow trunks of old trees. When someone finds a hive, he acquires the right to exploit it, but when he collects the honey and the beeswax he always leaves a few hives untouched so that the bees will return to the same place and continue production — a rudimentary form of apiculture.

Money is not very often used in relations between different groups, nearly all commercial transactions being in the form of barter. To a certain extent the whole community constitutes a single socioeconomic unit on the basis of reciprocal relations in the interaction which maintains the nuclear families in the bosom of the extended families, and the links which these have with each other.

The sexual division of labor suggests very strongly a division also of *space*. The horizontal space of the Chiripá is on three different levels: the clearing where the dwellings are and the paths which cross it; the plantations (both of these being culturally defined spaces); and the forest. Beyond the most distant plantations there extends a homogeneous and infinite space characterized by the beginnings of the forest. Crossing this barrier are routes which lead to known destinations but there are also routes which lead to unknown places populated by mythical or supernatural beings. On leaving the village in which he lives and crossing the barrier of the forest, the Chiripá disappears into the universe. The spaces for women and children are the house space where the domestic chores are done and cleared areas and paths as well as the plantations where they work. These areas are shared with the men, but theirs also includes the forest. Women and children can take part in gathering without moving away from the clearings and tracks, but men are often absent for days at a time, checking their traps, engaging in hunts of one sort or another, or seeking a special type of wood for a house or to exchange for something else.

Relations with the DAI and the Region's Wider Society

The Avá-Chiripá come under a loose form of guardianship exercised jointly by the DAI and the Cáritas Paraguaya, a charity organization. These supply food, clothes, and medicines at regular intervals on condition that the Indians carry out improvements on their lands. At the time of writing the DAI has two Creole officials in Fortuna: an administrator, Francisco Ezcurra, and his son Ricardo. Both speak Guarani. (Ricardo was my friend and translator before I mastered the Guarani language.) Both enjoy a relatively high level of interaction with the Indians, having *compadre* ties with several of them. In spite of Ricardo Ezcurra's common-law marriage to one of the granddaughters of the shaman/chief

Avá-Nembiará his and his parents' position in the community remains that of "friendly outsiders."

In theory, the group is governed by a council under the chairmanship of a high-level official of the DAI (who pays irregular visits to Fortuna), and including the administrator and the two chiefs who brought their bands together. But the decisions of this council affect the group only in those areas of activity where their status as "wards" is concerned, while internal political power continues to lie in the hands of their own chiefs. Generally speaking, the exercise of political power does not assume any great significance, and therefore there are not too many reasons why conflict should arise between the local leaders and national officials, except in the area of work.

The infrequent contacts between the Chiripá and the regional society relate basically to the socioeconomic system of the surrounding area as represented by the small town of Curuguaty, which is typical of the small rural townships of Paraguay, with a tiny population of approximately 700. The houses form fairly regular blocks around an extensive main square in which stands the chapel. The population has no gas, electricity, or main drainage and the forest begins a little way beyond the last outlying houses.

Near Curuguaty, in the neighboring forests which enclose Fortuna, one can still see the remains of buildings and old bits of metal which belonged to the ancient city of Curuguaty. In its time it had more than 20,000 inhabitants and was destroyed by the Brazilian troops during the Paraguayan war (1865–1870). From that time the region became somewhat marginalized in relation to the rest of Paraguay until 1966 when a new road was opened linking it with the town of Coronel Oviedo and in the opposite direction with the falls of Guaíra, on the border of the Brazilian state of Mato Grosso.

With the opening of the roadway came a proliferation of timber works in the area. Sometimes their operations are hampered by the "wild" Guayakí reacting against Creole penetration into their territory. These timber firms have had as yet no need to recruit Indian labour since there are large numbers of Creole peasants in Paraguay now available for wage labor on a regular basis.

From what has been said it will be clear that the expanding national economy has only recently extended into this region, but, at this moment, it presents a serious threat to tribal integrity. Already the clamor for Indian land, from peasant settlers as well as from the big landowners of the region, has begun.

MYTHOLOGY AND RELIGION

If there is a single feature which characterizes Guarani culture — both among the Avá-Chiripá and among other subgroups — it is its extreme religiosity. Because of this, I consider it necessary to give special emphasis to this point before analyzing the role of the shaman, since it is this profound religiosity which legitimizes shamanistic activity. One of the greatest specialists on Guarani culture, Egon Schaden (1954), emphasizes this extraordinary characteristic:

Throughout the world there is certainly no people or tribe to whom the biblical phrase: "My kingdom is not of this world" is more applicable. The entire mental universe of the Guarani revolves round the concept of the beyond.

Christian Influence

For almost 150 years the Avá-Chiripá lived under the rule of the Jesuits in their missionary settlements. Yet, if we compare their rich mythology with that of other groups (e.g. the Mbya) who were not evangelized, we can appreciate that both oral traditions are basically similar. This persistence bears witness to the fact that there was little or no interruption in the transmission of tribal myths and cosmological concepts even within the missions. The proselytizing process produced a few syncretic manifestations but did not succeed in altering the symbolic content of the indigenous culture at the deepest level. According to Saguier and Clastres (1969:23), the Jesuits took only a few themes which corresponded to their own beliefs from the vast mythico-religious pantheon of the Guarani.

This superficial fusion (or confusion) of the two theogonies resulted in the emergence of certain syncretic figures, like the indigenous Tupá, who was rapidly assimilated to the Christian god. In fact, for the Guarani, Tupá combined a notion of the sacred allied to a specific celestial deity, usually identified as the "Lord of the West Wind" who brought rain and storms. As a result, he appears, in a manner not entirely in keeping with Christian ideas, as a supreme being who rides on the wind seated on his *apyaká* [zoomorphic stool] with his lower lip pierced by the *tembetá* which symbolizes and produces lightning. Doubtless it was the fact that Tupá possessed celestial attributes which made it easy for the Jesuits to link him to the Christian god without noticing that Tupá is only one of the sons of the real supreme being of the Guarani.

Another mythical Guarani figure reinterpreted by the Jesuits was the *añag*, whom they identified with Satan. The *añag* are creatures of ambiguous conduct, usually malign, and associated with jaguars, but whose roles and attributes in the cycle of the twins consists in serving their rivals Kuarahy and Yacy [sun and moon], who, for the most part, mock and ridicule them. The malificent side of their nature, as enemies of the cultural heroes, allowed the Jesuits to relate them to the devil, "the Evil One", of their own mythology. Although this identification persists to a certain extent in the peasant culture of Paraguay, the same cannot be said in the case of the Chiripá. For them it has become a single evil figure connected with jaguars who lives in heaven but has no influence in the world of the living.

Examples could be multiplied, but I shall content myself with emphasizing that not even the material artifacts connected with magico-religious ritual can be seen as Christian borrowings. This is the case of the feathered cross (*kuruzú ypoty*) used in rituals. This exists in the earliest Apapokuvá cosmogony (Nimuendajú 1944:78) under the name of *ywyrá joasá re-ko'ypy* [eternal wooden cross], on which Nanderú Guazú [our great father] built the Earth on which we live. At the same time the eternal wooden cross is symbolic of the four sacred cardinal points, each of which is related to a wind and a specific deity.

Perhaps one of the most interesting features of this process is that it also produced phenomena of reinterpretation in the opposite direction. Just as the Jesuits used indigenous deities to facilitate their preaching, so the Chiripá (and other Guarani groups) used Christian dogma as a means of reinforcing their own cosmology. That is to say that exogenous factors, introduced by Christianity, served not to adulterate but to strengthen to the full the central values of tribal doctrine (Schaden 1965:105), since the former were reinterpreted in accordance with the content of the latter. Thus it was that the figure of Jesus Christ was incorporated as a "savior" into an already established pantheon of "cultural saviors." Christ was thus identified with the *paí guazú* [great shamans] of the times of the earliest guardian spirits. Acceptance of Christ in this sense was facilitated by the fact that internal contradictions in Guarani society had already given rise, in pre-Hispanic times, to the emergence of messianic migra-tions (more numerous after the conquest) in search of the mythical *ywy mará ey* [land without evil]. These migrations were led by the *paí guazú*, in their capacity as saviors, who had received a mandate from the gods allowing their followers to cross the *pará guazú rapytá* [great primeval sea] by means of "magical flight." Thus they would arrive in the land without evil. It is therefore feasible to interpret the Christian message of "salvation" in this way, identifying the biblical paradise with the land without evil and Jesus Christ with a messianic savior. Notwithstanding, at least among the Avá-Katú-Eté, Jesus Christ is a relatively insignificant savior compared to the figures of the venerable *paí guazú* of antiquity.

Mythology

As will be appreciated, an exposé, however brief, of the Chiripá's extensive mythology would require more space than that given to the main
theme of this work, namely shamanism. But, in order to understand its
intimate connection with shamanism, it is necessary to be acquainted,
however superficially, with some aspects of the mythical world of the
Avá-Katú-Eté.

Of necessity, the descriptive summary which I propose will alter, by
synthesis, the real complexity of the mythological phenomenon, since the
legends will appear in an ideal order which corresponds to an external
model rather than to a real analysis of the correlations between the
legends and their numerous interconnections. This external model constitutes a classification by mythological types.

In the first place, we have the creation myth, the cosmogonic myth, in
which Nanderú Guazú creates the world and places it upon the eternal
wooden cross. Immediately his companion appears, Nanderú Mbaé-
Kua'a [our great father who knows all things], and together they fertilize
the first woman who, on becoming pregnant, is transformed into Nandé
Cy [our mother]. Then Nanderú Guazú creates *avatí* [maize] and Nandé
Cy provokes his anger by not believing that it can germinate in a single
day. In the heat of the divine anger, Nandé Cy is abandoned on the
recently created Earth and Nanderú Guazú returns to his celestial abode,
apparently accompanied by Nanderú Mbaé-Kua'a, since the latter disappears from the scene.

The final part of the cosmogonic myth serves as an introduction to the
heroic myth represented by the cycle of the twins to whom Nandé Cy gave
birth after her double copulation. Left alone on the earth, Nandé Cy is
devoured by the *añag* [jaguars] of the future, whose grandmother adopts
the twins immediately after attempting to kill them. The twins are
Kuarahy [sun] and Yacy [moon], and the cycle recounts their adventures
on Earth, fighting the *añag* who killed their mother, through a series of
episodes. A consequence of these adventures is the appearance of food
plants, fire, the bow, edible animals, and an extensive list of social and
kinship rules. Thus is made clear the role of Kuarahy and Yacy as cultural
heroes, true antecedents of man and charged with establishing the human
order on the Earth. The outline of a basic opposition can be seen in the
cycle: that of nature/culture, the former represented by the *añag* and the
latter by the cultural heroes who create a world meant for men while
evolving the fundamental norms and characteristics of human behavior.
The version of the cycle which I found among the Chiripá will be the
subject of a special study, but the essential features of it are given in a
bilingual form in Nimuendajú's work (1944) on the Apapokuvá.
Although Nimuendajú's transcription was made at the beginning of this

century, both versions are fundamentally the same, with the exception that, in the Chiripá cycle, Kuarahy creates his own brother Yacy, since Nandé Cy gives birth to Kuarahy alone.

Complementing the twin cycle is a wide-ranging series of etiological myths, or myths of origin which explain the mythological *raison d'être* and the origin of a great variety of plants and animals. In addition, the myths of this type include numerous astral myths which recount the origin of the stars and constellations: for example the Pleiades, which are seen as the "Path of the Primeval Tapir." As I have said, the myths of origin can be regarded as a complement to the twin cycle since in them is completed the concept of nature as sacred and linked to man. Thus, for the Chiripá, this sacred nature includes a great variety of animals and plants of divine origin which are the object of special consideration and to which are dedicated many of the sacred songs which form part of the cult. Each Avá-Katú-Eté lives in total awareness of the sacred nature of his environment and his sociocultural order.

The stories which would continue the mythical traditions of the Chiripá in ideal chronological form are those of the cataclysmic myth in which Earth is destroyed, sometimes by fire, sometimes by water, sometimes by Nanderú Guazú's overturning the eternal wooden cross which holds up the world. The variants correspond to the separate Guarani groups, and occasionally to the subdivisions within a group. It is probable that this multiplicity of variants is due to the differential influence of the biblical cataclysmic version of the Flood. In the case of the Chiripá, two earlier worlds were destroyed by fire because of the impious conduct of the human beings who lived in them. Nevertheless, Cádogan (1959:18) has recorded a flood version among the Chiripá. It is the myth of Chary Piré [the grandmother] and her son. When the earth was covered by water, Chary Piré beat her *takuapú* [rhythm stick] to the accompaniment of a sacred song. Thanks to her devotion, a *pindó* [palm tree] sprouted out of the water and she and her son took refuge in the top of it. I do not think there can be any doubt that this palm tree is the same one venerated to this day (*pindó vyjú* — eternal palm) which acts as the *axis mundi* or the bridge which joins earth and sky in the Chiripá concept of space.

Pantheon

I shall continue by reproducing a much simplified outline of the religious pantheon of the Avá-Katú-Eté (Figure 1), making allowance for the fact that its theogonic system, like that of other groups like the Ñandeva, Paí Cayua, and Mbya (Schaden 1965:106), shows frequent duplication of deities, linked to each other by kinship ties, but with differential attributes. Another source of confusion lies in the separate names with which

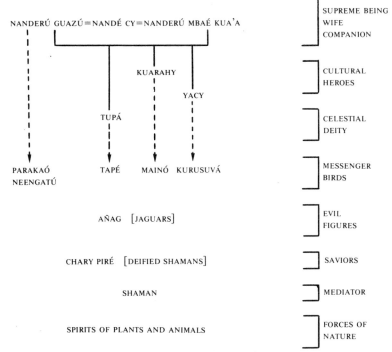

Figure 1. Outline sketch of the Avá-Chiripá religious pantheon.

the Chiripá can designate the same mythological figure in accordance with whichever of its functions the individual or the group considers most important.

At the apex of the pantheon stands the figure of Nanderú Guazù, whose activities date from the very earliest times: creator of the Earth, of agriculture, and of maize, he is the father of the twins and is responsible for cyclic cataclysms. He does not usually intervene in human destiny, but is represented by his mythical messenger the *paraka'o ñeengatú* [the parrot which speaks discreetly]. His companion Nanderú Mbaé-Kua'a performs a role in earthly life which is difficult to determine although it is possible that it is he who is responsible, as the transmitter, for the acquisition of knowledge through the sound of the *mbaraká* [rattles] used by the shamans in ceremonials. Nandé Cy following her tragic death at the hands of the *añag*, lives in the Chiripá paradise, awaiting the arrival of her sons, in the shade of the eternal palm.

Kuarahy [sun] is the principal figure of the cult in his capacity as cultural hero and man's ancestor. He is the first *paí guazú* [great shaman] with whom present-day shamans identify. He communicates with them through his messenger bird, the *mainó* [hummingbird]. The veneration in which he is held is so great that the Chiripá-Guarani term for the east is *ñandé rovai* [that which faces us], since during rituals and acts of prayer and ceremonial, they have to be able to look toward the place of the rising sun. The other twin, Yacy [moon], although he possesses certain "trickster" characteristics (starting menstruation, violating virgins, initiating adultery, and so on), is also venerated as the lord of cultivated plants and the vegetable world in general. His assistant is Yacy Tatá Guazú [great star of fire — Venus], and his messenger bird is the *kurusuvá* which begins to sing when the maize comes into ear. The same bird is invoked in prayers for the expediting of this process (Cádogan 1959:29).

Next, in order of importance, is the abovementioned Tupá, a sky god, lord of the west wind and of the tempest. His *tembetá*, a lip ornament of yellow resin, symbolizing lightning, is still the sign of tribal identification for various Guarani groups, like the Apyteré. His emissary bird is *tapé*, a bird similar to a giant swallow, whose name is frequently used as a patronymic among the Chiripá. The parents of Tupá are Nanderú Guazú and Nandé Cy, Nanderú Mbaé-Kua'a having played no part in the matter. Finally, in this sketch of the Chiripá pantheon, we meet Chary Piré who has already been mentioned and who inaugurates the figure of the savior.

Mythical figures with evil attributes are led by the *añag*, rivals of the twins whose mother they devoured, but whom they adopted in their capacity as uncles. When the twins avenge themselves on them, the only survivor, a pregnant female, is punished by being transformed into, or giving birth to, a jaguar. The Paí Cayuá still retain a memory of this deed (Cádogan 1968:79), for, in order to frighten away jaguars they invoke them in sacred language, calling them "uncle": *"She tuty tekerese marangatú"* ["My uncle jaguar full of good fortune"]. However, these *añag* are completely inactive in man's earthly life although they play a role in his destiny after death.

This mythico-religious pantheon can be completed with a large number of "spirits of nature" whose characteristics may be either vegetable or animal. Their power is influenced by that of the great shamans (historical or mythical) who have been deified. The great shamans of the present continue this interaction and so unify the religious pantheon through their role as mediators between the "spirits of nature," men, and the gods.

ANIMISM AND ESCHATOLOGY

The notion of the "soul," and all its implications, is the vantage point from which we must conduct a thorough survey of the activities of the Chiripá shaman. I shall make frequent comparisons between Chiripá concepts and those of other Guarani groups, in order to underline the fact that they are derived from a common substratum. I intend, therefore, in spite of circumstantial differences (caused by missionary activity, group fragmentation, and contacts with the dominant culture), to speak of a relatively homogeneous Guarani culture, at least in the area of South America which includes southern Brazil, northeastern Argentina, and eastern Paraguay. I shall not include other southern groups such as the Chiriguano and the Guarayo since there is not sufficient ethnological data to make comparisons possible.

The Notion of the Soul

For the Mbya of the Ivy Pyté (Paraguay), a Guarani group studied by Cádogan (1952:1), *ang* is the shadow, the trail of the human being, his echo: "Our word is the manifestation of our soul which does not die." In classical Guarani, *ñeé* means "speech," human language, though for some Mbya groups it signifies the barking of dogs, birdsong, and so on, that is to say, the language of irrational beings. But for the Chiripá, the Mbya Jeguakává, the Apapokuvá, and others, "language" (*ñe'e*), and "soul of divine origin" (*ang*) are synonymous. In addition, for the majority of the Mbya subgroups (Apyteré, Tavyterá, Jeguaká-vá, and so on), *ñe'eng* signifies "divine human soul" or "human voice," or, put another way, "the vital word."

In one of the most important mythological texts collected by Cádogan (1949b), called *Ayvu rapytá* [Origin of the word], it is recorded that the first work of Myba the creator was the "vital word," the *ñe'eng*, which constitutes the divine part of the soul sent by nē'eng rú eté [true father of the vital word] to be incarnated in a creature (Cádogan 1949b:23).

To the vital word of divine origin is added another soul which develops as the individual grows. This "second soul" is the *tekò achy kué* [product of the imperfections] and is responsible for the base passions and evil appetites of humans. This product of the *tekó achy* is known as *tupichúa* [animal soul] (Cádogan 1968:81) which remains with a man all his life and orients him toward acts of "animal" behavior (i.e. behavior which violates the sociocultural order). The Mbya-Guarani notion of the soul can therefore be summarized as positing the duality, *ñe'eng/tupichúa*, the first being the vital word of divine origin, and the second the negative terrestrial soul.

Egon Schaden, in his studies on the Guarani groups of southern Brazil, (Schaden 1954:132), discovered that the Ñandeva recognized three souls which could be visualized as shadows: *nane'a* [our shadow]. Shadows cast in front or behind are called *ayvú-kué-poravé* [the good word which we speak] and form the soul which returns to its divine origin when a person dies. The shadow cast to the left is the *atsy-yguá*, considered as the biological basis of man and of the "animal" aspects of his behavior. The shadow cast to the right is the *ayvú-kué* [the word which sprouts] and is limited in function to being a sort of companion to the *ayvú-kué-poravé* which it implicitly obeys.

Another subgroup of the Paraguay Mbya, who call themselves the Apyteré, also conceptualize the soul in a tripartite form (Bartolomé 1969b:64). The Apyteré possess three souls which are introduced into the unborn child and gave life to him from the moment he is born. These three souls are (1) *ñe'e porá* [good word]; (2) *ñe'e yoybuy* [words placed crosswise]; and (3) *ñe'e raroba* [the word held in waiting]. The first soul is of divine origin and flies away during sleep, accompanied by the second which corresponds to the negative aspects of behavior. On returning from their nocturnal journey, they recount to the third soul the visions, events, and revelations which they have witnessed or acquired. When this account is being given to the *ñe'e raroba*, the individual remembers (is aware of) the dreams which he has had.

For their part the Apapokuvá (Nimuendajú 1944:16) refer to the divine soul as *ayvú-kué* [the word which sprouts]. It is therefore also a "vital word." At an individual's birth, his *asynguá* [animal soul] appears and is responsible for his ordinary behavior

Finally, the Avá-Chiripá call the divine vital word *ñe'eng* and, like the Apapokuvá, the animal soul, *asynguá*. The *ñe'eng*, as man's divine soul, guides him in carrying out the acts sanctified by mystical rules, like the practice of vegetarianism, meditation, and spiritual tranquility. On the other hand, the *asynguá* suggests to a man that he may eat meat, commit sexual excesses, adultery, and so on. The *asynguá* is usually defined as "a sort of monkey which we carry on our shoulders and which we cannot see." This description and other attributes which it is held to posses show that it is seen as a sort of alter ego in animal form.

It is clear from the evidence that each group and subgroup has its own special way of characterizing the soul. However, they all coincide at two fundamental points: the identification of the soul with the spoken word and the existence of an internal duality — even in the tripartite conceptualizations — which governs the cultural definition of behavior as positive or negative.

Soul and Name

An individual's "vital word" and his name are closely linked, so much so that it is more precise to speak of a totality of soul and name rather than of a unification of the two. A name is not just the form by which a person is designated, the name *is* the person, given that it is the name of his soul and that his soul's attributes are his personal attributes as well. This identification is maintained until death and can only be modified in times of extreme crisis such as the approach of death. When an Avá-Chiripá is seriously ill, an attendant shaman, if there be one, will, as a last resort, change the individual's name to "put death off his track." When a dying man receives a new name and subsequently recovers, neither he, nor his family, nor the members of his community, will ever again say his old name since to do so would be to renew the threat of death.

The "vital words" of living beings are sent by the gods and it is the responsibility of the officiating shaman to decide which deity it is who is sending the new essence of life which will take shape and become incorporated into humanity. The "vital words" may come either from the abode of the gods or from the *ñe'eng-güery* [country of the dead] — the place of previous souls where live those who are destined for reincarnation.

In the ceremony of baptism, *mitá-mbó-ery* [naming of children], the officiating shaman, by means of his chants and his previous dreams, seeks to identify the name and provenance of the vital word in question. During the ritual the shaman sings to the accompaniment of his *mbaraká* [rattle], seeking divine inspiration and assisted by a prayer which the women intone. Not all shamans can officiate at this ceremony — only those who possess the "baptismal prayer," the *mitá-reno'i-há* [baptizers of children], who are able to invoke their "helping spirits" or the messenger birds which transmit the name.

The *mitá-mbó-ery* takes place in the so-called "season of good weather" (November-March) and is generally a collective affair with several children receiving their names at the same time. While the ceremony is taking place, the child's mother weeps as an expression of anguish. I could not determine, nor would they tell me, the exact reason for this. It is possible that the distress is provoked by fear that an error in the ritual or in the mother's behavior might cause an animal's soul to enter the child in which case he would be considered insane. Or, it could also be a ritual expression of anguish before the powers and forces in play and influencing her child. When the name has been identified, the shaman sprinkles the child with sap of *ygarí* [sacred cedar — *Cedrela fissilis*]. This second part of the ceremony is apparently syncretic with Christian baptism.

According to Cádogan (1968:101), the *apyaká* [zoomorphic stool] on which Nanderú Guazú and Tupá are seated is the Guarani symbol of incarnation and emblem of the animal kingdom to which man belongs. To be born is therefore "to take a seat" among humans, and this "taking of one's seat" is done on the *apyaká* made from the wood of the sacred cedar.

It has to be explained that, nowadays, Chiripá have two names. The first is the sacred soul name which they call *re'ra kaa'güy* [forest name] and which is used only in ceremonial and among the extended family. The second name, to which they attach no great importance, changing it frequently, is a Christian name which the parents themselves give to the child when it is born. When asked his name, a Chiripá will always give his "Christian" name, since knowledge of the other is forbidden to strangers. It was only after I had become extremely friendly with the Chiripá that I was told some of the *re'ra kaa'güy* of the individuals with whom I had most dealings. The most usual patronymics, for both men and women, are taken from animals, plants, or other sacred attributes: for example, Ava-Tapé [man who is the messenger bird of Tupá]; Avá-Nembiará [man who plays or jokes]; Kuñá Takuá Ywy Verá [woman bamboo of the shining earth], and so on. A man whose child has been baptized is referred to as *mitá-reno'i-há* [baptizer] with the title of *tyvasá* which Cádogan derives from *tovasá* [to give benediction] (1959:19).

Death and Resurrection

Then Kuarahy spoke again: "We shall try once more. I am going far away from this place while you must stay here quietly praying. When she begins to get up, pay no attention. Remain quietly where you are and do not call out 'Mother!' " But hardly had the flesh begun to develop on the bones, than Yacy ran toward them shouting, and the bones again fell to the ground. It is because of Yacy that we, too, are unable to rise up. It is Yacy's fault that we cannot live forever nor remain eternally young. Because of Yacy, Kuarahy could not raise up his mother. If he had succeeded in doing so, we should no longer have to die. It is because of Yacy that life comes to an end. . . .

In this fragment of the cycle of the twins which I recorded from Chiripá informants, it can be seen that death is not regarded as a "natural" phenomenon but as the result of the action of the cultural heroes in trying to revive their mother's bones after she had been killed by the jaguars. Yacy's conduct, from which death originates, cannot be regarded as a human sin, since human beings played no part in the events. Yet this mythical origin of death provides an explanation for its presence on the earth of the sort that legitimizes the forms of behavior that take place at death's approach.

In all the cases which I have witnessed, the dying man remains relatively calm while his kinsmen give themselves up to every imaginable manifestation of grief and pain. A shaman is usually present and, to the sound of his rattle, he intones a funeral chant whose rhythm increases as the sick man draws closer to death. The shaman's chant serves to guide the dead man's divine soul (vital word), which must now leave the body and attempt to return to the abode of the deity by whom it was sent.

Different types of souls have different fates. The *ñe'eng* [divine vital word] has to pass through a series of tests before it can make its way to the home of the deity who sent it, or arrive at the *oka-yusú* [paradise]. For the Apapokuvá (Nimuendajú 1944:20–21) the divine soul must pass near the dwelling of the *añag*, one of whom is asleep in his hammock; should the soul waken him, it will be devoured. After clearing this obstacle, the soul arrives at the place where Urukera, and owl, lives. On seeing it the owl screeches and summons the souls of all the other dead, which receive the new arrival with a great show of affection, but are reluctant to let it leave again preferring that it should stay and live with them as it did on Earth. The only souls which pass freely are those of children since they have no *tekó-achy* [imperfections] to impede their flight. The more imperfections a soul has accumulated in its earthly life, the more difficult will it be for it to traverse these obstacles.

The negative part of the soul, the *asynguá*, the earthly soul with its many imperfections, is transformed into the *angüery* [the spirit of death], which roams the earth molesting the living, causing disease, madness, and even death. The main purpose of the *angüery* is to usurp the place of the divine soul in a living person whom it therefore torments in the hope that his *ñe'eng* will flee before its presence. Nothing is more feared by the Chiripá than these *angüery* which wander through the forest and near the burial places of those to whom they belonged. One precautionary measure is to treat a dying person with all possible attention and show great grief so that his *angüery* will not be able to bear a grudge. It is thanks only to the most complex rituals, requiring the presence of a shaman, that an *angüery* can be persuaded to move away from the neighborhood of the living, at least temporarily, or to stop molesting them. Nevertheless, however hard an *angüery* tries, it can never be reincarnated.

Only the *ñe'eng* can be reincarnated (*oikove yevi*) and only in certain circumstances. One of these arises when the dead man himself has desired reincarnation, if for example he has left loved ones behind on Earth or died without fulfilling a great ambition. They can also obtain reincarnation in cases of violent death, or if a shaman was not present at the moment of death to assist the *ñe'eng* on its journey to the beyond. These divine souls are those which, according to the Apapokuvá, are detained by the owl and reunited with those who have died earlier. Their dwelling place is known to the Chiripá as *ñe'eng-güery*, which can literally be translated as "country of the dead." It is here that the divine "vital words" await an opportunity to be reincarnated and be born again from a human womb.

In those cases where a reincarnation occurs in the course of a baptism, the shaman lets this fact be known at once and informs both the child's parents and the relations of the reincarnated person. Reincarnation most often takes place between members of the same family and as such may be considered an expression of lineage continuity (Eliade 1970:108).

For the Apapokuvá (Nimuendajú 1944:24), when a reincarnated child dies soon after birth, this is because he returned to visit his kinsmen and could not readapt to earthly life. Among the Ñandeva (Schaden 1954:130), there are propitiatory ceremonies to induce reincarnation of those souls to whom it has not occurred. During these ceremonies, the shaman is transported in his dreams to the country of the divine souls of unborn and stillborn children and selects one of them for the reincarnation.

The notion of reincarnation is closely allied to the pre-Hispanic cult of the dead, traces of which still remain among some groups, especially the conservative Mbya. The clean, unfleshed bones of the dead are kept in baskets and prayers are offered to them. Only when it seems certain that no reincarnation is taking place are the bones buried (Cádogan 1951:198–202). Although the Chiripá bury their dead quickly, in some tribal communities the bones of important shamans are kept for a time (this practice was observed during the time of the conquest) in the hope of reincarnation or failing that, of the soul finding a way back to Earth.

Paradise and the Land Without Evil

These two concepts are of great importance in Chiripá society although the two ideas often merge, probably as a result of early missionary influence.

The Chiripá paradise is called *oka-vusú* (Cádogan 1968:83); on the verge of the road which leads to it grow the divine archetypes of all the edible or useful plants to be found on earth. Among these plants is the *mandyjú* [eternal cotton] from whose cocoons Nandé Cy sits weaving in the shade of the eternal palm, with her son Tupá beside her. This paradise is situated in the celestial regions and it is to it that unblemished divine souls make their way.

Those who do not succeed in entering *oka-vusú* remain in the *ñe'eng-güery* to which I have already referred, whither the shamans go in their dreams to seek advice from their sponsors and the great shamans who have died. Both *oka-vusú* and *ñe'eng-güery* are dwelling places of the dead and communicate with the Earth by means of the *axis mundi* represented by the eternal palm since both are celestial places.

Unlike *oka-vusú* and *ñe'eng-güery*, the *ywy mará ey* [land without evil] is situated *on this Earth*, away to the east, and to arrive there one must cross the *pará guazú rapytá* [great primeval sea]. It is in this mythical concept that we find the justification for the sacred nature of the cedar (*ygarí*), whose wood was used to make the canoes in which the migrations in search of the land without evil took place. The *ywy mará ey* is a place of abundance and prosperity where everyone can have his plot and work for excellent harvests without worrying about the future. Immortality is possible there and life proceeds under the protection of the "saviors" and the "great shamans." One need not die to reach this place, on the contrary, only the living can inhabit it. However, in order to have the right to gain the land without evil, an immense exercise in spiritual endeavor is necessary. This requires special techniques of concentration extending over the hours of sleep as well as periods of consciousness. It is also essential to maintain a strict diet of an almost totally vegetarian kind. As a result of both these practices and by a strict observance of ritual and sacred rules, the human body frees itself from its physical weight and the "animal" part of the soul from all its imperfections. Lightness of body and soul is the essential factor in reaching the state of *agüyjé* [spiritual perfection] after which comes the even more inaccessible state of *kandire*. When a man *is* or *is becoming kandire*, flames spring from his chest as evidence that his heart is illuminated by divine wisdom (*tatá-chiná*). Only then can a man reach the land without evil by flying over the great primeval sea (Cádogan 1950:242).

For all the Avá-Katú-Eté and especially for their shamans, to achieve the state of *agüyjé* is, at once, the purpose and the final goal of human life. This is why they insist on the urgent need to observe to the full the religious, moral, and social precepts which govern human life.

The *ywy mará ey* was the goal of all the messianic Guarani migrations pre- and post-Hispanic. Its characteristics finally came to include the total absence of whites and Creoles, so that it was a "promised land" exclusively for the Guarani. One of the main obstacles which, at the present time, prevent a Chiripé man or shaman from achieving the much desired state of *agüyjé* is the increasing pressure of the regional and national population. The Creoles and whites impede or scoff at the rituals and this inhibits strict observance of religious and social traditions. They also introduce strange and profane foods like noodles, olive oil, fats and — as always — alcohol. All of these contribute to the increase in *tekó-achy* [imperfections] since they were not specially created for men by any god or cultural hero. Thus we can see how the pressures of the dominant society attack the philosophical bases of Indian life and permeate the metaphysical aspects of Indian culture.

The Saviors

The saviors to whom I have already referred owe their exemplary character to the fact of having achieved *agüyjé*, thereby becoming capable of leading their people to the land without evil. The saviors include both mythological and historical figures, for they sometimes count among their number the great shamans and chiefs who led the initial struggle against

the Spaniards and those who, later, kindled the revolts against the conquistadores.

The presence and importance of the saviors is related to one of the
constant themes of Chiripá and Guarani religion in general, namely, the
ever-present threat of the end of the world, or *ará-kañí* [the fleeing of the
light]. Religious conversation turns continually on this theme:

> The Sun will disappear and then there will be nothing for us to do on this Earth.
> This will be the moment of the *ará-kañí*. This will be our last day, the time that
> we shall see this Earth . . .

The threat of the *ará-kañí* grows daily with the increase of *tekó-achy*
among men who observe the sacred, mystic rules less and less. The danger
of apocalyptic destruction and the land without evil as a place of refuge
determine the need for the saviors. The first kind of savior is one who has
achieved *agüyjé* and has been empowered to travel to the land without
evil, as he appears in the following account related by the Chiripá chief,
Avá-Nembiará:

> Our ancestor departed in life without dying, and left no trail for us to follow. It is
> he who thunders in the east, he who departed with our human body and, while he
> who went away, dances, we too shall dance. . . . Long ago the chief danced and his
> feet did not touch the Earth. This is why, in order to dance, we must not eat meat
> but only those things which Nanderú has commanded us (Bartolomé 1969a:57).

The other type of savior is from the ranks of historical chiefs and shamans
who have been deified and incorporated in this way into the mystical
period of man's origins. This is, for example, the case of Avá-Canindé, a
real-life chief whose deeds are recounted by a Chiripá chief as follows:

> Avá-Canindé remained when everything had been destroyed. He was the
> strongest of all. He fought with everyone who lived on the Earth. He fought with
> the Avá-Juguay, with the Guaná and with the jaguars. He fought with them all
> and conquered them all. Men said that he was Nanderú because everyone feared
> him (Bartolomé 1969a:58).

Here it can be seen that mythological time has been merged with historical time and subsequently unified in the same metahistorical period.

THE GUARANI SHAMAN

The Historical Importance of the Shaman in the Guarani Culture

The oldest records which we possess concerning Guarani shamanism are
to be found in the chronicles of Thevet, Lery, Staden, and others. These

were recopied and analyzed by Métraux (1928) and refer to the Tupinambá of the Atlantic coast of Brazil.

According to these chronicles, the rank of shaman among the Tupinambá was not attained by initiation but by divine revelation. However, if there were many in each tribe who were granted the revelation or inspiration, only a very few reached the highest levels of the shamanistic hierarchy. These could be attained only through the efficacy of supernatural powers. All the others who "felt the call" were no more than second-class shamans in the face of the enormous prestige which a really distinguished shaman eventually came to possess. When an individual revealed an exceptional magical power, his relations with the other members of the community underwent great changes. He withdrew into solitude, he became extremely grave in character, he spoke little, and so on. When he developed this demeanor the community held him in great respect and all but venerated him. It was the same with the chiefs who consulted him in all affairs of state.

The principal functions of the shaman were to ensure fertility and safeguard crops from disease; to bring the rains; to cure the sick; to foretell the future by means of his dreams; and so on. There were also negative aspects to his power, for he could induce pestilence, disease, or death in his enemies, always taking into account the support of his "helping spirits" which could be either "spirits of nature" or those of the dead with whom he communicated.

Thevet observes (1878:174) that the Tupinambá exhibited great fear and reverence toward their shamans. When a shaman of renown returned from a voyage or visited a village, the people cleaned the path where he was going to walk and everyone pressed to meet him to present requests and seek his advice.

One of the attributes of the Tupinambá shaman was his ability to transmit his magic power by allowing it to travel along tobacco smoke or on his breath. The disciples who received the "magic breath" immediately manifested great emotional disturbance and their bodies were shaken by tremors as forces of great magnitude began to operate on them. Such demonstrations would allow the shaman to increase his authority.

In eastern Paraguay, the large units of settlement (*teko'a*) were organized under different systems of leadership which determined their internal and external dynamic, the impetus toward expansion, and their conservative tendency. There were warrior chiefs, agricultural chiefs, and shamanistic chiefs. The *teko'a* led by agricultural chiefs had a tendency toward conservatism in terms of their territory and size. On the other hand, settlements led by warriors generated a dynamic of expansionism with a tendency to incorporate the greatest possible number of hands for cultivation, thus increasing their economic and numerical strength.

The most prestigious shaman, the *paí guazú*, disputed these leaderships and became the absolute chief of his people (Susnik 1969:107). Thus while the warrior chief was organizing his council of war the great shaman assembled his council of shamans, whose decisions were much more important than those of the warriors. The same author emphasizes that the shamans participated in sociopolitical life by means of the powers invested in them, among which was one of fundamental importance for an agricultural people, that of control over crops (Susnik 1969:18).

This economic control at the magico-religious level was the determining factor in their assumption of outright leadership of a community which depended on agriculture for its survival. Métraux (1967:14) suggests that it is almost possible to speak of a theocratic system among the Guarani of Paraguay, but he also stresses that the term *theocratic* is not very apposite to the much looser social structure of the Guarani.

The Shamans and the Conquest

After a series of military encounters, the Jesuits came. They were entrusted with the task of pacifying the Guarani. The well-developed sense of the sacred which these tribes possessed made them first of all reject, and then accept, the preaching of the Gospel, whilst the same notion of the sacred allowed their own cosmic vision to persist in the very heart of the missions. When we trace this process we can see the figure of the shaman as the chief protagonist in Guarani resistance to change in their traditions and socioreligious system. Rejection of the Gospel as the basis of shamanistic activity is documented by the chronicler Nicolás del Techo (1897: vol. 3, p. 227) in the following account:

Before the foundation of Santa María la Mayor by fathers Ruger and Boroa, they were resisted by a sorcerer, who painted his body most terrifyingly and to whom the devil frequently appeared, sometimes in the form of a tiger. He would present himself to the fathers and suggest to them, in different voices, that they should not uproot the customs of the country.

There are numerous such examples of the shamans' resistance to Christian teaching even when the latter had begun and was well under way:

The sorcerer, Niezú commanded that the baptized children be brought to him, and, disdaining the sacrament, he washed them with warm water as if to erase its effects. He also scraped their tongues with a rough shell because of the holy salt which had been placed there. . . . Then he initiated them into idolatry with certain rites. He pretended that his body was giving off a liquor of some kind with which he anointed the children while their mothers performed a sacred dance (del Techo 1897: vol. 3, p. 333).

Missionary preaching only started to become really effective when, later on, a few shamans accepted Christianity and life in the reductions. Del Techo confirms this:

Father Simón Mazeta, besides *reducing* numerous Indians, converted a famous magician who burnt to the ground the village where he had lived and brought its inhabitants to San Ignacio. Not only did the former sorcerer do this, but having sworn many Indians against the missionaries, he now contained them with his authority (1897: vol. 4, p. 221).

Factors (other than fear of the land trustees) which contributed to the initial success of the missions were the fact that preaching was done in the native tongue; and the stand which the missionaries took on the idea of paradise and the continual allusion to salvation (Saguier and Clastres 1969:25). As I have said, these concepts were already present in the tribal religion, so that it was relatively easy to see the Jesuit priests as bearers of a new cult whose eschatology could be identified with the local one; who communicated with their gods by means of complex rituals; and some of whom, having a knowledge of contemporary Spanish medicine, effected cures with remedies which were strange but nevertheless included prayers and benedictions.

None of this excluded the periodic recurrence of "paganism" among the shamans, who felt themselves to have been displaced, and the groups which managed to coalesce around them. Thus the messianic revolt of Overá was started and there was an increase in migrations led by shamans who had achieved *agüyjé* and who received divine inspiration in their dreams.

The Guarani quickly began to understand that their ancient order was starting to crumble inside the missions. The only people capable of restoring this sacred, traditional order were the shamans, above all the great shamans who had died before the advent of Christianity and who were therefore the archetypal sustainers of the social and cosmic order of mankind. Thus various cults arose, one of them observed by de Montoya (1892:112), who describes how the bones of the dead shaman Yryvutú were worshiped in the hills of Ivytirizú. A hut had been erected there, and inside it, the shaman's bones were kept, wrapped in a hammock covered with a mantle of feathers. Next to the head, another shaman distributed fruit among the sowers, as amulets to ensure the fertility of the soil. As one might suppose, when this was discovered by the Jesuits, hut, bones, and all were destroyed.

Throughout the missionary period the attempts of the shamans to reinstate the old order were as futile as they were dramatic. Despite various efforts, they only managed to begin the process of reimplantation when the missions came to an end in 1767. But the struggle to maintain this process continues right up to the present.

AVÁ-CHIRIPÁ SHAMANISM

The brief summary of information which precedes this section, ambitious in the range it tries to cover, is simply an attempt to introduce us to the universe of the Avá-Katú-Eté. I wish to make it clear that in analyzing a phenomenon like shamanism both factual information as well as imaginative interpretation have a part to play. Shamanism, in spite of its clear social role and the sociological interpretations to which it lends itself, is nevertheless a cultural manifestation whose study goes beyond the limits of observation and investigation. It requires a continual process of drawing inferences from the data. These inferences involve a measure of subjectivity on the part of the investigator who reveals his own experience of the phenomenon.

The Origins of Shamanism

According to Jenson (1966:267), the mystical foundation of shamanism is related to the communication which it establishes with the beyond. There is confirmation of this in the cycle of the twins where Kuarahy employs shamanistic practice in order to communicate with his father Nanderú Guazú: he makes a rattle (*mbaraká*) and dances until his father takes him away with him.

Although communication with the beyond is only one facet of shamanistic activity, the code of conduct, as presented in the mythology, allows the shaman access to the source of his own powers. In this, as in all other respects, the shaman's conduct recalls that of the cultural hero. The heroes established the religious and social order on Earth and the primary function of the shaman is to maintain the continuity of this order, in his capacity as a representative of the divine scheme. As Balandier (1969:117) shows, the relation between power and society is one which carries religious connotations since all human society links its own social order to a transcendent order of cosmic origin. In short, the shaman's power is seen to consist of forces derived from the powers that rule the universe and maintain earthly and human order. He is the mediator between men and the sacred origins of the world order while being charged at the same time with the preservation of that order.

One of the names given to their shamans by the Avé-Chiripá is *Nandé rú* [our father]. The significance of this is sufficiently explicit to require no further explanation. Another, much commoner term is *paí*. The meaning of this is much more ambiguous, but one explanation is that offered by Egon Schaden (1954:120), who points out that the word *paí* is linked etymologically to *mair*, the term applied to the French by the Tupinambá, and to *mbai*, the term applied by the Paraguayan Guarani to the Spanish.

Mair and *mbai* are both shortened forms of *mbae-ira*: "the solitary one," "the one set apart," "he who lives far away." Later *mbai* was transformed into *paí*, by reason of the common transposition of *mb* to *p* which takes place in Guarani — witness *mborahei* [song] to *porahei*. It thus transpires that the *paí* of the Chiripá is the "solitary one," the man who lives on the threshold between the world above and the world below, midway between man and the gods.

As far as the shaman's apparel is concerned, there is reference to it in this fragment of the twin cycle related to me by my Chiripá informants:

Nanderú Guazú took his *mbaraká*, put his *yasaa* on his chest, his *poapi-guaá* on his arm and his *acaan-guaá* on his head. He added to these all his ornaments of *guaá* [parrot] feathers and also carried his *kuruzú-ipoty*.

When Nanderú Guazú ceded to his son Kuarahy a portion of his powers, he also granted him the use of his apparel and this, in its turn, is used by the shaman who represents the figure of the cultural hero. The *yasaa* is a sash of cotton plaited with feather ornaments, which is worn across the chest; the *poapi-guaá* is a bracelet of the same materials; the *acaan-guaá* is a tiara of multicolored feathers which is placed on the head and, finally, the *kuruzú-ipoty* is the feathered cross which is sometimes replaced by a handful of large, red feathers.

However, the basic shamanistic tool is the *mbaraká*, the ritual rattle, whose use in Guarani culture is attested by references as old as the texts synthesized by Métraux (1928) from the chroniclers of the Tupinambá. For the Tupinambá, the *mbaraká* was the receptable of a spirit and was held in the hand or on the ground with the aid of an arrow which pierced the gourd from side to side. According to the chroniclers, the *mbaraká* owes its importance and its sacred character to the fact that its sound was interpreted as the message of the spirit which inhabited it.

This practice, known of the Tupinambá nearly four hundred years ago, is still very much in force among the Avá-Chiripá with the exception that they do not pierce the gourd with an arrow, but with a wooden rod decorated at the top with a handful of feathers. For the Chiripá, the *mbaraká* does not only contain a spirit but can invoke others by means of the sound produced by the little fruit inside it. The small, black fruit used are those of the shrub known as *ibahú*, the archetype of which is to be found in *oka-yusú* [paradise].

León Cádogan (1962:48–49) suggests that the *mbaraká* receive messages from Nanderú Mbaé-Kua'a, and thus are the repositories of divine wisdom. Every adult male of the tribe has a *mbaraká* which he uses during rituals, but these lack the "potency" of the shaman's *mbaraká*.

Recruitment

In his classic work on the Apapokuvá [the people of the long bow], Nimuendajú says:

The *paí* of the Apapokuvá differs in various ways from his colleagues in other tribes. The most important difference is that no one can become a *paí* by apprenticeship, not even under the direction of the great initiates. It has to be by inspiration. It must not be thought that the *paí* constitute a closed or hereditary caste (1944:43).

Notwithstanding, among the present-day Chiripá, of whom the Apapokuvá are a migratory subgroup, it is possible to accede to shamanism through teaching and apprenticeship although neither is as decisive as divine revelation. In many cases, election and inspiration go together but it is possible to become a shaman by inspiration alone. In addition, selection and apprenticeship must later be followed by divine revelation in order that the existence of a new *paí* may be confirmed.

In most cases, selection of an heir by a prestigious shaman is simply the confirmation of a vocation which the individual has already manifested. This vocation is revealed in his personal behavior, in the observance of the socioreligious rules, and by participation in the *ñemboé kaagüy* [prayer of the forest], a ritual to which I shall refer later and which is the most important collective ceremony of the group. Ritual, as ordered and led by shamans, apart from its many social and religious functions, carries a commitment of a pedagogical nature. It must teach the religious songs and dances to the young. In this way, ceremonial has some of the characteristics of a school of religion in which young people participate entirely voluntarily. It is therefore normal for the most exceptional graduates of this school to be chosen as disciples or heirs by those shamans who feel or know that their own end is near. The young man so chosen may not refuse to assume his new role and, indeed, when one takes religious vocation into account, it is unlikely that he would do so . On the other hand, given the prestige which shamanism enjoys, it may be that someone who does not feel a true vocation may consider himself obliged to take the first steps along the difficult road which he must travel before being considered a *paí*.

It is possible that the choosing of an heir, a practice which contradicts Nimuendajú's account (1944), is a relatively recent phenomenon which can be explained in terms of the Chiripá's strong reaction to cultural assimilation. In this respect, the choosing of heirs would be a way of forcing the young to continue tribal traditions and avoiding the westernizing influences of the regional society. This would be yet another example of the way in which the Chiripá's quest for survival is based on the legendary figure of the shaman.

Yet, regional and national society continue to exert pressures on the indigenous culture and the shaman also has to consider how to respond to this penetration, especially as it is now not possible to respond in terms of a new messianic migration or some warlike alternative. As the shaman is responsible for the social cohesion and cultural continuity of the group as well as being mediator between his community and the universe, at the present time he must be capable of giving direction to his people in dealing with the new relationships arising from the situation of contact. These relationships are not only economic; they exist at every level, produce chaos and conflict in the Indian's universe, and make reality seem daily more unfamiliar and hazardous.

This mention of what we may call the shaman's intercultural role will serve to justify my description of the ritual of initiation since I myself was chosen as his heir by the *paí guazú* [great shaman] of the village, Canuto Sales (Avá-Nembiará). The others chosen were Ricardo Ezcurra, the young Creole who lived in the community, and Bruno Sales, the *paí guazú*'s grandson and the only member of the group to undergo military service (through the influence of the DAI). When I asked Avá-Nembiará why I had been chosen, seeing that I was not Chiripá and did not even speak their language well, he replied that since I had all the knowledge of the *karaí* ["whites," literally "masters"] and since he in the course of our interviews had taught me many of the "things of the Avá-Katú-Eté," I was well equipped to become a great *paí* of unrivaled knowledge. The same could be applied to Ricardo Ezcurra who had completed primary school, and to his grandson Bruno who had learned to read, write, and speak Spanish in the army. It is therefore clear that he hoped our function would be to act as mediators between the tribe and the regional society. Such a function could only be carried out by men who could sail in the frontier seas of both worlds, the Western and the traditional.

Initiation

I shall now describe my own initiation as it actually took place. It corresponds to that of my companions as we discovered when we exchanged notes about our experiences. I have elected to describe my own, since, as might be expected, it is the one of which I can give the most direct account.

I returned to Colonia Fortuna one day with a colleague, Odin Toness, after a short trip to Asunción. Avá Nembiará received me with a show of great happiness telling me that he had dreamed of my return and had even known that I would be accompanied by a friend. On the following day, while we were talking at the door of his hut, he revealed to me that he wished to designate me as his successor for the reasons already mentioned.

When I had accepted his proposal, he led me into his house in the company of Ricardo Ezcurra, allowing no one to enter except the large number of doves who shared it with him. Once inside, he made me sit on a kind of stool made from crisscrossed strips of deerskin. He took his seat on my right while Ezcurra remained standing. Immediately, he opened my shirt and began to breathe on my chest intoning all the while a *guaú eté* [sacred song] in the form of a litany. While he was praying, he acted as if he was holding something in his right hand and appeared to take this thing with his left hand drawing it along the trajectory of his breath. (This thing was subsequently described to me as a "kind of flower." This operation continued for about fifteen minutes after which he spread over the stool a *yasaa* [sash] to which he attached a small bunch of parrot feathers without ceasing to intone his litany. Then he took the sash, breathed on it, and placed it on my chest. Then he began to trace circles above my head with both hands whilst still continuing to pray. At the conclusion of this brief rite, Avá Nembiará, in a state of great emotion which I fully shared, enjoined me never to be parted from the *yasaa*. I did not have to use it continuously but I had to put it on from time to time. The most important precaution I had to take was never to have sexual intercourse while wearing the sash.

On the following day, he invited me to go hunting with him, but halfway through the morning, and after bagging a few pieces, he told me that hunting had only been a pretext to allow us to be alone in the forest. We then sat on an old tree trunk and he asked me to think about the animals I had just killed. He made no suggestion as to whether it had been a negative or a positive act; he simply invited me to reflect upon it and we remained, thus, in silence, for half an hour. Then, almost until nightfall, he spoke to me of the destiny which he hoped would be mine from that moment on. He told me what my attitude toward life should be and that it was preferable that my diet be chiefly vegetarian. He stressed that a *paí*'s mission is to help rather than deceive the people, that he should never commit evil deeds, and that, when I became a healer, my acts should be governed only by love (*sic*). He also indicated to me that my faith had to grow, without specifying any deity, and that I must transmit it to the people so that they could all respect me. I should avoid excess of both alcohol and women and try to get the *karaí* [whites] to help *our* people. This last detail was very significant for he used the term *ñandé* [we (inclusive)] and not *oré* [we (exclusive)]. He thus included me in his own community.

He then told me that his sacred prayers had been taught to him during the journeys which he made to the *ñe'eng-güeri* [country of the dead] by means of his dreams. He predicted that when he died I would have my first dream in which he would appear and speak to me, teaching me my first prayer and my personal chant. The dream would provoke great anguish in me and I would cry on awakening while trying to remember the chant. After the dream, however, I would be able to use bunches of feathers all along my shaman's sash as a symbol of my higher rank. The song which I would receive would be the one which I should always use to call him (invoke his divine soul) before I went to sleep and he would appear in my dreams to offer me his advice and to help with the problem which had been presented to me. However, if my prayers were to be effective they had to be preceded by noble and correct behavior, like a deep meditation in which I should evoke his image.

Shamanistic knowledge would be revealed to me through his teaching, but the chief source of knowledge would be the messages which I would receive in dreams. This would be the case until I had enough "wisdom" (lightness, purity) to be able to travel in my dreams to the country of the dead where I would have access to the wisdom of other dead shamans as well as to his. The process would continue through the years until my knowledge was such that I could receive visits from the *mainó*, the sacred hummingbird, messenger of the sun. He would give me still more wisdom until I could communicate with the "spirits of all things" (plants and animals) and have a "helper" (auxiliary spirit) who would collaborate with me. With the passage of time and as my knowledge increased, I would be entitled to use the double crossed band of feathers which indicates the highest shamanistic rank, that of the *paí guazú*. When my knowledge was such that I could act as a healer, I would also employ sleep. For example, if I did not know the right treatment for a sick person, I would have to intone my chant with great sincerity, to the sound of the *mbaraká*, a present from him, before going to sleep. As I slept the treatment would be revealed to me. Should it be necessary to use herbs, the dream would tell me which ones and where they could be found. On the following day, I should go to the place indicated and if I did not find the herb immediately it would be pointed out to me by means of a *sign* of some kind, like a broken branch, or a bird sitting on the plant in question. Avá Nembiará then gave me an immediate demonstration of his own exceptional knowledge as a herbalist, by beginning to gather all the plants about us, calling each by its name and mentioning its specific qualities. For that day we were united in a relationship of sponsor and protégé.

The Acquisition of Powers

As we have seen, initiation must be followed by mystical experience taking place during sleep, in the course of which a man acquires his shamanistic chant. Realizing that I shall probably never experience it, I shall illustrate it by means of separate accounts which I have collected.

Bruno Sales, who was initiated by his grandfather during a period of leave from the army, had an abortive revelation when he returned to barracks. One night, the late *paí* Juan Martinez, whose assistant Bruno had been in the *ñemboé kaagüy* [prayer of the forest], appeared to him. When he awoke, in a state of great anguish, he could not remember the chant he had received because it was not possible for him to recite it in the company of his kinsfolk, collective praying by the extended family being necessary for the proper receipt of the chant. At the moment, Bruno does not expect to be given a second opportunity.

In the case of another shaman of the tribe, Quirino Lopez (Avá-Tupá-Karaí) the mystic experience took place with no difficulty since he could count on the company of his family and friends, as he tells us in his own account:

Yhiapú guasuva [the great sound] is in the east and Tupá is in the west. During my sleep I talked with Tupá who ordered me to be a *paí* among my people. That day I began to pray in the morning and my people began to surround me. There were my people all around me. Then I told them all why I was praying, told them that I had spoken with Tupá. That day there was a feast with chicha to which all my neighbors came. My neighbors came to the feast which is called *aty-guazú* and from that day I became a *paí*.

Similarly, in another account, Adriano Portillo (Avá-Tapé), chief of one of the bands which make up Fortuna and a *paí* of lower rank, tells how he received his prayer:

Nanderú Guazú sent me a messenger to teach me to pray. For this is our life, because prayer is the only thing of value on this Earth. It is for this reason that the messenger came to me so that I could remain, so to speak, Nanderú's envoy on this Earth, so that I could look after the people and instruct them in their dealings with earthly matters. In order that I may know the designs of Nanderú Guazú, I must not eat meat or fat, and I must carry out his orders so that I may care for my people. He made me listen to his prayer so that I could chant it. In my dream he made me listen to it, and so I prepared and made ready my ears. My kinsfolk came and made preparations for me to pray. They placed lighted candles of beeswax around me, and then I was able to pray and the god released me. It is thus that we live on this Earth and my people ask for my advice and I try to give them satisfaction. I follow the orders of Nanderú Guazú and, in my dreams, he listens to me and gives me knowledge.

The great shamans who have died can also appear during sleep to make revelations to future shamans. This happened in the case of Florencio Portillo (Avá-Tapé):

In my dreams I saw Avá-Mainó and Avá-Guiracambí. They were *paí* like ourselves and did all kinds of good works, caring for the sick, and things like that. I saw them dressed in dirty, old clothes, holding in their left hands the *mbaraká*, and in their right hands the *kuruzú ypoty* [feathered cross]. They had *poapi-guaá* on their arms, *yasaa* on their chests, and *acaan-guaá* on their heads. They were sent by Kuarahy to tell me that I had to be a *paí* of the cult on this Earth.

In some other cases, the acquisition of the shamanistic chant takes on the characteristics of the "magic flight," as can be seen in this unusual account given by my sponsor, Avá-Nembiará:

I walk a little way, toward the east, and there I see a beautiful house with its doors all the same. I arrived there, at this place which we call *ñe'eng-güeri* [country of the dead]. It was there in *ñe'eng-güeri* that I learned my prayer. There I met my brother-in-law and my grandfather. My brother-in-law took hold of my left arm and my grandfather took hold of my right and together they revealed to me the ladder which joins earth and sky. Then I noticed that there was dancing, and the place of the dancing was the beautiful house like a church of the type attended by you [whites]. Then I asked what it was and my sponsors told me that it was the place where prayers are learned — I can hardly tell you about these things since merely thinking about them makes me want to weep. As the dancers turned toward us, I noticed that there were no young men or women among them. Therefore I do not like to look at the women when I am praying since, in prayer, we are concerned with things of true worth. After I had seen the men dance, I looked toward the sun in the east. I looked to see if it was going to rain but I knew that it was not going to rain. In the midst of all this, I was taken to a mountain to hear the chant. On descending I saw a dead man in a pit. The body was distended and flies swarmed round his grave. Then my sponsors, who were still with me, said to me, "Protégé, you are the one who must cure this man," to which I replied that I could not since I did not know how. Then my sponsors made me listen to the prayer which I had to say [at this point he chants a little and sobs a little saying that in telling these things, he relives the experience] and made me walk three times round the tomb. I chanted and breathed on him and the man was cured. It had been a man who had been buried there in the forest and he arose and began to speak. Sometimes Our Father, when he hears these prayers, will even restore the dead to life. On the following day, I chanted early in the morning as I had been taught and every night my sponsors showed the remedies by which I could cure the sick. To get this knowledge I went to the east and that is how I know the love of all things.

As these accounts show, the revelation of shamanistic powers, and the receipt of the chant which will serve as the basis of the shaman's activities by allowing him to communicate with the gods, take place in two ways. The first, illustrated in the cases of Bruno Sales, Quirino Lopez, Florencio Portillo, and Adriano Portillo, consists of a passive acceptance of the enlightenment and source of divine power as transmitted by Nanderú Guazú's emissaries, Tupá and Kuarahy, or by the great shamans of the past. The second method, as related by Avá-Nembiará, also takes place during sleep but the attitude of the shaman-elect is clearly an active one since he is transported by "magic flight" to the "country of the dead" where he receives the power from the spirits of two of his kinsmen (themselves shamans during their lifetime) who sponsor him. Yet both types of experience have a number of characteristics in common and merge at certain points; both take place during sleep with the participation of emissaries or "auxiliary spirits" who execute the transmission of the prayer or act as intermediaries in the process.

It is the reception of the chant which initiates shamanistic power. Thereafter, the higher or lower rank bestowed upon initiates depends on the effectiveness of their powers of healing and prophecy. Social consensus, in its turn, has a role in determining this.

The Chants

Before going any further, it is necessary to define some of the principal characteristics of shamanistic chants and prayers. Although Nimuendajú (1944) calls them "chants of the *paí*," all my informants referred to them as *guaú* [sacred songs], clearly distinguished from the *koti-hú* [profane songs]. *Guaú* in their turn can be either *guaú eté* [true sacred songs] or *guaú-aí* [little sacred songs]. In the first, the words are unintelligible, even to those who say them, and in Cádogan's opinion (1959:13) constitute the remains of a sacred language whose meaning has been lost. Archaic Guarani terms are often used in the *guaú-aí*. The interpretation of these both by Guarani scholars and by the people themselves is ambiguous, neither party being able to agree as to the meaning of them.

In any event, and as my informants assured me, the words have less importance than the *tone* of the chant as it is received during sleep. It is this that defines the individual nature of the personal *guaú*. During my stay among the Avá-Chiripá, I had the opportunity to record many *guaú* and to listen to many more belonging to different individuals and shamans. In a great number of cases these personal *guaú* consist of the repetition of a single word *engay*. Cádogan (1959:21) translates this as "yearning." This word is repeated continually but with great changes in rhythm and melody in each individual case. Sometimes, the chants mention Nanderú Guazú, Tupá, or Kuarahy.

Every man or woman possesses, or can possess, a lifelong personal chant or prayer. In terms of chants and prayers, the people of Fortuna can be divided into four groups, as can the Apapokuvá (Nimuendajú 1944:41). The first group is made up of those, of either sex and any age, who have no personal chants and only sing the collective chants during rituals. The second group consists of those who possess a chant but one of limited use; they perform them in ceremonies or at times of personal or social crisis, invoking the deity from whom the chants are derived. The third, much smaller, group is composed of those who can be included in the category of shaman by reason of having received "power" at the same time as their chant; they can use it in healing practices and in helping to lead collective ceremonies. The fourth group, which has few members, consists of the *paí-guazú* [great shamans], the only people with the power to initiate and lead ceremonies and to function, too, as prophets, doctors, and spiritual leaders of their people.

The difference between the chants of individuals and those of the shaman is basically a difference of "potency." The shaman's chant is more potent than those of noninitiates. This "potency" comes from the fact that the performer of the chant is a person who possesses a special "mystic force." The rhythm heard in sleep is closely bound up with mystical experience and with it is associated the receipt of the chant and shamanistic power, so that the shaman's experience is of a much more intense kind, both individually and culturally, than that of noninitiates — that is to say that the shaman legitimizes his activity by linking it to an experience which is seen and lived out as reality. Thus the shamanistic chant is a resurrection and revival of the sanctity which is present when he sees and has contact with the divine messengers who present themselves to him.

Finally, I must point out that each individual chant is performed to the same deity who either appeared or sent his messengers to bestow it in the dream. Thus Chiripá shamans dedicate their chants to Yacy, Kuarahy, Tupá, or Nanderú Guazú. The shamanistic chant or prayer is like a bridge which permits communication between the world above and the world below. By means of this, the shamans can carry out their various activities and also increase their knowledge through their relationship with godly wisdom.

THE SHAMAN AS HEALER

The factor which most contributes to a shaman's reputation and to his ascendancy in terms of rank is the success of his cures. As his reputation as a healer increases, the whole community reacts by seeking to establish friendly relations with him, offering him presents and treating him with great respect. The growing prestige of the acknowledged healer allows him to climb the shamanistic ladder right up to the rank of *paí guazú*.

Of all shamanistic functions it is that of healer which constitutes one of the most important forms of group solidarity and cohesion, given that the whole community is conscious of the fact that the negative forces of nature can be controlled by one of its members. This awareness strengthens the bonds of union between the separate extended families which make the tribe. They know that the presence of a *paí guazú* provides constant reassurance as far as their relations with their environment are concerned and are aware that the forces of that environment can attack the whole group as well as individuals.

The Concept of Illness

The Chiripá distinguish between two basic types of illness: (1) the result of increased discord between the "negative" and the "positive" souls; and (2) the result of the activities of the "spirits of nature." In the first case, responsibility rests with the individual, whose improper social behavior increases the imperfections of his "animal" soul to the point where it becomes overloaded with "negative forces" which have to be removed before he can be cured. The second type is a case of a negative element or substance being introduced into the body by the "spirits of nature" who invisibly attack, taking advantage of the circumstantial weakness of those souls who lack piety.

In both cases it is clear that illness is conceptualized as the consequence of an imbalance in the relations of the individual with himself and with society. Illness is therefore a crisis or breakdown in the social and natural order which rules human life. It is therefore much more a social than an individual phenomenon.

In addition, both concepts of illness contain the idea of the presence of alien elements inside the body. These must be dislodged by the healing shaman before health can be restored. As the opposite of illness, health represents a state of internal harmony in the individual as the consequence of fulfilling his social roles.

Healing Techniques

All techniques employed by shamans are standard ones exemplified in mythology. The cultural heroes were the first to apply them, so the shaman, whose figure of reference is the hero, is simply reproducing remedies established in early mythological time by the hero twins, especially Kuarahy. To demonstrate this more clearly I shall quote several fragments from the twin cycle, collected among the Chiripá, in which reference is made to these techniques. All the fragments are translations of accounts originally recorded in Guarani.

TREATMENT BY SUCTION. Kuarahy and Yacy then repented that they had killed all those birds as food for one who had killed her own mother. Kuarahy then desired to bring them back to life, so he made a basket of *wembe'pi* [philodendron] and, with Yacy's help, placed all the dead birds inside it. Then he took them out, one by one, and sucked their throats to revive them. He sucked their throats and the birds revived. The first bird he took out was the *yacú* [pheasant]: he sucked his throat and the *yacú* revived. It is for this reason that, to this day, the *yacú* has a bare neck where no feathers grow, because that was the spot where Kuarahy sucked it to bring it back to life.

Following this precedent, persistent illness is removed by the shaman's sucking the affected part. Frequently more than one session of treatment is needed. During the night preceding each treatment, the shaman dreams about the victim's health in order to discover the cause of illness. His dreams will also tell him when the infection has been completely removed, if his healing efforts prove successful. The ancient nature of this practice is attested by one of the chroniclers of the Tupinambá, who observed it in 1613. Here is his account:

I see the shaman at work, sucking up the patient's illness, as hard as he can, into his mouth and throat, pretending to hold them full and distended and then quickly spitting outside the enclosed space. He spits with great force, making a noise like a pistol shot and says that it is the illness which he has sucked (d'Evreux 1864:308).

The power with which the shaman is imbued prevents the poison which he absorbs from entering his own body. Among the Chiripá there exists the curious practice of taking shots of alcohol immediately after sucking a sick person. A new element comes into play: alcohol functions as the "purifier" of the shaman's throat, rather than as a disinfectant, since this latter idea is not very clearly understood.

TREATMENT BY BREATHING. The following fragment of the cycle of the twins occurs after an *añag* has killed and eaten Yacy:

Then Kuarahy said to the *añag*: "I beg you to leave me the bones. I do not like fish, I am only asking for the bones." The *añag* left him the bones and a small portion of prepared maize flour. Kuarahy put the bones and the flour together and went off into the forest. There he prayed and breathed on Yacy's bones and upon the maize flour. He breathed until flesh returned to Yacy's bones. His flesh returned again and, with it, his life.

As the vessel and heir of this divine power, the shaman can transmit it on his breath. The emission of the shaman's magic breath may be assisted by tobacco smoke. In the cures which I witnessed tobacco was not used, but the technique is not unknown. The healing process (number of sessions and the patient's state) is also determined during the sleep of the officiating shaman. Usually, the area upon which the shaman breathes is the upper part of the head, the spot where souls enter, but any other affected part can be breathed upon. This "magic" breathing represents the introduction into the sick man's body of a "potency" emanating from the shaman which will struggle with the "spirit of nature" which produced the illness until it is dislodged from the body which it is infecting.

TREATMENT BY PRAYER. Then Kuarahy went away and again began to pray. He prayed to the flower of the *mburukujá* asking it to help him raise up his mother's bones and restore her to life. The *mburukujá* is Kuarahy's favorite flower which he frequently invokes in his prayers. Then Kuarahy began to pray once more in order to raise up his mother's bones.

The prayer or chant is usually employed in the most serious cases, since it is a question of directly invoking the "auxiliary spirits" of the deity who granted the shaman his power, so that they may combat the disease. It is the form of treatment most commonly given for snakebite, with no use of herbs and no touching of the wound. Surprisingly, the outcome is often successful even in the case of very poisonous snakes. These "antibite" prayers are acquired during sleep, each shaman having his own particular one.

Lévi-Strauss (1968:175) suggests that that chants are a form of psychological treatment, and refers to them as a "psychological manipulation" of the infected organ. Although this explanation can be sufficiently justified in terms of psychosomatic suggestion in the case of human beings, it is still difficult to explain the cases of cure by chant in the case of animals, where it is unlikely that "suggestion" could be a factor. On more than one occasion I saw a castrated pig whose wound had become maggoty cured by chant. As the shaman chanted, the maggots fell off without any sort of powder having been applied. I believe that these phenomena deserve more attention then is usually paid to them without resorting to parapsychological or esoteric explanations. This lack of attention is due to the fact that they cannot be explained by reference to our own system of logical and causal principles although they are part of observed reality.

TREATMENT WITH HERBS. Nearly all the Avá-Chiripá possess some knowledge of a series of plants for everyday complaints which they plant in the vicinity of their houses. Only a shaman, however, can diagnose (in his sleep) cases of more serious illness and indicate which herb should be used in each specific case.

It was again Kuarahy, the cultural hero, who revealed the therapeutic qualities of herbs to men (Cádogan 1949b:25). According to him, Kuarahy showed men how plants should be used and also taught them the invocation which must be recited when they are being gathered. The invocation concludes as follows: "I entrust myself to thee as I gather this remedy, so that thy many messengers may ensure the success of it . . ." As this passage shows, it is the "spirits of medicinal plants" which are invoked to attack the "spirits of disease." It is therefore a question, as so often in shamanistic practice, of a struggle between spirits which determines the success or failure of the treatment. As Jenson (1966:262) observes, understandable facts and phenomena of this world are interpreted as having parallels of a spiritual nature. Thus, shamanistic treatment, based on the idea of psychophysical dualism, interprets illness not only as an organic process, but also, and more importantly, as a parallel spiritual process with organic manifestations.

The Effectiveness of the Healer

The existing literature on shamanism is so abundant that I would not claim to be adding anything really original at this point. I shall merely reiterate some of the key points for an understanding of it.

For the Chiripá the result of the treatment does not depend exclusively on the attendant shaman, but also, and in great part, on the conduct of the community. Every failure is attributed to a lack of genuine religious feeling on the part of the members of the community, and to the arguments and disputes which spring up in their midst. Social conflicts alter the sociosacred order in which the shaman functions. His success requires social cohesion. Any contravention of the social order alters the equilibrium and the legality which govern cultural life. The shaman works with the material the community offers and needs its trust. That is to say that, from a sociological perspective, shamanistic powers are granted by the community and if they are to be maintained the population has to believe in the need for their existence. Hence, any loss of unity affects an activity which fundamentally requires a collective consensus, as Lévi-Strauss (1968:164) puts it:

... Failure [the shaman's] is secondary to and, in all their comments is perceived as being the function of another phenomenon: the disappearance of social consensus ...

Among the Chiripá, however, shamanistic failure is much less frequent than success. The mechanisms which the shaman puts into action during the process of healing correspond not only to his own living out of the myth which gives meaning to the practice, but also to the patient's participation in the known process. Hence the sick man must be aware not only of the effect of a charismatic personality acting upon him, although this is important, but also of his own conception of the universe which gives meaning to the sickness as well as to the cure. The patient is therefore conscious that the whole cosmic order is acting on his behalf. This order is represented by the figure of the shaman who guarantees that the archetypal relationship between sickness and disease can be effectively repeated. The agent as well as the patient possess the same lived experience of the process. This experience is intensified by the shaman through the ritual of treatment which dramatically revives the powers he has acquired and projects them onto the sick man, ensuring all the while that the latter's perceptions and feelings remain strictly tied to the ritual being performed. Suggestion is too simplistic a formula to designate a process in which the actors are aware of a cosmos in which the correspondences to themselves are direct.

SHAMANISM AND CEREMONIAL

Ritual

The Avá-Chiripá's most important ceremony is the *ñemboé kaagüy* [prayer of the forest]. I shall give a brief account of it before passing on to the shaman's participation in it and the significance which it holds for the community. I shall not give too many descriptive details (in spite of having taken part in several) because there is already a detailed exposition of it (Cádogan 1959).

The ceremony takes place in the House of Dances, situated in the center of the little village. It is bigger than ordinary houses (six meters by four) and one side of it, the one facing east, is totally open. In front of this open space is a large trough (*yvyra ña'é*), which holds the ceremonial drink, *kagü* [chicha]. This trough is made of the sacred cedarwood, *ygarí*, and is in the shape of a canoe, approximately four meters wide. Although its only function is to hold the *chicha* its canoe shape recalls the craft used by the Guarani during the migrations. In front of the trough there are three cedar posts, about 1.20 meters high. The two outer ones are known as *tatáendey* [candle holders] since each has a hole at the top into which is placed a feathered stick hollowed at one end. Candles are placed in these hollows. The center post is called a *kuruzú* [cross]. A branch, taller and thinner than the ones used for a feathered cross, is placed next to it, together with a little arrow (*ju'g miní*). The little arrow is apparently of more ancient origin and is symbolically linked to the story of the twins' ascent to heaven by means of a ladder of arrows. All the ritual objects are decorated with bands covered with feather ornaments.

The ceremony lasts for a total of nine days. In the early days only a few people attend but their number increases as the days pass. The ritual is enacted in front of the trough and the posts, the men — each one with his rattle — forming a line with the shaman in the center, and his helpers and assistants on each side. Behind the men, the women spread out in their line, with their cheeks painted red and beating their *takuapú* [rhythm sticks], which are exclusively for female use. The prayers take place mostly during the night and last until the sun comes up. The shamans take it in turns to chant with men and women joining in the chorus.

From the third day on, the crowd becomes massive. On the fourth day the chicha is made. To make it, the women pound the maize to powder, mix it with water and leave it to ferment. Chicha can also be made from sugarcane or honey. After it has been made it is left to ferment until the end of the ceremony.

The *ñemboé kaagüy* is divided into two parts. During the first eight days it is eminently sacred and only sacred chants are intoned. But, on the ninth day, the shaman intones a chant which signifies that the deity who had been present during the prayers has left, and that therefore the fiesta, with the ritual drinking of chicha, can begin. During the "profane" part of the ceremony, chants of a festive nature, *koty-hú,* are sung. There is thus a division when the shaman's chant acts as a sort of "threshold ritual" between two sections distinct in type: the sacred time of the *guaú eté* and the time of the *koty-hú.*

To begin the drinking, the officiating shaman takes a little in a small gourd and breathes into it. In the case of honey chicha, a bee should fly from inside the "cup." In the case of cane chicha, a white flower should appear. These signs mean that the sacred part of the ceremony has been successfully performed, since they are signs of the deity's pleasure. After drinking himself, the shaman gives the sign for the other participants to start drinking. After drinking they begin to dance in circles and criss-crossing groups of men and women.

In the course of a *ñemboé kaagüy*, the community's entire surroundings have all the characteristics of a sacred space, since, in its center — in the House of Dances — a god is to be found. Therefore every aspect of behavior tends as far as possible toward purificatory norms. Sexual relations do not take place; meat and fat are not eaten; voices are kept low and the silence is broken only by the voices of the singers and the sounds of the *mbaraká* and the *takuapú.*

The date for the ceremony is determined by the dream of the highest-ranking shaman responsible for leading the ritual. According to some sources, the ceremony used to take place once a year and was designed as a ritual inauguration of the maize harvest, to bless the first fruits. In recent years, however, the number of celebrations has multiplied. Thus, in the period from January 1968 to January 1969, there were six: (1) in May, during a swamp fever epidemic; (2) in June, to chase away "evil spirits"; (3) in August, a shaman being very ill; (4) again in August, a second shaman being ill; (5) in September, for the maize harvest; and (6) in November, for the gathering of fruit.

Each one of these reasons for the ritual involves incidents which play an important part in maintaining social order. This includes the cases of illness since the sick men were shamans of great prestige with all the social importance that that implies. If we take into account the fact that the *ñemboé* lasts nine days, on which it is not possible to work, and that six were performed in one year, new evidence emerges for the significance of the shamanistic dream with reference to the economy, given the total of 54 nonworking days set aside for ritual. The existence of two Houses of

Dance is significant. The second, of more recent construction, is situated in the middle of the population center farther away from the seat of administration and from the junction with the Curuguaty road. Thus the ceremonial center is clearly being moved as far as possible from Creoles and whites.

Mythology and Ritual

It comes as no surprise that the ethnographical literature reveals a close connection between the religious ceremonial and the mythology. When we consider the rituals as dramatic representations of events occurring in a specific myth, it follows that we have to discover which myth it is that gives meaning to a particular ritual.

According to Cádogan (1959:18) the *ñemboé kaagüy* represents the myth of Chary Piré who escaped from the flood thanks to her faith in the use of the *takuapú*. However, in my opinion, there is no specific myth at the origin of this ritual. Rather, it contains symbolic elements from the entire mythological spectrum of the group.

Ritual is founded on the belief that a community may be able to communicate collectively with the gods, a capacity which ordinarily only shamans have, and then only individually. The social and cultural system of the tribal community as standardized in mythology can be considered an adaptation of the known, universal order, as Jenson shows (1966:57). The cult, for its part, is a collective, social demonstration of this order. This demonstration is, as it were, a form of payment by which the community acquires reassurance about its place in that order. The presence of the god, usually Kuarahy, is a reaffirmation of the sociocultural order of the group, since the figure of the cultural hero on Earth brings with it a cyclical renewal of the order originally imposed.

In the case of those rituals designed to drive away "evil spirits," either of nature or of the dead, which threaten the community, the idea is that the danger will be removed by the deity who is invoked. That is to say that the rite possesses *a force of its own* (Eliade 1970:141), and also activates other forces which are summoned to help men in situations of crisis which they are unable to overcome themselves, like epidemics, incurable illnesses, and "spirits" with which the shamans consider themselves unable to cope.

It seems to me important to point out that the increase in the number of ritual celebrations implies a determined response in cultural terms to assimilative pressures. The society reacts by reaffirming its own identity as expressed in ritual through which they become, once more, participants in their own exclusive cosmos.

Ritual and Society

Although ceremonial is manifested as an objective, a personal form, it is, nevertheless, a social activity insofar as it functions as a conditioning agent of the individual's subjective experience. This experience is of a highly socializing nature because, although the individual's own need to participate may be lessened, the community endorses it by offering him a place within the ritual and within itself.

Another of the basic characteristics of ritual is the possibility which it offers for societal communication, by fostering feelings of communion brought about by shared experiences (Jenson 1966:58). In this way it maintains constant unity within the community and contributes to the notion of collectivity by offering activities and experiences in which all may share. The social order and system of authority thus seem to take material form in the collective presence of individuals interacting with each other during the ritual. All these practices contribute to social integration and promote cohesion by fostering solidarity (Sahlins 1972:152).

Thus, among the Avá-Chiripá, the *ñemboé kaagüy* may be regarded as a collective act of self-knowledge in which the rite allows the tribal community to be present in its totality. Apart from negotiating between man and divinity, it also operates between men and the society to which they belong, strengthening the ties which unite them.

The *ñemboé kaagüy* is, in fact, the only activity capable of assembling all the Chiripá in pursuit of a common objective. It is the time when they can use their sacred names and social interaction turns on notions of religious reverence and extreme formality. Even certain individuals who, for circumstantial reasons, have distanced themselves from the tribal community, reintegrate themselves into it by attending the ceremonial celebrations, thus recovering their ethnic identity and membership of the extended family. This return to the world of sacred things restores to the Avá-Katú-Eté a social order in which they are the principal protagonists.

The Shaman and Ritual

As I have shown, the considerable increase in the number of celebrations per year is proof of the internal tension provoked in Chiripá society by the growing pressure of the regional society. For this reason, it is necessary both to have the ceremonial reiteration of their ethnic identity as well as to search for the much desired "salvaltion" by means of increased ritual acts. The growth in the number of *ñemboé kaagüy* reflects the behavior of a society upon which weighs the threat of disintegration and which seeks, in its relation with the sacred, an alternative form of continuity.

By the ceremonial expression of the need for "salvation" and conserva-
tion of cultural identity, the figure of the shaman emerges still more
clearly since he can be defined as the mediator of "salvation" and the
agent of his people's cultural identity. In his capacity as ceremonial
leader, he reiterates his functions as agent of communal cohesion and
maintainer of the sociosacred order of the tribe, since he is an intermediary with the sacred world as well as between members of his group. Thus
as we saw in connection with his healing role, the society becomes the
shaman's *collective patient*, for his efficacy greatly depends on social
consensus, while his activity as ceremonial leader is a further expression
of the consensus of the whole group. No one has described this state of
affairs more clearly than Jenson (1966:270–271) when he says:

There is, in effect, no shaman who does not seek to procure salvation or to avoid
calamities. The basis of this lies in his special capacity, by which he alone can work
effectively within the framework of ideas which say something about where and
how salvation can be achieved and calamity avoided. And such representations
must be included in the world view of the people in question.

This allows us to define Chiripá shamanism as being increasingly important. The shaman mediates with the sacred; he heals and is the ritual
mediator in his dual sacred and social role. This is why tribal communities
which lose their shamans (through plagues and so on) tend to disintegrate
for the lack of someone to give a sense of cultural values.

SHAMANISTIC LEADERSHIP

Shamans and Chiefs

As is shown in the historical section, shamanistic leadership coexisted
with secular leadership, but, in our own time, has been acquiring increasing importance to the displacement of political leadership. This transfer
from secular to religious leadership although the chroniclers already refer
to conflicts between the two, is mainly due to the present situation of the
Chiripá.

The political system of the Chiripá community is ostensibly based on
the presence of a captain and a sergeant who can be appointed either by
the military districts in whose orbit the tribes live, or by the tribes
themselves. In this instance, the captain and sergeant of Colonia Fortuna
have been appointed by the regional authorities who have provided them
with the uniforms appropriate to their rank. The role of the captain is to
act as intermediary between his group and the Paraguayan authorities.
He also fulfills a certain political role since it is his duty to hand over to the

regional political authorities the perpetrators of serious crimes with which the group cannot deal.

The chief of ancient Guarani communities was succeeded by his eldest son (Métraux 1948:85), but an individual who distinguished himself in war could become chief. Under this system, the members of the village would build the chief's house and work his land. In contrast, contemporary Chiripá secular chiefs have little influence, apart from that bestowed by charismatic personal qualities, since their authority is merely nominal and controlled by the Western authorities. To these reasons may be added their absolute lack of control over economic production, which is governed by the extended families and ultimately guaranteed by the shamans. As Schaden (1954:116) points out, the office of captain is an institution which did not evolve within the culture but was introduced by the members of the dominant society. This situation generates a constant state of internal tension since the imposed system of leadership lacks a basis for integration into the cultural system.

I have already noted that each extended family is headed by its *ty'y rú* [common father], and, for this reason, the leadership of some shamans relates exclusively to the members of their own family group. This results in another factor which favors shamanistic leadership: the fact that the shaman possesses a leadership base founded on kinship, a situation which also existed among the Ñandeva, Cayuá, and Mbya studied by Schaden (1954:113). The shamans who head extended families come together in a very informal council, under the informal leadership of the shaman of highest prestige, Avá-Nembiará.

The shamans of Fortuna, like those of all the Guarani, are not only healers and ceremonial leaders, but also prophets and foretellers of the future while, at the same time, they can influence the fertility and success of crops. In this way they show their capacity to govern by means of the ritual power which they possess over nature. As Balandier (1969:120) showed, if the chiefs rule the people, then the shamans rule the chiefs, since the shamans' source of power is legitimately sacred and is not imposed by any social system either internal or external.

The latent conflict between shamans and chiefs diminishes in the light of the fact that the chiefs do not interfere in what for the Chiripá is the area of greatest importance: that of religious ideas. At Colonia Fortuna, the secular chiefs, the brothers Florencio and Adriano Portillo (sergeant and captain respectively), have sought to legitimize their power by acquiring access to shamanistic rank, but through psychological unfitness and by their failure to observe the strict standards demanded of a shaman, they have not acquired a rank high enough to give them status equivalent to that of some other shamans.

Shamanism, Social Relations, and Social Control

RITES OF PASSAGE. Throughout an Avá-Chiripá's life, from birth to death, and especially at these two extremes, as we have seen, the figure of the shaman is very important. There are, however, other stages when the shaman is also present.

The rite of passage corresponding to a girl's first menstruation has lost the historical form which it still maintains in some other groups. This consisted in the building of a little hut of palm branches (*oga miní*), inside which the girl remained spinning and plaiting plant fibers. At the present time, the idea of seclusion persists, but this takes place in a corner of the ordinary house previously "cleansed" of the "spirits of the earth" (*ywy ojá*) which might take possession of the girl at this time. The cleansing is carried out by the shaman who protects the girl while her period lasts.

Male initiation has lost its archaic feature which involved the insertion of the lip ornament (*tembetá*). But its characteristics have been recorded by Métraux (1948:87): the young man was put to sleep with beer, and a specialist shaman pierced his lower lip with a bodkin made of wood or deer's horn. Then the shaman invoked Tupá so that the rite might afford protection from death.

The shaman also has a role to play in marriage ceremonies. The young man asks the bride's parents for her hand in marriage. Once they have agreed (there are payments of chickens, fruit, and so on), the shaman is summoned to instruct the couple in the conduct of their future life. The rules are simple: they must build a house, cultivate a plot, behave well, never commit adultery, and so on. In this simple way, matrimony is consecrated.

ARTIFICIAL KINSHIP TIES. Sponsorship has great social importance and is established by infant baptism. The *godfather* holds the child aloft while the officiating shaman proceeds to baptize him in the manner already described. At the conclusion of the ceremony, he is officially confirmed as godfather with the obligation of giving presents to his godson when requested and of blessing him when asked.

Another very important social tie which the shaman helps to form is the *aty'vasá* [adoptive brother]. This fraternity is established when two men or women who are very friendly go to the shaman's house and asks him to recite the prayer which will unite them in brother- (or sister-) hood. From that moment, the property of the two becomes interchangeable and they owe each other reciprocal obligations. If one *aty'vasá* dies without leaving a family, all his possessions which are not buried with him pass to his adoptive brother. The *aty'vasá* may or may not be a blood relation of his "brother," but they must respect each other more than brothers. There is no prohibition of marriage between the children of *aty'vasá*, and indeed, there is a preferance for this type of alliance.

The shaman's connection with the vital cycle of social and family relations increases the links between members of the tribal community and strengthens the individual and collective experience of the institution of shamanism. That is to say, the individual's and the society's relation to the forces which govern their destinies always seem to be united in the person of the shaman.

ADMINISTRATION OF JUSTICE. Although the secular chief is ostensibly charged with the administration of justice, crime implies a violation of the established order and therefore, the shaman, as the agent of that order, is the person who really determines the punishment. Avá-Nembiará is therefore the one who judges internal matters of a minor nature. In a case of murder, the guilty party is handed over to the Paraguayan authorities, provided that the victim's family have not already taken vengeance, which is what happens in the majority of cases.

To settle cases of robbery and to identify the robber, the shaman pronounces his verdict after having *dreamed* about the events and having had the transgressor's identity revealed. The shaman is also brought in when a member of the community is lost in the forest or is wounded and fails to return. In these cases the shaman again resorts to sleep before indicating the place where they should search. In an urgent case when time is important he intones a short chant and points out the spot. Any mistake in the direction of the search is interpreted as the result of the activity of the *angüery* [animal souls of the dead], which mock at the living and make them lose themselves in the forest.

SOCIAL CONTROL. With typical ambivalence, the shaman's power can also manifest itself in negative ways by attacking an individual who has seriously transgressed the rules of conduct. This type of supernatural sanction is feared much more than the beatings or handing over to the authorities which accompany the committing of crimes. The shaman can discharge his negative power onto an individual by means of adverse prayers in which he invokes his "auxiliary spirits" to attack the victim by making him ill. Or he can use harmful herbs which he administers to the guilty party.

At other times, the shaman may employ his negative powers to attack personal enemies or he may be bribed by someone who wants to avenge himself on an enemy of his own. Although these events are very infrequent, since it is very rare for a *paí guazú* to act in this way, shamans of lower rank may be tempted to use their powers to these ends. Given this possibility, it is usual for the members of one extended family to unite itself by sponsorship to other family groups to preclude conflict. At the same time they have the benefit of a powerful ally if anyone should try to inflict harm on them by means of sorcery. So it is that the shaman, albeit through fear, fosters relations and unity between the extended families.

When the negative activity of a shaman is discovered, there is an immediate reaction against him because the community feels unprotected from the powers which he can set in motion. When an event of this kind occurs, all the victim's relations appeal to Avá-Nembiará to punish the person responsible. While all this is going on, the community lives in a state of great distress because of the proximity of evil forces which have been released.

Other cases of sorcery are attributed to the shamans of other groups who have sent "evil spirits" to attack the Chiripá. In these cases the shaman must not only treat the bewitched person but he must also avenge him by sending his own "auxiliary spirits" to punish the suspected adversary.

Shamanism and the Economy

The Chiripá *paí* do not exercise control over production but they guide economic activity by virtue of the relations which they can establish with the "world beyond" in their dreams.

In agriculture, it is necessary to point to the distinction which exists between what cultivated plants mean in themselves and the possible ways of controlling them. It is known that, in order to grow a certain plant, a special seed must be planted, at a certain season of the year, and in a particular type of soil. But it is also known that the world is full of contradictory forces whence the unexpected, in the shape of a plague or a drought, may appear at any moment. It is a world in which good harvests and the quality of fruit are not only the direct results of the combination of technique and labor, but are also dependent on the activity of existing forces, which tend to act in accordance with the relationships which men maintain with them. To control this random fate represented by the forces of nature one must resort to the person who specializes in controlling them, the shaman.

The *paí* is consulted to determine a suitable spot for cultivation. He chooses it after consulting his dreams. After slashing and burning and before sowing, the shaman is again called in to cleanse the plot of ants, vermin, and anything else, material or spiritual, which could be harmful to the crops. This he does by surrounding the area with an imaginary line, one section of which is left open so that the vermin can get out. It is on this spot that the *paí* takes up his position, praying to the sound of his *mbaraká*, until they have all fled. The most auspicious time for the harvest is also chosen by the shaman in accordance with the indications given in his dreams.

No activity is more subject to chance, even for the expert, than hunting in the forest. It is possible to go for days without seeing a single animal, but the hunter may quickly chance upon an area where animals are abundant. The shaman's indication is the hunter's only guarantee.

Like hunting, the gathering of precious honey, of tender hearts of palm, and of fruit in general is guided by the dreams of the *paí*. Given that women and children play an active part in gathering, the dream must also predict the presence or absence of danger (in the form of snakes or other animals) in the relevant area of the forest.

Exchange of goods within and between extended families is subtly directed by the *ty'y rú* [common father] of each one. They also control the distribution of game and products which have been gathered.

The Intercultural Role

The relations of the Avá-Chiripá of Colonia Fortuna with the regional society cannot at the moment be described as interethnic relations, not at least in the terms of Cardozo de Oliveira's definition (1968:341) as "two groups of people dialectically unified through diametrically opposed but interdependent interests, however paradoxical this may seem." The Chiripá of Fortuna, because of their status as "wards," are in a different situation from that of other groups of the same tribe. The interaction of the other groups with regional and national society is much more evident and can be defined in terms of economic domination. In our case, the two systems, the tribal and the regional, are still not sufficiently interdependent at the economic level to be seen as a unified system. That is to say, the Indians are not dependent to any great extent on the regional society's consumer products, nor is the latter dependent on the lands or labor of the Indians.

Nevertheless, in a national society which does not allow for cultural pluralism and which does not consider the Indians as "citizens," it is inevitable that domination resulting from asymmetrical cultural relations in which the Indians are the cultural and sociological minority will be exercised in social and political terms. The first steps in this domination seek to prepare the Indians for their future role as wage earners. Although this result is not the express policy of any one person or group, it is the logical development of the national system which is extending its control into the marginal zones into which the ethnic minorities were pushed. In this process of social and political domination, an important role is played initially by "intercultural agents" who act as bridges between the two cultures in contact. These agents come from both the regional and the national society, but the Indian subsystem also has the capacity to react and to produce its own agents or mediators, diametrically opposed to those designated by regional or national society.

In the Chiripá's present situation, there are three different types of mediators, which I shall call manipulated agents, acculturating agents, and representative agents:

MANIPULATED AGENT. As Gluckman shows (1954:78), where there are no native chiefs, national society has no really effective means of penetration, since it is unable to manipulate the loyalties of kinship and religious groups to serve its own interests. As a logical corollary of this, the regional authorities (the military) appoint and recognize the leaders, "captain" and "sergeant," it thinks will be easiest to manipulate. Those who usually accept these posts are those members of tribal communities who are not very representative and who lack real prestige. They try to compensate for this by assuming the role of representatives of the group in the outside world. But, as I have said, these manipulated agents lack real authority within the tribal community and their powers are merely nominal. This colonial technique of domination is not in the least surprising since it is the one used in America since the beginning of the conquest.

ACCULTURATING AGENT. This is the case of the employees of the DAI, whose primary motivation is not to *modify* the cultural distances which separate the subsystems, but to maintain them in a position of subordination by means of the institution of "guardianship." However, as a secondary motive, the exogenous elements which they introduce into the native culture following the policy of the "development of the community" make them into agents of pure and systematic ethnocide.

REPRESENTATIVE AGENT. Here once more appears the many-sided figure of the shaman fulfilling his role as mediator between the community and the universe, in this case the social universe, which surrounds it. I have already indicated some aspects of the intercultural role in referring to the process of my initiation, but I have to make it clear that its function is totally different from that of the agent of acculturation. Basically the intention is to reinterpret the new sociocultural contact reality on the basis of the culture's own symbolic code. As such it hopes to influence new conditions by following traditional cultural patterns. Thus shamans express the need for "more dreams" to enable them to face the problem of interaction with Creoles with a guarantee of security and effectiveness which the supernatural character of honorific knowledge alone can offer.

REFERENCES

BALANDIER, GEORGE
1969 *Antropología política*. Barcelona: Península. (Originally published 1967 as *Anthropologie politique*. Paris: Presses universitaires de France.)

BARTOLOMÉ, MIGUEL A.
1969a Notas sobre el cambio cultural Guaraní. *Revista del Museo Americanista de Buenos Aires* 1:47–61.
1969b Notas sobre etnografía apyteré. *Suplemento Antropológico de la Revista del Ateneo Paraguayo* 4(2):63–75.

CÁDOGAN, LEÓN
1949a Creencias religiosas de los Mbya Guaraníes. *Boletín de Filología* 5:671–682.
1949b Síntesis de la medicina racional y mística Mbya Guaraní. *América Indígena* 9(1):21–35.
1950 La encarnación y la concepción: la muerte y la resurrección en la poesía sagrada "esotérica" de los Jeguaká-va Tenondé Porá-gué (Mbya-Guaraní del Guairá, Paraguay). *Revista del Museo Paulista* 4:233–246.
1951 Mitología de la zona Guaraní. *América Indígena* 11(3):195–207.
1952 El concepto Guaraní de alma. *Folia Lingüística Americana* 1:1–4.
1959 *Como interpretan los Chiripá (Avá-Guaraní) la dansa ritual*. Asunción: Zamphiropolos.
1960 En torno a la aculturación de los Mbyá-Guaraní del Guairá. *América Indígena* 20:135–150.
1962 Aporte a la etnografía de los Guaraní del Amambái, Alto Ypané. *Revista de Antropología de São Paulo* 10(1–2):43–91.
1968 Chonó Kvbwirá: aporte al conocimiento de la mitología Guaraní. *Suplemento Antropológico de la Revista del Ateneo Paraguayo* 3(2):55–158.

CARDOZO DE OLIVEIRA, ROBERTO
1968 Problemas e hipótesis relativas a fricção interetnica. *América Indígena* 27(2):339–379.

CHASE-SARDI, MIGUEL
1972 "La situación actual de los indígenas en el Paraguay," in *La situación del indígena en América del Sul*. Edited by G. Grünberg, 237–306. Montevideo: Tierra Nueva.

DEL TECHO, NICOLÁS
1897 *Biblioteca Paraguaya: historia de la provincia del Paraguay, de la Compañía de Jésus*, five volumes. Translated by Manuel Serrano y Sanz. Madrid. (Originally published 1673).

DE MONTOYA, ANTONIO R.
1892 *Conquista espiritual*. Bilbao: Sagrado Corazón.

D'ÉVREUX, YVES
1864 *Voyage dans le nord de Brésil fait durant les années 1613 et 1614*. Paris.

ELIADE, MIRCÉA
1970 *Lo sagrado y lo profano*. Barcelona: Barral. (Originally published 1965 as *Le Sacré et le profane*. Idées 76. Paris: Gallimard. (Translated 1968 by Willard Trask as *The sacred and the profane*. New York: Harcourt Brace Jovanovich.)

GLUCKMAN, MAX
1954   "Political institutions," in *The institutions of primitive society*. By E. E. Evans-Pritchard et al., 66–80. Oxford: Basil Blackwell.
JENSON, ADOLF
1966   *Mito y culto entre pueblos primitivos*. Translated by Carlos Gerhart. Mexico City: Fondo de Cultura Económica. (Originally published 1951 as *Mythos und Kult bei Natürvolkern*. Studien zur Kulturkunde 10. Wiesbaden: Steiner. Translated 1963 by Marianna Tax Choldin and Wolfgang Weissleder as *Myth and cult among primitive peoples*. Chicago: University of Chicago Press.)
LÉVI-STRAUSS, CLAUDE
1968   *Antropología estructural*. Buenos Aires: Eudeba. (Originally published 1958 as *Anthropologie structurale*. Paris: Plon. Translated 1963 by Claire Jacobson and Brooke Grundfest Schoepf as *Structural anthropology*. New York: Basic Books.)
MÉTRAUX, ALFRED
1928   *La religion des Tupinambá et ses rapports avec celle des autres tribues Tupí-Guaraní*. Paris: Leroux.
1948   "The Guarani," in *Handbook of South American Indians*, volume three. Edited by Julian Steward. 69–94. Bureau of American Ethnology Bulletin 143. Washington D.C.: Smithsonian Institution.
1967   *Religion et magie indiennes d'Amerique du Sud*. Paris: Gallimard.
NIMUENDAJÚ, CURT
1944   *Leyenda de la creación y juicio final del mundo como fundamento de la religión de los Apapokuva-Guaraní*. São Paulo: Recalde.
SAGUIER, R. B., H. CLASTRES
1969   Aculturación y mestizaje en las misiones Jesuiticas del Paraguay. *Aportes* 14:7–27.
SAHLINS, MARSHALL
1972   *Las sociedades tribales*. Barcelona: Labor.
SCHADEN, EGON
1954   *Aspectos fundamentais da cultura Guaraní*. São Paulo: Facultad de Filosofía.
1963   Aspectos específicos de la cultura Mbüa-Guaraní. *Revista de Antropología de São Paulo* 2:83–94.
1965   Aculturacão indígena: ensaio sobre os fatores e tendencias de tribos indias em contacto com o mundo des brancos. *Revista de Antropología de São Paulo* 13:1–317.
SUSNIK, BRANISLAVA
1969   *Apuntes de etnografía paraguaya* (fourth edition). Manueles Museo Barbero 11. Asunción: Museo Barbero.
THEVET, ANDRÉ
1878   *Les singularitéz de la France antarctique*. Paris: Maisonneuve. (Originally published 1558.)

Effect of Rural-Urban Migration on Beliefs and Attitudes Toward Disease and Medicine in Southern Peru

A. QUINTANILLA

The Indians living in the high plateau of southern Peru belong to two different linguistic groups: Quechua-speaking and Aymara-speaking. From the point of view of conceptualization and practices related to disease and medicine there are no major differences between them, and in the subsequent discussion no attempt is made to distinguish between the two populations.

One of our working hypotheses is that disease and medicine in the Quechua-Aymara world are understood by the Indian within relatively coherent conceptual frames of reference. Even though the Indian interpretation of the causes and nature of disease falls, to a great extent, in the realm of magic thinking, it has a certain coherence and logic. The categories of disease among the Quechuas and Aymaras of Puno have been well described by several authors, particularly Frisancho (1972). I do not intend to repeat those descriptions here except as necessary to illustrate certain postulates. A few broad generalizations can be offered.

1. In the Indian culture diseases are defined in accordance with a certain primitive nosology. In this nosological classification, some diseases are categorized as a cluster of symptoms and signs with more or less defined causes, treatment, and prognosis. Another group of diseases is identified not by a set of symptoms but rather by a common etiology, usually magic. This will be discussed further.

2. Indians are not entirely opposed to Western medicine. In fact, it is accepted that Western medicine may have some usefulness along with traditional medicine. Modern medicine has made inroads into what once was the exclusive domain of the local healer or witch doctor (*laikka* or *jampicuc*).

The integration between traditional conceptualization and treatment of disease and Western medicine has evolved slowly, over many years, and in this way without noticeable disruption of the traditional beliefs.

3. Their system is coherent inasmuch as their concept of diseases integrates well within the context of their whole cosmic interpretation. The explanation of the causes of disease makes sense within their conceptual world, and treatment is the logical application of remedies designed to neutralize or counteract the forces believed to be the causes of disease.

THE IDEA OF DISEASE IN THE RURAL QUECHUA-AYMARA WORLD

In order to study the impact of migration I will review briefly some concepts of disease and medicine held by the Indian in the rural community as opposed to the Indian transplanted to the city. I refer to the Indians who are minimally exposed to the Westernizing influence of the coastal city as the rural Quechua-Aymara world. Spread over a vast area, grouped in small hamlets or in isolated communities, with no knowledge or only minimal knowledge of the Spanish language, they present to a marked degree the theoretical characteristics of the *Gemeinschaft* [community]. Rural, communal, patriarchal, preliterate, homogeneous, ruled by custom and tradition, isolated, their economy is one of subsistence, static and self-sufficient.

As pointed out by Martínez (1961), this Indian has developed a more or less clear distinction between diseases which are amenable to the therapeutic tools of the physician and those which are not. These categories correspond more or less to diseases believed to be caused by natural agents and those of preternatural or magic causation, for which the physician has neither powers nor insight.

Examples of some of the diseases listed by Martínez as due to natural agents and treatable by physicians are the following:

Costado: Disease believed to be due to exposure to cold or a chilling wind; it is characterized by chest pain, cough, and sometimes hemoptysis. (It probably includes most forms of pneumonia, pleuritis, epidemic pleurodynia, occasional cases of herpes zoster, intercostal neuritis, and other diseases characterized by chest pain.)

Puraka usu: Abdominal pain believed to be the result of dietary indiscretions. (It may include any of the myriad of diseases where the presenting symptom is abdominal pain.)

Caju usu: Disease characterized by persistent cough and thoracic pain; it affects mainly children and is believed to be caused by cold. (It probably includes most cases of whooping cough, as well as banal bronchitis.)

Nayra usu: Encompasses diseases of the eyes characterized by reddening, soreness, pain, and lacrimation which in rare cases may lead to blindness; it is believed to be due to wind, heat, or smoke. (It includes most cases of conjunctivitis, keratitis, uveitis, and probably many other diseases of the eyes.)

Of more interest is the group of diseases which are not considered amenable to Western medicine. The following are important examples in this category: (1) A group of closely related disease entities or variants of the same entity, variously known as *jallpa jappiskka* (Quechua), *orakke mankantihua* (Aymara), *urahuena kkatua, katkja* (also Aymara); (2) *Animu karkkuska* (Quechua), *ajayu sarakkata* (Aymara), *susto* (Spanish).

Phenomenologically I call them disease entities because that is what they are within the context of the Indian conceptual universe. If we put ourselves in the position of the Indian, with his cognitive elements and mechanisms of causation rooted in magic thoughts and beliefs to which he strongly adheres, we cannot help but see them as disease entities. This is important, because a disease entity is a defined type of health disorder which calls for specific diagnostic and therapeutic measures.

Jallpa kappiskka (Quechua), *orakke mankantihua* (Aymara): In a myth common to many primitive peoples, the earth, the mountains, the springs, and rivers have a spirit which under certain circumstances may take possession of a person and cause him to become sick. *Jallpa kappiskka* applies particularly to possession by the spirit of the place where one lives. The clinical manifestations are loss of appetite, general malaise, muscular aches, nausea, vomiting, and headache. Since these are universal symptoms, it is obvious that *jallpa kappiskka* can correspond to almost any of the diseases as we know them. The singularity of *jallpa kappiskka* as a nosographic entity is given, for the Quechua-Aymara, by the specific causation as indicated by Frisancho (1972). In reality, probably the majority of cases of *jallpa kappiskka* are infectious diseases and most of them viral, particularly in children. Those cases of *jallpa kappiskka* manifested chiefly by gastrointestinal disturbances may correspond to simple acute gastroenteritis, whose viral etiology has been recently established. Many cases are functional disorders such as irritable colon. Others correspond to shigellosis, salmonellosis, and staphylococcal food poisoning. Occasionally, more serious or even fatal surgical intra-abdominal conditions may be responsible for the disease.

Animu karkkuska (Quechua), *ajayu sarakkata* (Aymara), *susto* (Spanish): The disease is believed to result from detachment of the spirit or abandonment of the patient by his soul, which wanders aimlessly in the area where a frightening episode took place. The person who lost his soul develops symptoms which are remarkably reproducible and allow the diagnosis to be made easily, often without the benefit of coca divination by the *laikka*.

It is noteworthy that this syndrome has been described in virtually all Latin American countries and even in the United States (in Texas), among Spanish-speaking people of Mexican descent (Rubel 1964:268). There is a remarkable coincidence in the description of the disease by different authors. The patient has a restless sleep, nocturnal fears, lack of appetite, loss of weight, loss of interest in attire and personal hygiene, depression, and introversion (Sal y Rosas 1958; Martínez 1961; Frisancho 1972; Rubel 1964; Vellard 1957). The treatment, with minor local variations, consists basically in the identification of the place where the soul was lost and the performance of a ritualistic ceremony in which the *jampicuc* or *laikka* entices the soul to follow him from the place where it is wandering to where the patient lies so that the two are reunited; all this is accompanied by the proper incantations and magic ritual to assure the success of the treatment.

EFFICACY OF THE NATIVE HEALER

The *laikka*'s approach to disease reassures the Indian and allays his anxiety because it is the logical answer to his concept of disease. The crucial difference between the Indian's concept of disease and ours is not so much in the kind of factual knowledge but in the mental categories in which we believe.

In our quest for explanations, modern medicine has painstakingly established the physical causes of an ever-growing number of diseases. The primitive mind, on the other hand, has solved its quest for the cause-effect relationship by attributing causality to forces which we call magic but which for the primitive mind are in a way more real and credible than our medical answers. Belief in the explanations offered by Western medicine requires a high degree of faith in explanations which are utterly meaningless except for the initiated. Today, germs and microbes are commonplace concepts for the occidental layman, but there was a time when it was not so and to believe in them required an act of faith far greater than to believe in the spirit of the earth doing harm to a child. Today there is a host of diseases for which modern medicine is beginning to describe the causative mechanisms in terms of molecular diseases, autoimmunity, failure of self-recognition, immune complexes, membrane phenomena, messenger RNA (ribonucleic acid), and what-not. In these areas even the average medical practitioner does not understand what the specialist is talking about, let alone the layman. Yet, the medical practitioners and the layman believe the conclusions of the researcher because modern medicine has such a distinguished record of accomplishments that it is easy to believe.

For the Indians who live in isolated huts in the high plateaus of southern Peru, this act of faith is neither easy nor warranted. They have undoubtedly observed that in certain cases the Western doctor has a greater rate of success than the local healer (*laikka, jampicuc*, or *yatiri*), but this observation has not shaken their faith in the healer, because they have also observed that in certain diseases the modern physician was utterly incompetent while the *laikka* was often successful. In consequence, the popular wisdom has concluded that some diseases are amenable to treatment by physicians while others are not, as previously described.

Acceptance of the physician in a limited role has not been disruptive because it resulted from the slow realization of his powers over certain types of maladies. Modern medicine was never forcibly imposed upon the Indians — the option was open to the sick Indian and his family. The Indians opted to seek the physician's help only when they had reason to believe that he would be more successful than the healer, while they called the *laikka* for those diseases caused by spirits, mountains, the earth, or malefic actions of witchcraft or *brujería* (Spanish). The Western physician is considered, and correctly so, hopelessly ill-equipped to handle these disease entities.

When modern medicine was made available in the rural communities of Puno, the Indian was not deprived at any time of the local healer, who was available as he had always been, and with him the comfort and security offered by a man who can understand the obscure forces at work and can command healing powers. Whether or not the healer's treatment is effective depends on as many variables as our own therapeutics. Failure to achieve a cure does not necessarily diminish the prestige of the healer, just as unavoidable failures do not destroy the prestige of our clinicians.

Many of the disease entities which are not considered within the realm of occidental medicine are psychiatric disturbances, particularly certain forms of neurosis. It seems likely that most cases of *susto* and *animu karkkuska* are neurosis of anxiety with organic manifestations conditioned by the firm belief prevalent in the group that the episode of fright *will* produce such symptoms. *Susto* in infants is more difficult to interpret, and probably encompasses a variety of conditions. To the best of my knowledge, patients with *susto* do not have organic disease, and their manifestations are only the functional disturbance associated with neurosis of anxiety (López Ibor 1950; Álvarez 1958). It is noteworthy that the concept of detachment or loss of the soul is akin to the sensation of *déspersonalization* (French) or loss of "self" (Dugas and Montier 1910). It is well known that neurotic manifestations may assume peculiar and reproducible characteristics conditioned by the culture of the group. The symptoms can be learned and the pattern transmitted by imitation. The clinical picture, reproducible and similar in patient after patient, can be explained because there are institutionalized expectations of behavior of the person with *susto*, analogous to the institutionalized expectations of the sick role as described by Parsons (1952:436).

Examples of similar syndromes peculiar to certain groups are the *ufufunyane* of the Zulu-speaking peoples and the *ukuphosela* of the Xhosa (Loudon 1965:137); the possession syndromes described among the Teita by Margetts; and the frustration syndrome of the island of Tikopia (Firth 1959:328). There are even epidemics of *susto*, as there are of *ufufunyane*, and as there were epidemics of dancing mania in medieval Europe (Rawnsley 1962:49).

Given the psychiatric nature of the disease, it is not surprising that the *laikka* should be more successful than the Western physician in treating this disease entity. The physician is likely to be lost in a sea of obscure symptoms, will want to have a variety of laboratory tests, and will finally be unable to establish a precise diagnosis, much less effect successful treatment. In contrast, the *laikka* will be speaking the same conceptual language as the patient; he will establish rapport with him at a deep emotional level and, through powerful suggestion, will usually succeed in ridding him of his imaginary symptoms.

EFFECT OF MIGRATION TO THE WESTERNIZED CITIES OF THE COAST

Indians have been migrating to the coastal cities for many years. When the impoverished lands of the altiplano cannot support more than one family, the growing children are forced to abandon the native village and seek a better living in the Westernized cities. The profound psychological impact of migration and the slow process of adaptation termed by some Peruvian sociologists as the process of "cholification" (i.e. the Indian becoming a *cholo*, or acculturated) have been described many times. I will not delve into these changes except as concerns their effect upon health and medicine.

Rotondo (1960) has pointed out that one of the salient traits in the Indian migrating to the city is an excessive, almost pathologic fear of becoming sick. We have confirmed this observation. In a survey among a group of natives of Puno villages who had migrated to Arequipa within the previous five years, the following question was asked: "What are you most afraid of?" The number one fear was of falling sick. Not even the loss of job was feared so much. This cannot be explained solely by the financial implications of sickness. In Peru, any impecunious person is eligible for medical attention in the hospitals supported by the Ministry of Health. The same fear of sickness is frequently observed among Indian girls working as domestics in the city. In most cases the fear is unwarranted, because in the event of disease, the family will take the necessary steps to assure her medical attention. In general, primitive people are more aware of how precarious the state of health is, and the ever-present possibility of disease causes a great deal of anxiety; however, in the case of the migrant Indians, there is more to it than that.

One clue to the nature of this fear is provided by our observation that the diseases or symptoms of disease which were most feared were not necessarily those of serious physical nature. Often there was more concern over minor skin blemishes, questionable reddening of the eyes, questionable paleness, etc. Many of these "symptoms," often imperceptible to myself, caused the individuals great anguish. A girl insisted on going back to her native village to seek a cure for darkening of her skin which I could never detect. A young man left his job and returned to his village because of some vague aches and insomnia. Another girl was extremely worried about a "spot" in her eye which I could never see. Cases like these were seen time and again.

On the other hand, I have often seen Indians in the city who have arrived at the hospital *in extremis*, who had continued to work until they physically could not stand on their feet because they had not paid much attention to the progressive worsening of their condition.

The explanation for this anomalous perception of the severity of one's disease seems to be related to the Indian's categorization of diseases as amenable or not amenable to Western medicine. If they fear that their disease may be one of those which is not due to natural agents, and therefore not understood by physicians, they become extremely worried and feel abandoned among people who lack insight into the problem.

Migration to the cities in itself seems to increase the incidence of the psychiatric maladies described above, perhaps in relation to the cultural clash.

It is noteworthy that the *ufufunyane* syndrome of the Zulus occurs with higher incidence among those who live and work on farms run by Europeans (Loudon 1965:137). Another example of the same pattern is the case of laughing disease, which occurs in epidemics among tribes of Lake Victoria. This is a form of hysteria which is much more prevalent among girls receiving education in Christian schools (Lambo 1965:162), probably in relation to the change in cultural setting.

Another factor of the cultural clash which compounds the Indians' fear of disease is their inability to play the sick role in the urban setting, a role which would have been expected and approved in their native community. They rapidly learn that their symptoms are considered imaginary and that reassurance and support will not be provided by the outside world, so they will have to brood over their troubles alone with themselves.

The urban lack of resources to cope with their traditional diseases may be extremely disruptive and incapacitating, to the point that sometimes they cannot think about anything else, and yet will be reluctant to communicate their fears.

REFERENCES

ÁLVAREZ, W.
1958   *Practical leads to puzzling diagnoses.* Philadelphia: Lippincott.
DUGAS, LUDOVIC, FRANÇOIS MONTIER
1910   La déspersonalization et la perception intérieure. *Journal de Psychologie* 7.
FIRTH, R.
1959   *Social change in Tikopia.* London: George Allen and Unwin.
FRISANCHO, D.
1972   *Creencias y supersticiones relacionadas con las enfermedades del altiplano puneño.* Puno, Peru: Los Andes.
LAMBO, T. A.
1965   "Comments on Loudon 'Social aspects of ideas about treatment' " in *Transcultural psychiatry.* Edited by A. V. S. Reuck and R. Porter, 162–164. Boston: Little, Brown.
LÓPEZ IBOR, JUAN JOSÉ
1950   *La angustia vital.* Madrid: Paz Montalvo.
LOUDON, J. B.
1965   "Social aspects of ideas about treatment" in *Transcultural psychiatry.* Edited by A. V. S. Reuck and R. Porter, 137–161. Boston: Little, Brown.
MARTÍNEZ, H.
1961   Enfermedad y medicina en Pillapi, Bolivia. *Revista del Museo Nacional* 30:178. Lima.
PARSONS, T.
1952   *The social system.* London: Tavistock.
RAWNSLEY, K.
1962   *Sociology and medicine.* Sociological Review Monographs 5. Keele, Staffordshire: University of Keele.
ROTONDO, H.
1960   *La personalidad básica del mestizo peruano.* Lima.
RUBEL, A. J.
1964   The epidemiology of a folk illness: *susto* in Hispanic America. *Ethnology* 3:268–283.
SAL Y ROSAS, FEDERICO
1958   El susto. *Revista de Sanidad de Policía.* Lima.
VELLARD, J.
1957   La conception de l'âme et de la maladie chez les Indiens américains. *Travaux: Institut français d'Etudes andines* 6:5–33.

Learning of Psychodynamics, History, and Diagnosis Management Therapy by a Kali Cult Indigenous Healer in Guiana

PHILIP SINGER, ENRIQUE ARANETA, and JAMSIE NAIDOO

THE EDUCATION OF THE HEALER

The "education" was a process of interaction among three men, during which it was often not clear who was the psychiatrist, who was the healer-informant, and who was the anthropologist. Indeed, the healer has now visited the United States four times as a result of the anthropologist's and psychiatrist's initiatives. In 1970 and 1973 he came as a visiting lecturer to the anthropologist's university. In 1969 he was invited to participate in an Agency for International Development conference in Wisconsin on the problem of gaining cultural acceptance for unconventional high-protein foods. In 1967 he spoke before the American Academy of Psychotherapy on religious healing.

By now, the role of anthropologist and informant, psychiatrist and healer, are so blurred that one may justifiably ask "Who is the anthropologist, and who is the informant?" This in turn raises serious questions about the nature not only of anthropological ethical behavior "in the field" (Where is that?) but of medical ethics as well. But these questions will have to be dealt with in another place.

Cooperation between the Mental Hospital in (British) Guiana and the East Indian Kali healers, most notably Jamsie Naidoo, began in 1963, when the anthropologist lived at a Kali temple located about fifteen miles from the Mental Hospital. The psychiatrist-director of the Mental Hospital, or "the Mental" as it is locally known, was Dr. D. Panday, himself a Guianese of East Indian origin and trained in London's Maudsley Hospital. He was succeeded as director in 1964 by Dr. Araneta. During the years 1963–1966, until Dr. Araneta left, a great deal of cooperation developed between the anthropologist, healer, and psychiatrist.

In 1963, all diagnoses, as far as the healer was concerned, were "working" diagnoses, involving reality problems and treatment. The diagnostician-healer is very concerned with the motivation of the patient and his sincerity in coming for treatment. Little or no attention is paid to the differential subtleties of diagnosis as regards the patient's behavior. This is because outside of motivation, *prognosis* does not depend upon diagnostic shadings in Kali work, which is basically concerned with functional-emotional disorders. These differentiating symptoms are the equivalent of scientific detail for the Western psychiatrist. For the Kali healer it was foolishness because he already knew, as a member of the culture, what could go wrong with persons in the culture.

The Goddess Kali, or the Divine Mother, is believed to have originated among the pre-Aryan Dravidians as they changed from food gatherers to cultivators. All growing things were regarded as representing the female principle, and the earth mother gradually became the Mother Goddess.

Psychologically, Freudian-oriented psychiatrists believe Kali represents a derivative of an infantile, ambivalent image of the mother, that her grotesque endowments are the expressions of aggressive feelings derived from anal, urethral, and phallic phases of psychosexual development, and that the gnashing teeth, protruding tongue, and blood coursing down the cheeks relate to cannibalistic wishes of the child to the mother figure. Further, the blackness of the skin is an overall "investment" of the mother figure with cruelty and ill-feelings. These are derivatives of the anal-sadistic phase of development, etc.

The Kali healer-pujari's explanation is as follows:

He holding head because when de country was all shake up, de *rakshasa* come, he cut off de neck. [There is no consistent gender in local patois] That show he destroy all the evil people. At that time he show no sympathy for anybody at all. He have four hand to show you are a man, you have two hand, so he have four, double amount you strenth. One hand hold cutlass, one holds *tirsul* [trident], one holds head, one holds *udkay* [drum]. When he wants to enjoy, he plays drum. When he stick out tongue, he have power to kill.

Diagnostic categories were always related to specific, stereotyped dreams. This type of stereotype is similar to the symbolism of the orthodox analyst. The ability to produce a particular dream for a particular therapist is also a common phenomenon in Western psychiatry, although not interpreted as such.

The diagnosis bears the name of two major dreams:

1. Kateri. (This is the Madras name. The Hindu name is Churyl.) The Kateri may be a man or a woman and is associated with negative aspects of sexuality. A pregnant woman often has a particular dream, followed by spontaneous abortion. Sometimes the Kateri "can take a man shape" which "dreams her." When the Kateri "interferes" with a man, there are usually sexual problems, including impotence.

2. Dreaming Dutchman. (This is more common among men.) Here the assumption is that the individual has rested or napped in a spot where a Dutchman was buried, or where he buried his wealth after the British defeated the Dutch. The healer says:

The Dutchman hold you because you don't give anything, not even a little rum. Den you get fever. Go to doctah. Doctah do injection, medicine, tablets etc. De Doctah say he can's manage, "me no find you complaint." Neighbors tell go see priest. Me go devote de mudder. Me ask: Can you remember where this bai go shot or where go walk and so on: Whilst me talk, Dutchman come and start to play pon de bai. Den me put some *babut* [sacred ash] on he forehead and me telle he what work he got to do.

The healer's therapy, which basically has not changed over the years, consists of having the patient come to temple, or church, for a designated number of Sundays. This is because everyone, including the healer, works six days a week in the sugar fields, and Sunday is the free day.

In brief, although there are different kinds of "work" to be performed, all have the following elements: preparations by the patient-devotee before going to church: these include abstaining for three days before Sunday, from all "rank," i.e. rum, fish, meat, and sex. Clean "garments," (and sometimes new ones depending on the case) are also required, along with new cooking utensils. The patient will also bring *prasad* [food that will be blessed and offered to the deities (*deotors*)]. This includes sweets and all varieties of fruits. Sometimes sacrificial animals (ram-goat, fowl-cock) are offered (for a fuller description of the therapy, see Singer et al. 1967:103–113).

The most significant innovation over the years has been the most recent one (1973) introduced by the healer, which is that the patient-devotee may now speak *directly* to Kali Mai (Mother Kali) herself ("played" in trance by a healer) *in English*; formerly it was necessary to have a translator who would speak the sacred language (a South Indian dialect, "Gouri") and "interpret" to the patient from the Kali trance-healer-diagnostician and back again. Jamsie Naidoo justifies this innovation on the grounds that people want to know directly, and in English, what is being said to them, without the need of an "interpret."

However, over the years of contact with the psychiatrist, the healer observed that the psychiatrist would always ask the patient, "What will you do when you get better?" Initially, there was resistance to asking or answering this question. Patients would interpret it as meaning, "What are you going to give me in return for my making you better?" They would reply, "Doctah, me nah got nothing. You like fowl, you like sheep, fish? Me nah got no money." The healer eventually put the question in the following form: "Doctah want to know, what you going to do to make youself happy. What kind of work you like to do?" Of equal importance was not only the "translation" of the question, but the fact that it came from the healer and not the doctor. Sick people are all too used to doctors demanding fees before service.

After the healer finally learned the importance of the question in relation to the concept of motivation, that, for example, a patient might not want to get well because of the attention the sick role was providing him, he incorporated it into his own therapy. This awareness has resulted in his insistence that Kali work be *consciously* family-oriented, instead of just culturally family-oriented, which it largely was. Today the healer tells his patients, "You cannot get well unless you live good with each other."

An example of the healer's growing awareness of behavior is seen in the case of a fifty-six-year-old widow who practiced moneylending. She was postmenopausal and suffered from headaches (head-a-swing, head-worry), insomnia, general weakness, and depression. The healer recommended electric shock (after having seen its effect in cases of depression in many instances) saying:

I don't think she can get well because she wants love and nobody loves her. She has too much money but she will not help any relatives. That's why you must take money. Give electricity, she will feel a little better and if she feels better, she might get some friends. This person loves money more than people.

After five treatments of electroconvulsive therapy (ECT), the woman's depression lifted, although she had continued spells of severe depression. The healer's comment was that "she doesn't want to live again, because she doesn't want to give up money."

Dream Work

The healer has also increased his understanding of dreams and has enlarged his dream repertoire beyond that already discussed. Although he would always ask the patient about his dreams and expect one of the standard replies, he noticed that the psychiatrist would sometimes ask in cases of patients with repressed hostility: "Do you dream as though a lot of people are fighting each other, or meeting accidents?" This would often result in the patient describing dreams of those sorts.

In anxiety cases, the psychiatrist would ask whether the individual had "running" dreams, or "falling from heights," or "being late for the work bus." There would usually be positive responses with personal detail.

The healer, after observing this for some weeks, asked the psychiatrist why he would ask for such dreams instead of the Kateri or Dutchman dreams. It was explained to him, with many examples, that many persons have a great deal of anger which they are not able to express openly. Some familiar examples would be a young man complaining of headaches who was facing the prospect of an arranged marriage he did not want. Now, when the healer asks for dreams and does not receive the usual cultural response or is told that the person did not dream at all, he probes for hostility and anxiety dreams involving falling and violence. Dreams of violence have been integrated with the Dutchman dream, requiring Dutchman work (therapy). Retroflexed rage dreams are also incorporated into the Dutchman diagnosis.

Electroconvulsive Therapy (ECT)

Although the healer had witnessed many cases of ECT successfully applied to cases of depression, he did not make it part of his own therapeutic, recommended armamentarium until he was personally involved in a special case. A twenty-six-year-old man was brought to him by a well-known family. The patient had been married four months and was showing paranoid schizophrenic behavior. He had poorly systematized delusions and auditory hallucinations. There was no previous history before the onset. The healer brought the young man to the psychiatrist who hospitalized him. The patient refused to stay and escaped on several occasions returning to his family, which, in each case, brought him back to the hospital. Finally a series of five ECTs was administered. After the fifth treatment, the family, accompanied by the healer, came to the psychiatrist and requested release of the patient who was showing marked improvement. The psychiatrist told the healer that the patient had indeed improved, but required additional treatment. Against advice, the patient was discharged. Two weeks later, the patient was returned, and was given another course of ECT (six treatments) until a degree of memory loss ensued. He was then released into the healer's Kali care, improved steadily, and has maintained himself without problems since.

The therapeutic formula evolved here between the psychiatrist and the healer was that in severe psychotic cases not amenable to Kali cultural reinforcement, ECT would be administered up to memory loss, then reintegration would proceed via Kali reenculturation. Later, the psychiatrist developed the technique of unilateral ECT without resulting loss of memory.

REASON FOR COLLABORATION

Having accepted a new country as one's milieu for psychiatric investigation and therapy, a psychiatrist cannot but commit himself to the values and culture of the population; otherwise he would suffer culture shock. This is because he cannot escape the fact that "mental disorders" or syndromes can only be adequately defined, recognized, evaluated, and appreciated through the understanding of the functional interrelatedness of the environment with the inner motivation of the individual and the "accepted" community goals. In other words, "mental disorders," have meaning only in the society in which they manifest themselves. In view of this, the opportunity of forming a working relationship with the local Kali healers, initiated by the anthropologist, was a most welcome recourse in the efforts to identify the problems, define goals, and conceive plans for a mental health program of the host country. The working relationship was therefore initially sought with the following objectives in view: (1) It supplied the psychiatrist with the means of learning the cultural patterns, the existing social institutions and organizations along which he might direct his (patient) therapy, which perforce must take cognizance of the attitudes of the community to be effective. (2) The fantastic inadequacy of the psychiatric facilities (one psychiatrist for the whole country) was such that the reorganization of this exploration was an inescapable, if not frantic, move to meet the psychiatrist's own desperate plight. (3) It showed promise of evolving methods of evaluating techniques of community psychiatry, while at the same time, discovering, testing out, and articulating psychodynamic principles that may be operating in the Kali healing methods, affording an invaluable, preexistent laboratory and calling for no additional responsibility from the psychiatrist. (4) The relationship also afforded the psychiatrist a chance to introduce Western psychiatric concepts where he felt these might be of help to the healer in dealing with mental disorders. (5) To prepare the community, it afforded a chance for the psychiatrist to effect such change in cultural awareness and attitudes in coping with the anticipated cultural impact of increasing Western infiltration into the socioeconomic structure of the country. (6) The prospect of utilizing the healer's help for specific psychiatric syndromes, in which the anthropologist had reported amazing results, offered the desired resource for the already impossible work schedule of the psychiatrist. (7) The need to control the operations of the healer, who had no training in the recognition of somatic disorders, demanded the relationship as an urgent humanitarian medical responsibility. (8) The collaboration also offered a social rehabilitation facility, which had been nonexistent up to the time of the psychiatrist's involvement with the service. (9) The establishment of a liaison with the leaders of the communities, among whom the Kali healers involved were found to be most influential, afforded the mental health service an opportunity to evolve into a culturally modifying institution that contributed to allaying the social ills of the community. (10) With such an evolution, it was hoped that insights could be gained into preventive measures against mental illness through the elucidation in greater depth of the personal and environmental interrelationships that were predisposed to regression.

THE WORKING RELATIONSHIP ESTABLISHED WITH THE KALI HEALERS

A series of visits to the Kali temples and observations of the healing rituals, followed by discussions with the healers on the theories behind their practices, was undertaken. After a solid personal relationship (which is the only meaningful relationship in the personality-oriented, rather than object and role-oriented Western pattern of culture) was established, the healer was invited to assist in the evaluation of new cases at the Corentyne clinics and the Mental Hospital. This consisted of having the healer help in the history-taking, which was a tremendous asset because of his mastery of the peculiarities of the idiom characteristic of the district. A conference on the emotional needs of the patients, as brought out in the interviews, followed, and a comparison of the theories of management that were felt to be indicated was then undertaken. This provided the psychiatrist with insights into the patterns of cultural expectations, the traditions and myths that underlie the "accepted" community goals, and the functional interrelatedness of the environment and the inner motivations of the individual; it also shed some light on the factors that predispose to functional regression.

The healer also made periodic visits to the Mental Hospital to bring patients for evaluation (1) as to whether or not organic problems existed, or (2) as to whether his methods had or had not produced the desired results on "mental" cases. In these instances, diagnostic and management conferences were undertaken, wherein the healer was afforded some insights into signs of organic disturbances and also some information on how drug therapy, used in the clinic, could assist the patient in responding better to the healer's predominantly cultural reinforcement therapy (directed at bringing about order and organization out of emotional chaos). In these visits, the healer also was enabled to follow up cases that he had referred for admission, and the therapeutic procedures employed in the hospital were explained to him. The unilateral electroconvulsive therapy to the nondominant hemisphere of the brain, which proved more effective in calming patients than the conventional bitemporal placement, was developed and had dramatic effects in that it involved no memory impairment. This afforded the patient the continuation of the value-reinforcing therapy of the healer, through "devotion."

The healer's collaboration with the psychiatrist also took the form of management conferences for cases to be followed by the Kali healer and for cases that were ready for discharge.

Another form of collaborative therapeutic effort consisted of cases on which the psychiatrist had used drug and supportive psychotherapy but had then referred to the Kali healer because, being deficient in his appreciation of the cultural value of the symptoms, he had been unable to decipher the hidden motivation for their retention.

Furthermore, due to the relative lack of mobility in the social system prevailing in the district, the role-assigning process within the family has been observed to be extremely therapeutic, and family participation advocated in the Kali form of healing has been utilized to great advantage by the service.

WESTERN THERAPEUTIC MODALITIES EMPLOYED BY THE PSYCHIATRIC SERVICE AT THE MENTAL HOSPITAL AND PSYCHIATRIC CLINICS

Comprehensive mental health care, as it is generally conceived in the Western world, has had to be modified in the absence of trained staff. The service was geared to the economic realities of the situation, and remained at the level of "emergency psychiatric measures"; the objectives were mainly preventing chronicity, providing symptomatic relief, and lowering the inpatient population to reduce hospitalization costs. Toward this end, ECT and drugs were the main therapeutic measures employed. These measures seemed well-adapted to the situation because the majority of the patients belonged to the lower educational and socioeconomic group, and seemed to have their awareness of self based mainly at the sensory level rather than at the symbolic level. Complaints of "feeling broken up," "me head a worry me, like things crawling inside," and "me skin a tremble and me burn all over" are presented by depressives as well as by schizophrenics. The expectations therefore of having their "weak nerves" and "bad blood" relieved by somatic procedures were well conditioned by the culture to help them respond to the procedures forced upon the psychiatrist by the circumstances. The focus of effort was directed toward the following goals: (1) Early detection of psychotic processes by admonishing the general practitioners to refer at their cases' beginning stages and treating these cases as intensively as possible with electrotherapy and drugs. (2) Discharging patients to their families as early as possible; this was done to minimize feelings of rejection. The promotion of readaptation rather than institutionalization was also encouraged. There is a tremendous stigma attached to hospital "madness" in Guiana and families fear being identified as having madness in the family lest their other children lose their opportunites to get married. The short hospitalization, therefore, can easily be explained as "nervousness needing a rest cure" and the stigma is avoided. (3) Keeping admission rates at a minimum by encouraging daycare, whenever this was possible. (4) Improving the living conditions of the hospitalized patients and intensifying occupational and recreational activity programs; this helped to improve the atmosphere of the place very much. The enhanced self-image resulting from the patients' awareness of their productivity as well as the reawakening of their interest in their environment created a social milieu that proved more therapeutic than originally anticipated. (5) Persuading the custody-oriented staff to accept the open wards which were introduced. (6) Holding group discussions centered on the inpatient occupational and recreational activities, with occasional reference to difficulties in readaptation upon discharge, in lieu of an organized psychotherapeutic program which time would not permit. Outings for patients, organized by religious leaders and individual families in the community, were encouraged in the absence of an organized readaptation and rehabilitation program. (7) Undertaking, at least occasionally, supportive, and integrative, reality-oriented interviews with clinic patients in conjunction with drug therapy.

Due to the time limitation and the ever-increasing case demands (which occurred as hope of recovery for the mentally ill broke down the social stigma attached to seeking psychiatric help), the Kali healers' help became very important to provide the much-needed culturally oriented psychotherapeutic assistance.

The indigenous Kali healers of Guiana relieve symptoms through private and public rituals. They do not use herbal medicines as a rule, and patients usually see the Western-trained physician before going to the native healer. The healers' diagnoses are related to specific, stereotyped dreams, and are "working diagnoses" concerned with "reality" problems and treatment. Motivation of the patient and his sincerity in coming for aid are an important prerequisite for his acceptance into therapy. Little or no attention is paid to the differential subtleties of the diagnosis regarding the patient's behavior. This approach prevails, because outside of motivation, prognosis does not depend on diagnostic shadings in Kali work, which is basically concerned with emotional disorders associated with attitudinal maladaptation, as expected in the culture, and the Mother Goddess Kali.

The healer does not make any prognosis. He does not accept the principal responsibility. His job is to assist in the devotion by his encouragement and his understanding of the resources available in ritual and devotion for combating emotional deprivation among the devotees. Occasionally, as in the Kali Puja, which is the public healing ceremony, he will invoke the gods. A clear distinction is made between invoke and devote. When the mother is invoked, she must help. She then moves through the body of the healer, who is in a trance. The mother must now speak and say what is wrong. The people devote. The effectiveness of the therapy is always the patient's responsibility. Thus, the patient participates directly and *works actively in his therapy.* His contribution depends on his sincerity and zeal at reintegrating his values; it has nothing to do with his material offering, i.e. his gifts to the temple, which are given after the devotee (patient) gets better. Because of the nature of the transaction, the healer is never manipulated. He does not make promises and is not "bribed" or "bought." This therefore places the responsibility for emotional or life-style modification where it properly belongs.

There is no overt countertransference. The transference is to the mother, Kali. The healer is only the agent. Together, the healer and the patient both beg the mother and are ready to "regress," i.e. to prostrate themselves before the mother, assume temporary dependency to proceed along the path of accepted cultural functional evolution. Guilt is always turned inward, unless this could be displaced to the bad spirits. In any case, the patient is always at fault in the performance of his "devote," which can never be perfect. There is introjection of the good object (spirit) in the ingestion of the food prescribed by the healer, blessed by the mother, and cooked and eaten by the patient.

Family members are encouraged to participate in the fasting, the confession of their shortcomings, the renunciation of their bad habits, and in devoting. In the process of sharing the work, a better understanding of the role-assigning and role-assuming process within the family often comes about.

INDIGENOUS HEALER–PSYCHIATRIST COLLABORATION

As a result of growing experience in the collaborative efforts in therapy, a group of problems and situations were identified as showing good response to Kali healing methods and their modifications described above. These situations and problems have these features in common: (1) The patients must be sensorially intact, so that they can be aware of and respond to the rituals. (2) The patients have defined their goals to the psychiatrist and healer in relation to what they would do for themselves should their affliction be healed. (3) The patients of the rural areas are more responsive (irrespective of diagnostic category). (4) The patients are usually consciously and/or unconsciously embracing the Hindu value system. (5) Patients' families are willing to participate in the patients' treatment.

DIAGNOSTIC CATEGORIES

In relation to Western diagnostic categories, the following types of cases have shown good responses, as indicated by the data on cases that were followed up.

Neurotic Depressive Reactions Occurring During and After the Involutional Period

A typical case is that of a fifty-seven-year-old widow, Sumitra, who became depressed after her son and daughter married and left her home. Her illness developed rather abruptly; she had symptoms of insomnia, shakiness and weakness, loss of appetite, and loss of interest in her surroundings to the extent that she became bedridden for about two weeks before she was admitted to the hospital.

On admission, she showed psychomotor retardation and marked inattention, which caused her to give many irrelevant answers; she also suffered from severe depression, which was expressed by feelings of hopelessness and uselessness.

A course of six bilateral ECTs was given with good results. The patient recovered her appetite; her sleep improved, and she became active in the ward and joked and laughed with other patients.

She was discharged after twelve days of hospitalization, and placed in the care of her son and daughter-in-law. As an outpatient, she was maintained on Tofranil 25 milligrams and Librium 10 milligrams four times daily.

On her third visit to the clinic (twelve weeks after discharge) the patient again showed psychomotor retardation and had difficulty sleeping as well as a poor appetite; the daughter-in-law complained that the patient was very "passionate" (meaning easily provoked) and would get very angry, would curse, and threaten to harm herself.

The Kali healer was consulted and, after a joint interview with the patient, in which her relationship with her relatives and, particularly, her resentment of the fact that her married son had set up an independent household (contrary to Hindu tradition) were discussed, the patient was encouraged to report to the healer.

Subsequent follow-ups (one every four weeks) revealed steady improvement in the patient. She was again taking care of her garden and poultry, her daughter-in-law became more appreciative of her, and her medication was reduced to 10 milligrams of Librium in the evenings. When last seen, a year after her initial symptoms, she appeared to be contented and enthusiastic; she looked years younger, and contributed voluntary work at the Kali temple.

Of sixteen cases of this nature that were referred in 1964 to the Kali healer, about 40 percent of the patients (of all those who went for Kali treatment) showed complete recovery, as in the case cited above. Another 40 percent showed marked improvement, although in those cases the patients had to be maintained on antidepressant medications periodically. (Some had to report back to the healer.) The remaining 20 percent did not return to the clinic.

Most of the patients who showed recurrences of symptoms were those whose families showed little or no interest in participating in the Kali treatment.

Neurotic Reactions with (Hysterical) Conversion Manifestations, Usually with Hyperventilation

This condition is fairly common among the young, unmarried girls of the rural areas of Berbice and the Corentyne. A typical case is that of Elena, an orphaned East Indian girl of seventeen who was living with her aunt in Albion village. The girl experienced several attacks in which she would scream, curse, and then stiffen up and be temporarily withdrawn and unresponsive for a few minutes. This started about two months after her only brother died. She saw several physicians, all of whom prescribed tranquilizers (Librium, Valium, Chlorpromazine), and sedatives (phenobarbital), etc., but these gave her no relief. The patient became progressively more irritable and erratic; and the attacks became more frequent.

When seen at the Fort Canje clinic, this tall, well-developed, attractive girl appeared withdrawn and gave only monosyllabic responses. She was well oriented to time, place, and person. She expressed grief over her brother's accidental death, and was vague about her plans for herself. She described her relationship with her brother as a close one, although her brother had been strict with her, especially in her relationships with the opposite sex. She denied having any steady boyfriend, and said this was not a problem because her aunt was "reasonable." There was no gross thinking difficulty noted. The patient, however, appeared anxious and expressed fear over developing the "attacks," which she described as giving her very "bad feelings." She could not relate the attacks with any specific event or thoughts, although she said that she became irritable just prior to the attacks, and would cry, scream, and feel "short of breath." This would be followed by coldness and stiffness of the extremities, light-headedness, "bad feelings all over," and a sense of fading away and being confused, "like me head go swing me, and me can go out of me sense." An impression of hyperventilation syndrome associated with anxiety was made; and the possibility of a predisposition to seizures was entertained. The patient was placed on sodium amytal 65 milligrams, Mysoline 250 milligrams, and Librium 10 milligrams, three times daily.

A week later, the aunt brought the patient for admission because her erratic behavior and attacks persisted. On admission the patient showed tremendous emotional lability and had to be sedated with sodium amytal 250 milligrams intramuscularly (q.i.d.) for two days (neurological examination proved negative). She was maintained on sodium amytal 65 milligrams (q.i.d.) during the succeeding days of hospitalization and was encouraged to participate in the recreational and occupational activities. There was no recurrence of the attacks during her ten days of hospitalization. Her aunt, who visited her almost daily, then requested the patient's discharge so she could participate in the "Kali Puja," with which she was familiar.

After discharge, the patient reported regularly at the clinic for her pills, which were changed to Librium 10 milligrams at bedtime (just to keep track of her progress). There was no recurrence of the "attacks" reported during the subsequent year, and the patient's behavior stabilized. She was studying dressmaking and was quite content with her life with her aunt when last seen.

Many cases of this nature have been referred to the Kali healer for treatment and generally have shown remarkable improvement.

Compulsive Neurotic Reactions

Patients troubled by compulsive promiscuity and compulsive drinking, usually in response to restrictive authority or restrictive situations or physical handicaps, also respond well to Kali healing practices.

The case of Drupatie illustrates the condition referred to above as compulsive promiscuity. This girl was brought by her parents, who "begged" the psychiatrist to admit the girl because she brought shame to the family. Drupatie appeared as a very shy youngster although she was physically well developed for her fourteen years. The parents reported that the girl would run away from home and live with one man after another until she was located and brought back by the family. The mother revealed that Drupatie had always been a submissive and obedient little child. However, since the girl's menarche at age twelve and a half, she had become rebellious, and despite the parents' warning about doing "what black girls do" (meaning being flirtatious and going out with boys to dances as Negro girls like to do), Drupatie would run away and do these very things. As the restrictions were intensified, her behavior became worse.

The psychiatrist's interview with the patient was most unproductive, all she would do was cry and remain mute. An impression of compulsive neurosis was made, and the parents were made to understand that their restrictive attitude revealed to the girl that they anticipated this "bad" behavior. It was suggested that if they could show her more trust and discuss with her the consequences of her behavior, it would enable her to make up her own mind about what would be a more beneficial course of action for herself and she would be less likely to be "mannish" (meaning "wild").

Two weeks later the patient was again brought to the psychiatrist by her parents for the same reason. Because it was hard to establish a good rapport with this uncommunicative patient, it was decided that admission was worth a trial. During her two-week stay at the hospital, she cried continually, begging to return to her parents. She said that she did not know why she behaved as she did, that she was sorry because she knew it was not to her benefit.

On one of the parents' visits they brought the Kali healer, whom they had contacted for help. The healer examined the girl, placed his thumb upon the girl's forehead, and looked steadily into her eyes. The girl looked away, cried, and ran back into the ward. The healer diagnosed the girl as being possessed by "bad spirits due to a spell cast upon her by a black boy." (The girl always ran away with Negro boys.) Arrangements were then made to have the girl taken by her parents to the healer for a series of treatments extending from Thursday to Sunday for seven successive weeks. Discharge from the hospital was effected the following Wednesday and treatment by the healer began.

Two months later the patient reported back to the hospital clinic to "repeat her tablets" which consisted of Mellaril 50 milligrams, twice daily. The parents at this time reported that the patient was behaving better and that the family regularly participated in the Kali temple rituals. Medication was reduced to one dose at bedtime; and the patient was encouraged to report back to the clinic every three months. When last seen, seven months after the iniation of treatment with the Kali healer, the parents reported her to have been "behaving good." Later, arrangements were made for her marriage according to the accepted Hindu custom of having the parents choose the husband.

Of the seven cases of this nature referred to the healer, only three reported, and of these, two showed rapid improvement. The other one did not report regularly and eventually was lost track of.

The case of Bob Kisson, who was a twenty-eight-year-old married epileptic, exemplified a case of compulsive drinking. This patient was originally seen by the healer for "convulsive seizures" which started at the time of puberty after the patient suffered a severe head injury and was unconscious for about two hours. He was referred for evaluation from the Kali temple where he sought help for his "fits" on the advice of the anthropologist, who was at that time studying the Kali healing practices.

The patient's history revealed that he had seen several physicians and that the attacks had diminished to twice a month instead of ten to sixteen times per month. A neurological examination revealed no lateralizing sign; therefore, the patient's medication was increased to Dilantin 100 milligrams and Meberal 100 milligrams four times daily. Within six weeks the seizures ceased. The patient was strongly advised to take his tablets regularly, which he did. However, within another six weeks the patient reported recurrence of the fits again.

Despite a further increase in his anticonvulsant doses to five times daily, the fits continued, and the patient was noted to be depressed. Personal history showed that the patient had been unemployed since his marriage at age nineteen because of his frequent "fits." This forced his wife to work to support the family. The patient felt very badly about this; and because he was certain that nobody would employ him because of his work record, he felt he was a burden to his family.

His wife revealed that the patient had been a compulsive drinker since two years after their marriage. She also said that when he drank a lot, he would get very mean to her and would develop "fits" within the next twenty-four hours.

At the patient's next visit to the clinic he was confronted with his having failed to follow instructions to avoid alcohol. The patient cried and discussed his feeling of futility because of his "fits." He was reassured that he could return to work if his fits were controlled; but he would have to stop drinking. He was advised to report to the Kali healer to get treatment for his compulsive drinking.

During succeeding visits, no fits were reported, and within six months the patient was reported by his wife as having completely controlled his need to resort to alcohol. He was certified as fit to return to work, and has been symptom-free since.

There have been many compulsive drinkers who have sought help at the various psychiatric clinics operated by the psychiatrist. Two of these have consented to report to the Kali healer and both have done well.

Acute Schizophrenic Reactions Manifesting Marked Dissociation and Paranoid Ideation

Many such patients have been referred to the healer for therapy. A typical example is the case of Danny (a young married man of mixed East Indian and Negro background). He was brought to the mental hospital for treatment by his brothers, who described the patient as "talking stupidness." The illness started about two weeks before admission with sleeplessness, bizarre ideation, and erratic, irrational behavior. Gradually, the patient became withdrawn, suspicious, and more irrelevant in his responses. An interview revealed the patient to be anxious, suspicious, and grossly dissociated. He was given a course of unilateral ECT's, and, because he came from the area close to the Kali temple, the brothers were advised to contact the healer to help in the follow-up care, which they did.

Within two weeks, the patient was discharged much improved and was transferred to the outpatient clinic for continuation of drug therapy, which consisted of Stelazine 8 milligrams and Chlorpromazine 50 milligrams three time daily and 100 milligrams of Chlorpromazine at night. The patient also reported to the Kali healer.

Within six months the patient was completely withdrawn from medication. His performance as a farmer and head of a family exceeded his morbid norm, and he was not seen again until about ten months later when after hearing that the psychiatrist was leaving the country, he came to bid him farewell.

About sixty similar cases have been referred to the healer. Of these only two have had recurrence of attacks within fourteen months. Six have been completely withdrawn from medication; the rest were still reporting to the clinic for maintenance drug treatment at the time of the psychiatrist's departure from Guiana.

Phobic Reactions

These cases received the same treatment from the Kali healer as the schizophrenics with paranoid tendencies. They responded well to the exorcism of the Dutchman spirit in their bodies. Of four cases of phobic reactions that performed the Kali "work," two showed significant relief.

The case of Sookchan, a thirty-year-old married schoolteacher, is typical. He had a long history of being afraid of crowds. He would avoid meetings and would enter his classroom long before the class would start, so as to avoid being with people in the corridor. He managed to continue with his work by taking Libraxin continuously over a period of years.

When interviewed, the patient showed tremendous anxiety and expressed resentment over his father's lack of support of the patient's academic goals. He described himself as having always been a perfectionist and being overly concerned about what people thought of him. He showed a great sense of obligation toward his wife because she contributed to the family economy by working as a clerk at the town hall.

Many drugs were tried to reduce the symptoms. The combination of Librium and sodium amytal proved most efficacious. However, significant relief was experienced only after the patient underwent treatment at the Kali temple.

THE "WESTERN" PSYCHIATRIC DIAGNOSTIC CONFERENCE

A traditional, contemporary, Western, open-ended diagnostic conference in a teaching hospital may last between sixty and ninety minutes. The conference participants are usually the patient's assigned psychiatrist, a psychiatric resident or residents, sometimes a third or fourth-year medical student on the psychiatry clerkship, the psychiatric social worker who first interviewed the patient, and nowadays other members of the staff, students, other behavioral scientists including anthropologists, all of whom are jammed behind a one-way mirror and pretending invisibility. Relatives will usually *not* be present, either at the interview or behind the mirror. The rationale sometimes given for the exclusion is that the patient would not be frank if kin were present.

The history-taking is conducted by the patient's assigned psychiatrist; this may last about forty-five minutes or less depending upon whether or not there has been a previous history. The psychiatrist's supervisor may ask the patient questions. Other members of the staff may ask questions. The patient is then asked to leave the conference room. Then a discussion usually starts with the question of degree of rapport established between the patient and the psychiatrist assigned to the case. Other areas discussed will usually include the patient's complaints, the revealed and discerned life pattern of the patient, and speculations about the presentation of self by the patient before the professional group. Another element in the diagnostic conference is an evaluation of the patient's mental status, which is designed to "test" whether the patient perceives reality, reasons adequately, and uses good judgement. A discussion usually then follows in order to determine where the patient's pathology lies in relation to his "premorbid personality." A diagnosis is then usually proffered, discussed, and consensus sought from the rest of the therapeutic team.

Lastly, there will be a discussion of the therapeutic "management" of the patient. Usually, the concern here is to be "supportive," and there will be discussion of therapeutic "modalities" insofar as they concern "management" decisions over use of chemotherapy, electroconvulsive therapy (ECT), and various forms of psychotherapy.

DIAGNOSTIC CONFERENCE WITH INDIGENOUS HEALER

The patient (East Indian) is usually accompanied by relatives, including mother, father, mother-in-law, elder brother or other collateral, who almost always are overwhelmingly concerned and sympathetic. Generally, he will be brought to the psychiatric clinic *not* because of some overt act of behavioral deviancy, contrary to the norms of the larger community or the police, but because his immediate relatives have come to the conclusion that the patient needs sympathy and specialized help. In the course of the conference, the relatives play a useful role in *confronting* the patient with his behavior. Far from this being taken amiss, it serves to articulate the actual behavior causing concern. Usually, the only other professional personnel present are the Kali healer (Jamsie Naidoo) and the anthropologist.

In contrast to the Western psychiatric conference, this may be called a *selective diagnostic conference*, lasting between five and fifteen minutes. It is primarily meant to help the psychiatrist understand the cultural reality problems, to get the input of the indigenous healer into the patient's problems, and to point out to (teach) the healer how emotions, as well as cultural realities, may be utilized by the patient to withdraw from coping normally with reality. *History-taking* is brief and pointed and is concerned with the patient's chief complaint, its onset, and its development; how the patient spends his time now as contrasted to "before"; "now" aspirations contrasted to "before"; and when it was that the patient noticed in himself a change in his own ideas about the purpose of his life.

In the process of this history taking, the psychiatrist may "lose" his patient because of difficulties in phrasing. For example: the patient talks about changes in his life plans at about the age of twenty-five. The psychiatrist believes this may be related to the fact that he unwillingly married at that time due to family pressures. The psychiatrist says:

Sometimes, when one assumes responsibilities, one has to give up certain things, and sometimes it is quite painful.

[Deep silence follows. At this point the healer will intervene.]

You must answer Doctah or he cannot help you. What Doctah wants to know is you getting plenty, much too plenty pickny [children] now and things you like to sport before with sweet gyal and so on, you not able sport now!

The invariable effect of the healer's translation-intervention is to appropriately culturally force the patient to respond and verify the psychiatrist's inferences.

Thus, we can see that unlike the traditional psychiatric history, this history is undisguisedly directive and authoritarian. For example, based on the approach and interventions of the composite psychiatrist-healer, an interview would proceed as follows:

Psychiatrist: What you feel now?
Patient: Doctor, me head a swing me, me nah know what me can do with meself. Sometime me feel me body atremble. Me don't care for eat and me got too much passion [irritation, aggression].
Psychiatrist: Tell me when it is you notice feeling like this.
Patient: [Repeats same list of complaints and is interrupted].
Psychiatrist: How many weeks you now feel like this?
Patient: Two-three weeks.
Psychiatrist: Before this, you feel all right?

Patient: Me used to get this bad feeling and me head swinging two years now.
Psychiatrist: What you mean couple years now? Since you get you first pickny or since you got you last pickny? Answer truth. Nah be frightened!
Patient: Since me second pickny born.
Psychiatrist: Well, how much pickny you got?
Patient: Me got six.

                                [and so on].

The healer's specific interventions are made when asking details of the couple's sexual relations or of relations between the patient and the mother-in-law. If the healer cannot get the desired information from the patient, he will get it from the mother-in-law, who is usually present. He asks and receives frank answers to candid questions, such as: "When you husband go sporting and get drunk, does he beat you?" The wife will usually maintain a shamed, hung-head silence, but the mother-in-law will now tell her complaints about the son-in-law or daughter-in-law. She expects that the psychiatrist-healer (whom she sees as one in authority) will support the traditional authoritarian cultural norms.

When a patient does not directly or indirectly know of the healer, the psychiatrist will introduce him as "Uncle Jamsie Kali Mai Pujari. We work together." In this way, the psychiatrist is no longer perceived as a stranger-foreigner, and the healer at the same time is the recipient of some of the charisma of the doctor.

When the patients know the healer, they usually speak freely. Occasionally, a younger man will say, "Doctah. Me nah believe in Kali Puja. Why you bring this man?" The healer responds by saying, "Me come to learn from Doctah." This is usually accepted and problems are then freely discussed.

The healer will also frequently give a credentials boost to the psychiatrist in some of the remoter clinic areas by saying to the patient:

Me been with Doctah to Port Mourant [a well-known village associated in the minds of most East Indians as the birthplace of Cheddi Jagan] and everybody me and Doctah see is feeling better now.

The significance of this psychiatrist-healer interaction is to improve rapport with the patient, who sees the healer associating himself with "doctah work," and who perceives the psychiatrist according professional respect to the "bush doctah" in his performance of "Kali work."

After the history is completed, the psychiatrist asks the healer's opinion, in the presence of the patient and family, about why the patient feels the way he does. This results in the healer giving a cultural interpretation, or, if he feels he needs more information, giving him an opportunity to ask direct questions such as:

You does dream anyone comes to you when you sleep? You mess up you shorts [wet dream]? You got desire for you wife [husband]? You make enough money to circulate in the house? What you going to do when you get better?

These are standard questions put by the healer. It is interesting that they reflect cultural concern with dreams, sex, work, money, and the future.

After the healer has asked his questions, he will tell the patient he will get well if he goes to "doctah" and takes the prescribed "tablets." This is supportive and prognostic, which is directly contrary to Kali therapy ("work"), in which no prognosis is made and only the assurance of effort is made. The basis on which the healer feels he can offer prognostic assurance in the psychiatric setting is his understanding that the patient wants to get well and his future orientation, learned from the psychiatrist — "What you going to do when you get well?"

At the Kali Puja itself there is no prognosis; this is due to the fact that the patient may not necessarily be motivated because Kali Puja is a community, cultural participation, and not just a place to get well. Also, it may be a place of "last resort," where, after having been to many doctors, a patient finally goes without expecting to get well.

The character of the Kali Puja has gradually changed and now emphasizes the therapeutic aspect as well as the community cultural performance. Very often, because of the press of time, the psychiatrist and healer will interrupt the patient's discursiveness to force direct answers. Discursiveness, open-ended spontaneity is *not* encouraged. In short, the diagnostic conference is a *culturally deductive* session meant to test the reality of the cultural assumptions. This is very different from the Western psychiatric diagnostic conference, in which questions are phrased *as if* there are no assumptions, but in which the *diagnostic statistical manual* labels are very much in the forefront of the minds of the physician, psychiatric social worker, etc.

The patient's basic assumptions, in turn, and his presentation of self involve his desire to have the psychiatrist believe he is a poor unfortunate with absolutely no other resources. In order to reinforce this posture of helpless dependence, he will often present to the psychiatrist a letter of referral, given to him for a usual fee of four dollars from a Western-trained physician, which testifies to the fact that the patient's condition is chronic and nonorganic.

After the patient has left, usually with tablets (medication) and a follow-up appointment with the psychiatrist, there will often be a brief consultation between the psychiatrist and the healer. The healer may observe that the patient does not want to get well, and the psychiatrist observes that it is a matter that must involve the entire family. Together, they will agree that the entire family will be asked to go to the Kali temple where the work performed — prayer-devotion, anointing, circumambulation, and the cooking and eating of the sacred food — will be a family affair. All of this Kali "work" will often be performed, although not always, while the patient's emotional response is influenced by the drugs. At least, that is the theory.

THE MANAGEMENT-REEVALUATION CONFERENCE (M-RC) BETWEEN PSYCHIATRIST AND HEALER

Traditionally, in Western psychiatric settings the management conference follows the diagnostic conference and involves cases in active therapy. There are reasons for calling a management conference. It may be standard operating procedure in child guidance centers or community mental health centers after all reports and evaluations are turned in from the various specialists such as psychiatrists, psychologists, social workers, and others. It will follow an initial evaluation and two or more preliminary therapeutic sessions with the assigned psychiatrist. The M-RC in a psychiatric training institution is usually built into the continuous case conference, in which the interactions between therapist and patient are minutely examined. The M-RC in state hospitals takes the form of progress reports usually submitted every two weeks to the clinical director; these contain the recommendations made by the submitting psychiatrist.

Presumably a diagnostic conference is also a management conference. The major difference, however, is that the management conference constitutes a reevaluation, not in terms of diagnostic categories, but more in terms of "ego needs." The objective is to utilize the therapeutic relationships that presumably have come to be established between the therapist and the patient, the family and the patient, the family and the social worker, and all the rest of the therapeutic human and institutional armamentarium, including the nurse and the hospital milieu.

In the case of the psychiatrist and the indigenous healer, there were three kinds of cases involved:

1. Those brought to the psychiatrist by the healer for consultation and/or hospital admission;

2. Cases seen together at outpatient clinics by the psychiatrist and the healer;

3. Cases up for discharge from the hospital.

The greatest difference between the M-RC conducted with the healer, as distinguished from the Western approach, is that it was rarely "scheduled"; it was spur-of-the-moment and reflected process rather than bureaucratic organization and scheduled predictability.

For example, the healer might just "drop in" unannounced at the hospital or a clinic, alone or with a patient. He might inquire, as an interested friend and coprofessional, about the progress of patients with whom he had been involved. Should the healer come by the hospital in the morning, he would make rounds with the psychiatrist and possibly discuss some of the dynamics about particular patients at that time. If the healer arrived at the hospital in the afternoon, he would make his own ward rounds.

In all cases, patients who wished to might "devote" for a few minutes with the healer and make arrangements to be brought to the Kali temple for more intense devotions (and therapy) on Sundays.

During his time in the ward, the healer makes his own judgements which he then later reports to the psychiatrist. The healer's primary concern here is whether the patient seems to be sufficiently integrated to perform the simple Kali devotions and "work" at the temple. In summary, the following elements are present in the M-RC:

1. Psychiatrist and healer confer;
2. Healer and patient confer in the ward;
3. Psychiatrist and healer discuss healer's evaluation of the patient and knowledge of the family;
4. A decision may be made to discharge the patient and inform the family that they are all expected to go to the Kali temple for "work."

What is most unusual here, as contrasted with the Western-style M-RC, is that the healer plays a triple role — social worker, peer therapist, and cultural mediator-interpreter. As a result of his sustained contact with the psychiatrist, the healer has learned to evaluate patients behaviorally. For example, in the beginning he tended to be symptom-oriented, and to report that "this man complain all the time," but later he described behavior, such as "this man is now working. He do not run after sweet gyal, but he live good with he wife and money circulate in the house."

As of this writing, the cooperation with the Mental Hospital has broken down due to the deterioration of psychiatric services in Guiana. There is now no psychiatrist in charge of the Mental Hospital. However, the reputation established by the healer has continued to grow through the years and he estimates that on an average Sunday he personally sees between thirty and fifty patients. Also, he normally sees a number of persons every evening, after work, at his home. As always, no fee is charged.

REFERENCE

SINGER, P., *et al.*
1967   Integration of indigenous healing practices of the Kali cult with Western psychiatric modalities in British Guiana. *Revista Interamericana de Psicología* 1:103–113.

Effects of Behavioral and Ecological Variations upon the Incidence of Parasitic Disease Among la Gente of Concepción, Peru

JOHN M. McDANIEL, H. WILLIAM HARRIS, JR., and
SOLOMON H. KATZ

In recent years medicine and physical anthropology have become increasingly concerned with the investigation of disease using a "population" as the unit of analysis. In addition, one can no longer ignore the culture or subculture of the population undergoing analysis. Many previous studies should now be considered incomplete for although an epidemiological approach was used, numerous cultural groups were inappropriately lumped together as a single entity. Clearly such examples as those of Alland's description (1969) of parasitic susceptibility in Africa or Gajdusek's ingenious explanation (1964) of the disease Kuru present a more complete picture of disease phenomena.

Human parasitism is a particularly good example of a class of diseases that can only be fully understood and described at a population level. These parasitic diseases include the viruses, bacteria, fungi, protozoa, helminths, and arthropods. The study reported here is an examination of the incidence of helminth parasites among the people living in the settlement of Concepción, Peru. The purpose of this paper is to describe and integrate the cultural, environmental, and biological factors influencing parasitic populations. It was undertaken with the recognition that these factors cannot be treated separately, but are intimately associated with the complexity of the helminth parasites. With an understanding of these intricate relationships, one can begin to deal with the selective factors involved in the pathogenesis of human parasitic disease as well as potentially develop more effective measures to reduce its frequency.

THE POPULATION AND ITS ENVIRONMENT

Concepción is a recently founded, small (total population of 212), and isolated settlement. Located southeast of the town of Puerto Maldonado, Concepción is situated on the banks of the Madre de Dios river within that eastern section of Peru known as the montaña. This geographic zone is a tropical forest environment that is unique to South America. Its proximity to the Andes is attested to by the many surrounding hills and fast-flowing streams (see Maps 1 and 2).

The mean annual rainfall in Concepción ranges from fifty-nine to seventy-eight inches. Mean daily temperature varies from sixty-five to eighty degrees Fahrenheit. The soil is either a loose loam or clay. In those areas in which trees and low growth have been removed, small pools of water are regularly encountered. The combination of these climatic and environmental conditions produces an environment that is conducive to the proliferation of helminth parasites.

The settlement was established in 1956 by a secular Roman Catholic missionary. The population consists of three clearly defined cultural groups: the administrators, la Gente and los Serranos. The administrative element is composed of Spanish individuals who have come to the montaña to provide leadership to settlements such as Concepción. Los Serranos are individuals native to the sierra (highlands) of Peru who travel to the montaña settlements in search of economic opportunities. La Gente are natives of the montaña.

La Gente are the largest of the three groups living in Concepción. All members of this group are born in the montaña, have at least one parent who is a native of the montaña, and are fluent in Spanish. Living in isolated nuclear family units, la Gente clear and maintain small farms known as *chacras*. All families engage in slash-and-burn agriculture, and the agricultural harvest is supplemented by hunting and fishing. Within the settlement and in surrounding villages la Gente are beginning to augment their traditional economic pursuits by acquiring part-time jobs providing a cash income. The exposure to wage earning and the concomitant interaction with members of other cultural groups have resulted in increased acculturation of la Gente.

La Gente maintain a spirit of freedom and resourcefulness. Males, in particular, are quick to boast that no deep ties bind them to their families and present locations. They consider themselves highly adaptable and capable of adjusting easily to new environments and economic opportunities.

Members of la Gente display an impressive lack of concern for most health problems endemic to the area. In this context, children are taught to endure discomfort and pain with stoicism and courage. Adults tolerate problems that are culturally defined as being of "minor significance"

MADRE DE DIOS
DRAINAGE
SYSTEM

Map 1. South America

despite the frequent and severe discomforts these ailments may cause. Included within the category of "minor health problems" are those symptoms produced by helminth parasites. La Gente display little concern for sanitation. Only one family has built a latrine, others rely exclusively on open air locations near their homes. Shoes are seldom worn by most members of the group. Food is stored, prepared and eaten with little concern for possible disease transmission. Little care is displayed with respect to the purity of drinking water.

Despite the fact that la Gente of Concepción share many basic values and beliefs and engage in similar ways of life, there are significant variations in their behaviors and attitudes toward health problems. These differences arc apparent between ages, sexes, and specific families.

In order to carry out this investigation, McDaniel spent thirteen months in Concepción collecting relevant cultural data. Traditional ethnographic field techniques of participant observation were employed in this endeavor. Collection of ten gram stool samples was carried out during the last two weeks of field study. Samples were obtained for 136 or 91 percent of the 154 members over six months of age of la Gente in Concepción. We were unable to collect samples from infants under six months old. Each subject was provided with necessary materials and instructed as to their use. Immediately after collection, the samples were transferred to a prepared container filled with formalin. These were then prepared for transportation to the Pennsylvania State Parasitology Laboratories, Landis Hospital, Philadelphia, Pennsylvania. The samples were analyzed using the Faust Concentration Technique. Six helminths were studied: *Ascaris lumbricoides, Necator americanus, Trichurus trichuria, Enterobius vermicularis, Hymenolepis nana,* and *Strongyloides stercoralis.* Samples were scored on the basis of the presence or absence of any stage in the life cycle of the above parasites.

RESULTS

The la Gente possess extremely high incidence levels of *A. lumbricoides, N. americanus,* and *T. trichuria* (Table 1). The parasites *S. stercoralis, E. vermicularis,* and *H. nana,* however, are present at much lower frequency (Table 2). Similar frequencies of all six parasites have been documented in other southeastern sections of Peru (Cornejo 1959, del Rio 1960). Lumbreras (1963) suggests that frequencies documented for *S. stercorah's* result from the implementation of an invalid technique; moreover he supports the use of the Baermann Modified Cup Technique which he claims provides accurate results. Table 3 demonstrates the differences found, by the use of the Faust and Baermann techniques, in the prevalence of *S. stercoralis* infections of a given sample. From these data it may be inferred that the frequency of *Strongyloides* among la

Table 1. Infection with *A. lumbricoides, N. americanus,* or *T. trichuria* among 136 la Gente subjects

Intestinal nematode	Number of subjects	Number positive	Number negative	Percent positive
A. lumbricoides	136	108	28	79
N. americanus	136	105	31	76
T. trichuria	136	113	23	83

Table 2. Infection with *S. stercoralis, E. vermicularis,* or *H. nana* among 136 la Gente subjects

Intestinal nematode	Number of subjects	Number positive	Number negative	Percent positive
S. stercoralis	136	17	119	13
E. vermicularis	136	4	132	3
H. nana	136	2	134	1.5

Table 3. Comparison of the Baermann technique and Faust technique of analyzing stools of 114 hospital patients infected with *S. stercoralis;* $\chi^2 = 45.113$, p 0.009 (after Lumbreras 1963)

Stool technique	Number of subjects	Number positive	Number negative	Percent positive
Faust	114	22	92	19
Baermann	114	73	41	64

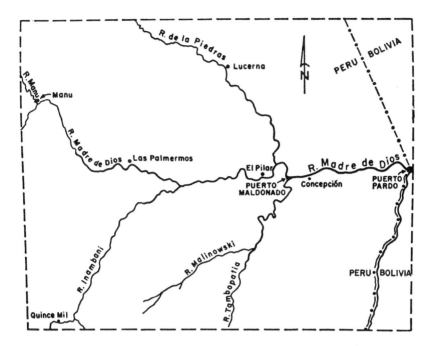

Map 2. Madre de Dios drainage, southeastern Peru

Gente may be much higher than recorded. The low frequency of
Enterobius v. may be attributed to the method of stool collection.
Enterobius deposits its eggs in the perianal region of the human host,
consequently fecal examination results in a distortion of the sample data
(Smyth 1962). The scarcity of *Hymenolepis nana* with la Gente remains
inexplicable. *Hymenolepis* is characterized as a "weak" parasite and is
known to elicit a particularly strong host immune response (Heyneman
1962), yet this does not explain its particularly low frequency in this
community.

Good sanitation and hygiene practices are most often cited as effective
methods of preventing the spread or maintenance of parasitic disease.
Interruption of a parasite's life cycle is the most effective way to prevent
its proliferation (Brown 1969). There is, however, only partial understanding of how much of an improvement in hygiene is needed to effectively reduce high levels of parasitism and what criteria should be used to
judge family hygiene on an overall basis. These questions were investigated in reference to the people of Concepción.

After termination of the fieldwork in Concepción, McDaniel rated the
hygienic practices of each of the twenty-two la Gente families into three
categories: Above Average, Average, and Below Average. This overall
assessment was based on the following criteria: cleanliness of the kitchen,

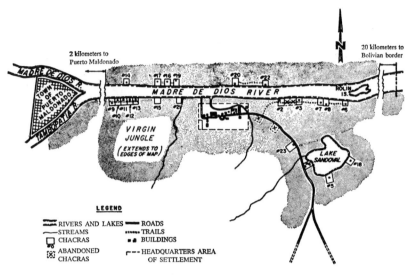

Map 3.   Settlement of Concepción (*Scale*: approx. 1 inch = 2 km.)

dining areas, and sleeping areas, personal cleanliness of the family, numbers of insects, vermin, and pets that gain ready access to the home, and the storage and preparation of food and water. The sum of these ratings determined each hygiene level. Difficulty was encountered because the level of hygiene and sanitation practiced by all was so poor that at first it was thought that interfamilial hygienic differences would be of little consequence. None of the listed categories could be described as having adequate hygiene as judged by Western standards. Even the Above Average hygiene group was continually exposed to risk of parasitic infection. However, Tables 4 and 5 demonstrate that there are differences in parasitic incidence as a result of these hygienic practices. When the frequency, as measured on a percent positive basis for each of the

Table 4.   The frequency of infection by *Ascaris l., Necator a.,* and *Trichurus t.* among 133 la Gente subjects according to hygienic practices

Intestinal nematodes	Hygienic practices											
	Above Average: number of subjects				Average: number of subjects				Below Average: number of subjects			
	Total	Negative	Positive	Percent positive	Total	Negative	Positive	Percent positive	Total	Negative	Positive	Percent positive
Ascaris l.	18	9	9	50	65	19	46	71	50	6	44	83
Necator a.	18	8	10	53	65	21	44	68	50	11	39	78
Trichurus t.	18	7	11	61	65	16	49	76	50	10	40	80

Table 5. Statistical comparison of the number of infected individuals among 133 la Gente subjects according to hygienic practices (see Table 4 for the numbers of infected individuals)

	Intestinal nematodes					
	Ascaris l.		Necator a.		Trichurus t.	
Hygiene comparison	χ^2	P value	χ^2	P value	χ^2	P value
Above Average versus Average number of infected individuals	1.870	0.172	0.458	0.499	0.810	0.368
Average versus Below Average number of infected individuals	3.971	0.046	1.025	0.311	0.130	0.717
Above Average versus Below Average number of infected individuals	9.016	0.0026	2.29	0.130	1.612	0.204

three parasites, is calculated, there is an increase in infestation as the estimated level of family hygiene decreases. The values are statistically significant for only some of these comparisons. *Ascaris* is significant for the comparisons between: Above Average versus Below Average and Average versus Below Average, while approaching significance in the third category. *Necator* and *Trichurus* approach significance only when one compares the extremes of hygiene practices.

The best explanation of these data can be found in the different modes of transmission of the particular parasites. *Ascaris* is contracted through ingestion of unclean food and water, *Necator* enters the host by boring through the individual's feet, and *Trichurus* is spread through both of these vectors. Therefore, the frequency of *Ascaris* is affected by changes in food preparation and household cleanliness, while *Necator* depends on

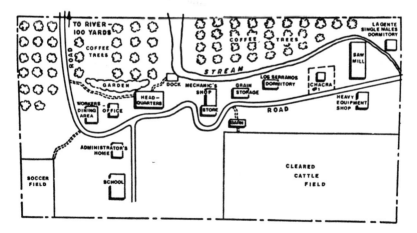

Map 4. Headquarters area of settlement: enlargement (*Scale*: 1 inch = 200 m.)

the soil conditions and the disposal of human waste. Since no la Gente families possess adequate waste disposal facilities, all are at high risk of contracting *Necator* and *Trichurus*. There do exist, however, variations in the soil conditions around la Gente *chacras*. Some families have cleared the land around their *chacras*, others allow the jungle growth to extend to the very edge of the dwellings. The comparison between the Above Average and Below Average hygiene groups does approach significance because the members of the Below Average group tend not to clear their living areas and are subject to greater *Necator* risk. The factors involved in this increased risk will be discussed in the next section. *Trichurus*, utilizing both oral and cutaneous entrances into the host, is only influenced by the combination of discussed hygiene differences and soil conditions. It therefore shows a negligible correlation.

Differences in the parasitic frequencies of these assigned hygiene groups are further demonstrated by scoring the number of individuals within a given hygiene rated family that are infected by one, two, or all three of the tested parasites (Table 6). The percentage of the family members with "high" infestation — all three parasites — was then ranked into three categories: Greatest, Moderate, and Least degree of parasitism. The Least category is somewhat misleading, for families ranked least averaged 40 percent of their members harboring "high" infestations. These assigned degrees of family parasitism were then compared to the formulated hygiene ratings. As Tables 6 and 7 demonstrate, one can judge the degree of parasitism of a family by its hygienic practices. This is indeed a crude estimating device, for many families gave partial agreement, but one can conclude that small differences in the hygiene levels of families produce significant differences in the prevalence of parasites whose life cycles are affected by these hygienic distinctions, e.g. *Ascaris*.

The la Gente families are scattered in a more or less random fashion throughout the area of Concepción (Map 3). The composition of the soil does not vary significantly over the settlement's expanse, but its condition varies markedly depending on each family's preference and economic status. All grow much the same crops: dry rice, yucca, bananas, beans, and some leafy vegetables using the standard methods of slash-and-burn agriculture. Families do differ in the amount of cleared area around their dwellings. Families with "cleared" *chacras* possess areas surrounding their living quarters where the soil is well drained, dry, and cleared of encroaching jungle growth. "Uncleared" *chacras* are characterized by the encroachment of jungle vegetation which results in the poor drainage of the area immediately surrounding the home. As a rule, families have defecation areas that are a short distance from the house, usually slightly beyond the immediate premises. Table 8 reveals that the families with "cleared" *chacras* have a much lower frequency of *Necator*, while *Ascaris* and *Trichurus* show no correlation. These data are compiled only from

Table 6. Nematodal infections by *Ascaris l.*, *Necator a.*, and *Trichurus t.* among the members of 22 la Gente families and the influence of hygienic practices upon the multiplicity of infections

	Family number																					
	1	2	3	4	5	6	7	8	9	10	11	12	13	14	15	16	17	18	19	20	21	22
Low infection (number without parasites or single species)	1	1	1	4	0	2	0	0	4	1	3	1	2	5	2	2	2	0	0	0	1	2
High infection (number with two or three parasitic species)	8	5	11	2	5	6	3	8	4	2	3	3	4	3	5	1	4	3	5	4	5	3
Number of family members	9	6	12	6	5	8	3	8	8	3	6	4	6	8	7	3	6	3	5	4	6	5
Percent of family members with high infestation	90	85	95	30	100	75	100	100	50	66	50	75	66	40	70	33	66	100	100	100	85	60
Assigned degree of family parasitism	G	G	G	L	G	M	G	G	L	M	L	M	M	L	M	L	M	G	G	G	G	M
Family hygiene practices:	A	A	A	A	A	BA	BA	BA	AA	AA	AA	A	A	A	BA	A	A	BA	BA	BA	BA	BA
AGREEMENT:	±	±	±	±	±	±	+	+	+	±	+	±	+	±	+	±	+	+	+	+	+	±

G = Greatest (80 percent)
M = Moderate (60–80 percent)
L = Least (60 percent)

AA = Above Average
A = Average
BA = Below Average

+ = agreement
± = partial
− = no agreement

Table 7.   The influence of family hygiene practices on the occurrence of nematodal infections in 133 members of 22 la Gente families

Number of infections in family members	Hygienic practices		
	Below Average	Average	Above Average
Greatest	7	4	0
Moderate	2	3	1
Least	0	3	2

Table 8.   The frequency of parasitic infections in the members of familes with cleared *chacras* compared with that in families with uncleared *chacras*

		Intestinal nematodes		
		Ascaris l.	Necator a.	Trichurus t.
Cleared chacra family members $n = 10$	Number positive	7	4	7
	Number negative	3	6	3
	Percent positive	70	40	70
Uncleared chacra family members $n = 55$	Number positive	39	40	42
	Number negative	16	15	13
	Percent positive	71	73	84
Cleared v. uncleared parasitic infections	χ^2	0.102	2.782	0.0009
	P value	0.749	0.095	0.976

families rated Average; all tested practiced much the same household sanitation. The infective larvae of *Necator* are known to migrate long distances through the soil whereupon they climb to the highest part of the moist ground and await their host (Chandler 1922). The physical appearance of the "cleared" soil indicates that the *Necator* larvae would be more restricted in their migratory movements and present less of an infective threat to the people nearby.

Six la Gente families (numbers 14, 16, 17, 19, 20, 22) live on the north bank of the Madre de Dios river. None of the six *chacras* are contiguous, and the few trails through the thick jungle provide for limited personal communication among the families. These families are then relatively isolated from each other and the community at large. In contrast, nine la Gente families (numbers 1, 2, 3, 4, 5, 6, 7, 8, 18) are located relatively close together within the busiest area of the settlement. A road and many trails make for frequent day-to-day contact between the members of all these families. These nine are termed "mobile" families. All fifteen families were selected with regard to hygiene practices, and an effort was made to randomize these selections. The "isolated" category numbers two average hygiene families and three below average, while the "mobile" had five average and four below average families. Table 9

Table 9.   Comparative frequency of parasitic infection among isolated and mobile la Gente families

Family characteristic		Intestinal nematodes		
		Ascaris l.	*Necator a.*	*Trichurus t.*
Isolated total = 29	Number positive	20	21	23
	Number negative	9	8	6
	Percent positive	69	73	79
Mobile total = 61	Number positive	52	49	43
	Number negative	9	12	18
	Percent positive	85	80	71
Isolated versus mobile	χ^2	2.318	0.328	0.396
	P value	0.128	0.567	0.529

presents data of the mobile-isolated comparision. None of the respective comparisons produce significant results. The parasites must therefore be effectively exploiting the vectors that are available to them in each case and the relative isolation of some families of Concepción confers no protection from these helminth parasites.

Originally compiled as part of the cultural data, the age and sex of each la Gente individual were then used in this investigation, and the prevalence of *Ascaris*, *Necator*, and *Trichurus* was tested accordingly. In Concepción, the females and males have very different social, economic, and household roles. The machismo concept is practiced among la Gente and the males are by far the more mobile and domineering sex. The females are sedentary, living on the *chacra*, engaged in childcare and domestic chores. La Gente women rarely go to the main settlement (Map 4) or to the larger town, Puerto Maldonado, ten kilometers away. The greater number of males (83) than that of females (53) is not a result of different survival, but is due to the wishes of some of the members of la Gente who leave all or part of their families in other towns. However, the parasitic data do show differences in the frequencies of infected males and females (Tables 10, 11). When individually tested, each parasite

Table 10.   The frequency of parasitic infections among la Gente males as compared with la Gente females

		Intestinal nematodes		
		Ascaris l.	Necator a.	Trichurus t.
Males total = 83	Number positive	63	64	70
	Number negative	20	19	13
	Percent positive	75	76	83
Females total = 53	Number positive	39	33	38
	Number negative	14	20	15
	Percent positive	75	64	73
Infected males versus infected females	χ^2	0.010	2.797	2.435
	P value	0.919	0.095	0.119

Table 11.   The proportion of infected and uninfected la Gente males as compared with la Gente females

Ascaris, Necator, and Trichurus		Number of subjects	
		Males (83)	Females (53)
	Present	79	43
	Absent	4	10
	Percent infected	95	83
Infected males versus infected females	χ^2 5.475		
	P value 0.0193		

shows no significance; however when grouped together and tested as a block for their presence or absence the results are significant. It is impossible to discern the specific causation(s) of the above difference, but both biological factors (Blumberg, personal communication, July 1972) and cultural practices (Alland 1969) have been shown to play a role in the type and severity of diseases that are experienced by both sexes. It is presumed in the case of Concepción that the reason for this frequency difference is a combination of culture and biology. Parasitic prevalence can also be found to be a function of the age of the individual (Tables 12, 13, 14). The presence of parasites is scanty in the category of ages one and two years, after which their presence rises rapidly and reaches a constant value of about 70 percent. *Ascaris* shows a slight decline starting at ages eleven to fifteen (Figure 1). This difference, like other smaller variations in the graph, is not statistically significant and may be biased as a result of sample size. The immune response of the host (Jackson et al. 1970),

Table 12.   Infection by *Ascaris l., Necator a.,* and *Trichurus t.* according to the age of the subjects

Age groups (in years)	Total	Ascaris l.	Necator a.	Trichurus t.	Not infected
1–2	15	7	2	8	5
3–5	15	14	10	12	1
6–10	34	26	26	24	4
11–15	22	19	17	17	0
16–25	20	16	12	17	2
26–39	17	11	14	14	1
40	13	6	10	10	1

Table 13.   Concomitant infections by *Ascaris l., Necator a.,* and *Trichurus t.* in la Gente subjects according to age

Age groups (in years)	Total	Number of individuals with:			
		Triple infections	Double infections	Single infections	No infection
1–2	15	2	3	5	5
3–5	15	10	2	2	1
6–10	34	20	6	4	4
11–15	22	12	7	3	0
16–25	20	12	5	1	2
26–39	17	8	7	1	1
40	13	4	6	2	1

Table 14.   Comparative frequency of parasitic infections of one-to-two-year and three-to-five-year-old la Gente subjects

Age groups (in years)	Total	Subjects	Intestinal nematode		
			Ascaris l.	Necator a.	Trichurus t.
1–2	15	Number positive	7	2	8
		Number negative	8	13	7
		Percent positive	47	13	53
3–5	15	Number positive	14	10	12
		Number negative	1	5	3
		Percent positive	93	68	80
Age (1–2)		χ^2	5.714	6.805	1.350
versus age (3–5)		*P* value	0.017	0.009	0.245

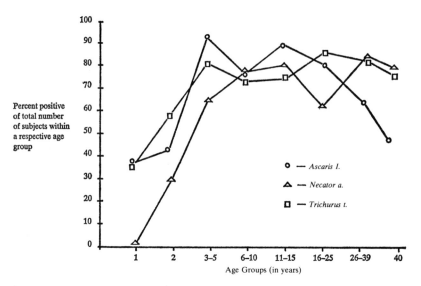

Figure 1.   Percent positive infections by *Ascaris l., Necater a.,* and *Trichurus t.* in respective age groups of la Gente subjects

improved hygiene upon reaching adulthood, and other host resistance factors (Larsh 1951) may contribute to this decline; however to our knowledge nowhere has it been documented that *Ascaris* is more suscept-ible to biological host resistance mechanisms than is *Trichurus* or *Necator.* Improved personal hygiene should certainly affect *Ascaris* fre-quencies, but no continuing improvement after the attainment of adult-hood was observed.

The marked frequency difference between age groups one to two and three to five years is directly attributable to cultural practices. The child under two years of age benefits from the attention of its mother or older siblings; moreover, the mobility of the infant is restricted, he is kept off the ground and is breastfed or ingests small quantities of food prepared separately from the main fare. Consequently he is afforded a degree of protection from the vectors of the helminth parasites. *Ascaris* and *Trichurus* spread by vectors such as contaminated food or play objects are present at a frequency of approximately 35 percent. *Necator,* contracted only by bare foot exposure, is not a danger at this age. The child between the ages of three and fourteen years is, in contrast, free to play anywhere in the *chacra.* His freedom and the relative neglect displayed by his parents subject him to an extremely high risk of infection. This immediate increase in parasitism in young children after their infancy has also been documented by De Rivas (1935). The subsequent frequency of infesta-tion does not vary markedly after this initial rise, but remains a relatively constant 70 percent with the exception of *Ascaris* as aforementioned.

This is in spite of field observation indicating a marked improvement in personal hygiene upon initiation into adulthood, about age fourteen. It is unfortunate that no longitudinal data are available to test whether the same individuals retain parasitic infections throughout their lifetimes or whether a dynamic equilibrium is established between infected and uninfected individuals.

DISCUSSION AND CONCLUSION

From a review of the data, it is apparent that host-parasite interactions are complicated and the investigation of these mechanisms is perhaps best carried out in a laboratory. However, laboratory results provide no information on the natural complexity of living human communities where a multiplicity of interrelationships is involved. These relationships are best investigated on a local level. For example, large random sampling over a wide area of the jungle will result only in the discovery of the frequency of a particular parasite, which alone is of little value since helminth parasites are already well known in this ecosystem. However, study of parasitism on a local level yields parasitic frequency data, possible modes of transmission that exist in that specific community, and insight into the nature of the people who are infected. The latter is especially important in parasitic disease for the existing culture propagates and maintains the people of Concepción and results in significant differences in the observed parasitic infestation of the community. A major concern at the inception of this investigation was the failure of all studied hygiene groups to practice adequate sanitation as judged by Western standards. The data strongly suggest that to achieve a large reduction in the frequency of helminth parasites, small changes such as cleared, dry areas around an individual's dwelling do make a significant difference.

In a community such as Concepción, parasitism must represent a strong selective force. *Necator* and *Trichurus*, which ingest large quantities of blood, can produce anemia and are particularly dangerous to growing children. *Ascaris* can produce intestinal obstruction and pneumonia (Phills et al. 1972). During the period of field study a death of a juvenile was directly attributable to parasitic infection, while many more children suffer from chronic diarrhea, stomach pain, and loss of vitality. The parasitism of these children must also have harmful effects on their growth and development (Robbins and Stanley 1967).

Much of the recent work concerning culture and disease has been oriented to a consideration of the way in which "the culture" of a group influences the health problems of its members. However, it has been the attempt of this study to clarify the way in which the cultures of subgroups within a community can influence the disease susceptibility of their membership. The concept of subcultures within a group which may exhibit significant variations in values and practices is pursued in detail by Goodenough (1963). The data from Concepción demonstrate that the members of subcultures within this small la Gente community are exposed to varying risks of parasitic infection. It appears that variations in the behavior of members of this cultural group are, in part, responsible for the documented variations in parasitic incidence.

From the perspective of human evolution, these variations in behavior among subcultures suggest that they are capable of imposing unique selective pressure upon the membership. While the biological anthropologist has pursued the effects of physical environmental variations upon the biology of human populations, these data suggest that examination of small variations in cultural behavior are also essential in understanding biological adaptation and evolution of human populations. Investigation of disease within a cultural group by an interdisplinary team of specialists should provide detailed data relevant to the problem and, one would hope, improve the life and public health of the residents of communities such as Concepción.

REFERENCES

ALLAND, A.
1969   "Ecology and adaptation to parasitic diseases," in *Environment and cultural behavior*. Edited by A. P. Vayda, 80. New York: Natural History Press.
BROWN, H. W.
1969   *Basic clinical parasitology*. New York: Appleton.
CHANDLER, A. C.
1922   *Animal parasites and human disease*. London: John Wiley and Sons.
CORNEJO, D.
1959   Incidencia de parasitismo intestinal por helmintos y protozoos en el Departamento de Madre de Dios. *Anales Facultad de Medicina* 42:281. Lima.
DEL RIO, GONZALEZ
1960   "Cinco anos de medico en el Madre de Dios." Instituto de Estudios Tropicales, Pio Aza.
DE RIVAS, D.
1935   *Clinical parasitology and tropical medicine*. Philadelphia: Lea and Febiger.
GAJDUSEK, C.
1964   Factors governing the genetics of primitive human populations. *Cold Spring Harbor Symposium on Quantitative Biology* 29:121–136.
GOODENOUGH, W. H.
1963   *Cooperation in change*. New York: Russell Sage Foundation.
HEYNEMAN, D.
1962   Studies on helminth immunity: comparison between lumenal and tissue

phases of infection in the white mouse by *H. nana. American Journal of Tropical Medicine* 11:46–63.

JACKSON, G. L., R. HERMAN, I. SINGER
  1970   *Immunity to parasitic animals*, volume two. New York: Meredith.

LARSH, J. E.
  1951   Host-parasite relationships in cestode infections with emphasis on host resistance. *Journal of Parasitology* 37:343–346.

LUMBRERAS, H.
  1963   Strongyloidosis: I: Evaluación de la "técnica de Baermann modificada en copa" en el estudio de la strongyloidosis. *Revista Medical Peruana* 32(334).

PHILLS, J. A., A. J. HAROLD, G. V. WHITEMAN, TARELMUTTER
  1972   Pulmonary abnormalities and esosinophila due to *Ascaris suum. New England Journal of Medicine* 282:18–23.

ROBBINS, S., B. STANLEY
  1967   *Pathology.* Boston: W. B. Saunders.

SMYTH, J. D.
  1962   *Introduction to animal parasitology.* London: English Universities Press.

PART THREE

Spirits, Structures, and Stars

Introduction

DAVID L. BROWMAN and RONALD A. SCHWARZ

The intimacy and subtlety of relations among man, nature, and the supernatural in tribal communities contrast sharply with the fragmentation and specialization of industrialized societies. Even the anthropologist trained to expect the unusual cannot avoid surprise and wonder as he begins to identify the elements, structures, and processes which make up the world view of the people he studies.

Reporting on the content and structure of cosmology and ritual has long been a major concern of ethnographers. Past consideration of these areas of belief has revealed the way in which illness and disease among nonliterate societies were linked to ideas of spiritual causation and moral transgression (e.g. Evans-Pritchard 1937). More recent anthropological investigations and structural analysis have added to our understanding of the ways primitive man organizes his experience of natural, social, and cultural phenomena into complex, systematic models.

The contributions in this section represent a sample of the diversity of perspectives and structures found among tribal groups on the continent. They are important not only for their detailed ethnographic content, but also for the analytical approaches used by the authors.

Taylor focuses on one category of spiritual beings (the faunal *hekula*) and the role of the Sanumá (Yanoama) shaman in mediating relations between these spirits and society. His analysis is particularly interesting since the *hekula* do not exist independently in the supernatural world, but depend on the shaman for their existence.

Sharon describes the structure and dynamics of a single séance of a Peruvian folk healer (*curandero*) in which elements of indigenous cosmology are syncretized with those of Catholicism. He provides a detailed analysis of the structure and content of a curing ritual in which the central goal is to achieve a balance of power.

Boglár concentrates on a Piaroa ritual and demonstrates the importance of examining the native's view of natural phenomena. He shows how the creative process of mask making is related to their conceptualization of the natural environment, their social system, myths, and ceremonial activities.

Dumont's paper on the Panare is a fascinating analysis of the relationship between astronomical and sociocultural phenomena. His research suggests that the Panare's view of astronomical events is linked with structural principles and transformations within and between a variety of sociocultural contexts.

REFERENCE

EVANS-PRITCHARD, E. E.
  1937 *Witchcraft, oracles and magic among the Azande.* London: Oxford University Press.

Body and Spirit Among the Sanumá (Yanoama) of North Brazil

KENNETH I. TAYLOR

This paper is a discussion of one aspect of the supernatural beliefs relating to the shamanism of the Sanumá Indians of the upper Auaris river valley in the northwest of Roraima territory in northern Brazil.[1] This has to do especially with the nature of the relationship between one category of the assistant spirits used in Sanumá shamanism — the faunal *hekula* — and human society.

The Sanumá are tropical forest slash-and-burn horticulturalists who also depend considerably on the results of regular hunting of game birds and animals and the gathering of wild forest products. Their main crops are bitter manioc, plantains, and bananas; their more important game animals are tapir, peccaries, monkeys, paca, agouti, and armadillos. They are still an isolated group, their only regular contact with outsiders being with missionaries and Makiritare Indians (known as Maiongong in Brazil). They are one of four main subgroups (Yanomami, Yanomam, Yanam, and Sanumá) of the Yanoama[2] of north Brazil and south Venezuela. This is a linguistic division, each subgroup consisting of the speakers of one of the four closely related languages of the Yanoama language family (Migliazza 1972).

[1] My understanding of shamanism as practiced in the upper Auaris region shows a number of differences of detail from that reported for other subgroups of the Yanoama, and even for other Sanumá. It should be understood, then, that this paper is based on my own data and observations. My information was collected primarily in two settlements (Auaris and Kadimani) and is based on regular observation throughout a twenty-three-month period of fieldwork (between April 1968 and September 1970), including five months during which I devoted some half of my interview work to certain aspects of shamanism.

The fieldwork was conducted jointly with that of Alcida R. Ramos, and I am much indebted to her for useful comments on this paper. Some preliminary results of our research are: Ramos (n.d.;1972); Taylor (1971a, 1971b, 1972).

The research was financed by a National Science Foundation doctoral dissertation grant, which support is gratefully acknowledged.

[2] Also known in the literature as Waika, Shiriana, Guaharibo, Shamatari, etc.

202   KENNETH I. TAYLOR

The shamanism of the Sanumá of the upper Auaris region is based entirely on the use of assistant spirits (*hekula dɨbɨ*) to act on the shaman's behalf. Shamanism is used primarily in curing, which involves the destruction or chasing away, by the shaman's *hekula*, of those other spirits (which can be of several different types) which have caused or which intend to bring about sickness and death. It can also be used to ensure hunting success. Another possibility is to "shamanize," that is, to ask certain *hekula* (which can also be used in curing, etc.) to attack and kill the enemies of one's group. In each case the shaman's role is simply to call the appropriate *hekula*, from the many at his disposal, and present them with the problem at hand.

The relationship between the *hekula* and their shaman, and that between the people of his village and allied villages, is one of benevolent, helpful cooperation. With certain qualifications this seems to be true of all *hekula*, but it is particularly so in the case of those which are the spirits of dead animals.[3] It would not, however, be correct to say that these faunal *hekula* exist simply to serve mankind. In fact, by no means do all faunal *hekula* do so. The demography and life spans of animal and human populations are such that there are always more faunal *hekula* available than there are shamans to use them. This remains the case even after allowing for the fact that older shamans often have several *hekula* of a given animal species living in their chests — one, or one pair, from each of several specified distant territories. When it comes time for a shaman to call a *hekula* to his service, to come and live in his chest, there is always a plentiful supply of faunal *hekula* in any given house of their species. Nevertheless, those faunal *hekula* which do function as assistant spirits to a shaman do so in a highly cooperative, helpful way.

I am describing the faunal *hekula* of Sanumá shamanism as essentially helpful and cooperative. This can be compared with the equivalent information, where available, as contained in other researchers' reports. Zerries (1955:81) mentions use of the *hekula* only in terms of their being induced "to bring mishap and sickness to the enemies of the village." Wilbert (1963) speaks of both the killing and curing powers of the *hekula*, but explains that he has the impression that the actions of the *hekula* are only in response to the wishes and direction of the shaman. De Barandiaran, who criticizes other missionaries for calling the *hekula* demons or evil spirits, says that they are at all times on the watch and waiting for the shaman's call for help. His account deals almost exclusively with curing shamanism, though he does include the introduction of a "hostile" *hekula*

---

[3]   The Sanumá category which I refer to here as "animals" — *salo bi* — may be more accurately glossed as "edible fauna." It includes birds, mammals, fish, amphibians, some insects, snakes, etc. For a more detailed discussion of the concept, see Taylor (1972:217–220).

into the body of the patient, by an enemy shaman, as one possible cause of sickness (1965:26)

Chagnon emphasizes the contribution of the *hekula* to the pattern of intervillage hostility, in their causing sickness and death. Their function in curing he mentions only in passing, and evidently considers the *hekula* to be essentially evil, calling them "demons" and "evil spirits" (1968:24, 45, 51, 52, 90). The incidence of intervillage raiding and associated hostile relations is very much lower for the Sanumá than for the Yanomami of the Mavaca river area. Thus the enemy-killing function of the *hekula* can be expected to receive less emphasis among the Sanumá. Nevertheless, I would insist that the difference must be one of emphasis only and the general nature of the *hekula* (helpful and cooperative, whether in curing one's kinsmen or in killing one's enemies) remains the same for both the Sanumá and the Yanomami. Whatever evil is involved is human. The *hekula* simply oblige by doing what the shaman asks of them.

In the soundtrack to the film *Magical death,* Chagnon (1971) gives a more satisfactory impression of the *hekula*. The film is, of course, specifically about a session of shamanism for the purpose of killing enemy children, but in the soundtrack full recognition is also given to the curing function of the *hekula*, and it is also made clear that their action in either curing or killing is entirely at the behest of the shamans. Goetz (1969) gives a well-balanced account of the *hekula* as assistant spirits which help the shaman both in attacking and interfering with the food supply of his enemies, and in protecting, helping, and curing his own people. Helena Valero's information on Yanomami shamanism, in Biocca (1971), also tells of the *hekula* as spirits which are used by shamans both against enemies and in curing fellow villagers. Thus, in spite of differences of detail and fullness of information, and with the exception only of Chagnon (1968), there is general agreement that (at least for the Sanumá and Yanomami subgroups) the *hekula* act only at the request of the shamans and in such a way as to cooperate with them in their intra- and intervillage relations.

My purpose is, then, to attempt an explanation, within the terms of the Sanumá belief system itself, for the especially cooperative character of the faunal category of *hekula*. The explanation I shall suggest is not expressed as such by the Sanumá, but it is implicit, and can be readily discerned, in the series of beliefs concerning the mythological status, and the present-day life cycle of the faunal beings. In mythological times the ancestors of animal species, just as the other beings of that time, were corporeal, humanoid in both body and spirit, and indestructible. When they were transformed into animals they lost this condition, becoming animaloid and destructible. The cooperative nature of the faunal *hekula* can, then, be understood as part of an attempt on their part to reestablish, to the extent that present-day circumstances permit, the situation of their mythological ancestors, i.e. that of humanoid appearance, indestructibility, and corporeality.

GENERAL CHARACTER OF SANUMÁ SHAMANISM

The Several Types of Shamanism

I have data on five principal types of shamanism. These are:
(1) curing shamanism;
(2) protection from evil spirits, etc.;
(3) festival hunting shamanism;
(4) other hunting shamanism; and
(5) shamanism to attack enemies.

CURING SHAMANISM. A Sanumá becomes ill as a result of the action of evil spirits, ghosts, the spirits of dead animals offended by the breaking of taboos, or human enemies using supernatural means of attack. One of these means of attack is the type of shamanism in which certain *hekula* can be sent to cause sickness in enemy villages. Supernatural attack also includes that of night raiders (*ōka dɨbɨ*) using magical preparations and techniques. This kind of attack is not responded to with shamanism, and so does not relate to my topic in this paper.

In most cases of illness, where the cause is spirit action, the *hekula* used in shamanism are, if powerful enough in a given case, able to cure the victim by killing or scaring away the offending spirit and by extracting or ejecting the illness (which may involve a pathogenic object) from the patient's body. This shamanism for the purpose of curing is, in fact, a fairly constant occurrence. It was by far the most common type of shamanism observed during the fieldwork.

Curing shamanism is, however, only one of several kinds of shamanism used. These all follow the same basic procedure of calling the *hekula* for assistance, and turning the matter over to them for their action.

PROTECTION FROM EVIL SPIRITS OR ENEMY HEKULA. When there is reason to believe that *sai dɨbɨ* [evil spirits] are in the vicinity of the village (typically, if not invariably, with the purpose of causing sickness), shamanism is used to scare these spirits away, or at least to divert their attention to some other village. On one occasion when a neighbor had spent most of the night shamanizing, he said it had been because his *hekula* had awakened him to warn him that the *sai de* which causes malaria had been on its way to the village. He was able to persuade it not to harm anyone at his community (Auaris) and had sent it off to the north, to a village of Sanumá who rarely if ever have any contact with the Auaris people.

In certain circumstances *sai dibɨ* reveal their presence to humans. Once when a young man returning from evening hunting heard what sounded like a baby crying in an empty fieldhouse, it was realized that it must have been the *meeni dibɨ* (one type of evil spirit) on their way to cause harm at Auaris. To prevent this an older man shamanized that night. When a shaman's *hekula* warn him that enemy-sent *hekula* are approaching, he will shamanize to ward off their attack (see below).

FESTIVAL HUNTING SHAMANISM. We also observed numerous times the use of shamanism in preparation for the ritual hunt which is always a part of a "Festival for the Dead." Shamanism of this kind is always a group performance, during the day, and always with the use of snuff.[4] A supply of snuff is usually prepared especially for the purpose. It was only in performances of this kind of shamanism that we ever saw men who are not shamans (or novices) taking the snuff. Festival hunting shamanism is primarily to call on appropriate *hekula* to help ensure success in the hunt. Many of these *hekula* are of species which in their living (*salo*) phase do in fact kill the animal which is desired by the hunters. *Hekula* of this kind are called in connection with a long list of animals and birds which it is hoped may be caught during the hunt. For example: the *kokoimane* [buzzard] *hekula* can help the hunters catch the *paluli* (Portuguese *mutum* "bush turkey"), the largest and most prized game bird in the area; and the *kitanani* [cougar] *hekula* can help in the hunting of deer.

Other *hekula* called are those able to protect the hunters from dangers such as snakebite and the attack of evil spirits. For example, the *uli dili dibɨ* (one type of evil spirit) can be called, just as if they were *hekula*, and asked to refrain from their usual practice of blowing magic dust at hunters moving through thick undergrowth. Also called are spirits which can influence the weather for the duration of the hunt. For example, the *sano* ("thunder," Sky People) *hekula* can be called and asked not to make rain during the hunt. Again using appropriate *hekula*, the shamans will rid each other, and any nonshamans (especially young men) who are also going on the hunt, of "bad aim." This is considered a supernaturally caused condition (one possible cause is the nonobservation of certain food prohibitions by the hunter's wife). It can be dealt with, by *hekula*, in what is in effect a minor "curing" interlude in the hunting shamanism session.

---

[4]   Three varieties of snuff are used in the Auaris area. These are: *sagona sai*, made from the inner bark of a tree; *palalo*, from the seeds of a tree; and *koali nagi*, from the leaves of a small shrub. The generic term "*sagona*" is applied to all three. It is thus evidently the equivalent of the generic term "*ebene*" used by the Yanomami subgroup (see Chagnon et al. 1971).

OTHER HUNTING SHAMANISM. Shamanism can also be used for everyday hunting, calling the *hekula* which can ensure one's intercepting a particular kind of animal, or successfully killing a bird or animal if encountered. This is not a common practice, at least while the hunter is at home in the village. It is, however, made more use of when a family (or larger group) is on a hunting trip and staying at a forest camp.

SHAMANISM TO ATTACK ENEMIES. The people of Auaris have *hekula* sent to attack them, especially by the Samatali (possibly a Yanomami subgroup) to the southwest. They usually sent the *waduba ausi* ("vulture," Sky People), *modogi* ("sun," Sky People), and *sanuna* [supernatural jaguar] *hekula*. To fight off these *hekula*, one young Auaris shaman told me he would use the *soinan dibi* ("bee," Sky People) *hekula* and the *pasoliuwi* ("spider monkey" — not clear if of animal or mythico-ancestral type) *hekula*. A number of other *hekula* would also be called to encourage them. This same young shaman said that he himself did not know how to do this sending of *hekula* to attack other people, but that the Kadimani village headman's father, who died a few years ago, had been especially good at it, and that his own father, an old man and a very important shaman in his day, and another senior man at his father's village could both perform that kind of shamanism.

The Acquisition of Hekula

The initial transfer of *hekula* to the novice is typically done by a senior agnate, preferably the father or father's father, or else a classificatory father.[5] When the *hekula* donor is an elder brother, or classifactory brother, he should evidently be in the "middle-aged adult" population segment, or older.

Shamanism for this purpose is done at night, and snuff is used by all involved. There is often more than one experienced shaman present, and more than one of these may give *hekula* to the novice. There can also be more than one novice at such a session. The donor shaman calls his *hekula* in the usual way and then, by the novice also performing the chant(s), *hekula* are transferred or "cross over" to the novice. When the time comes for the transfer of the novice's first *hekula*, he is expected already to know the necessary chants. This is so in spite of the fact that, no matter how many sessions of shamanism he may have attended and at which he may have participated in the taking of the snuff, he will not have been given any opportunity for formal practice of these many and lengthy chants.

[5]   See Ramos (1972) for analysis of Sanumá social structure and kinship terminology.

Once a shaman has received an initial set of *hekula*, and if he goes on to become an active and effective shaman, he can then call new *hekula* to himself. This is done without necessarily using snuff. In some cases *hekula* will come to a shaman and offer him their services. *Hekula* are sometimes given, or exchanged, between experienced shamans as an act of friendship. Certain *hekula* (e.g. Sky People and evil spirits, when used as *hekula*) are considered particularly powerful and dangerous and will only be taken by an older shaman.

The Performance of Shamanism

The one invariable feature of Sanumá shamanism, of whatever type, is the chanting by which the shaman calls the *hekula* to his aid. This chanting (with interludes, as described below) is the main feature of the performance, whether this is done by day or at night, accompanied or not by the appropriate dances or with or without the use of the hallucinogenic snuff. The snuff is taken either by oneself sniffing pinches of the powder, or by having someone else blow a dose of snuff through a short tube into one's nostrils, each in turn. This snuff is much enjoyed, by both men and *hekula*. When the snuff is taken by the shaman, his *hekula* also enjoy its effects, become intoxicated, dance, sing, and are always more than willing to attempt whatever the shaman has in mind. In general, the snuff is only used in the daytime, in which case the participating shaman(s) usually do the dances of the *hekula* they are chanting to summon.

Shamanism at night (when the chest-dwelling *hekula* are in any case already awake and active) is usually done without any need of snuff. Sessions for the transfer of a novice's first *hekula*, however, are held at night and the snuff is used. Conversely, if curing shamanism, or shamanism to ward off evil spirits, is urgently needed during the day, at a time when there happens to be no snuff available, this can be done, thanks to the cooperative goodwill of the *hekula*. This, in fact, I did observe several times. Apart from the occasions of transferring *hekula* to a novice, when several experienced shamans may take part, shamanism at night, for what ever purpose, is typically a solo performance.

When the snuff has been prepared for a session of daytime shamanism, this is invariably a group session, with any visiting shamans invited to take part. This, of course, they always do, not only because the snuff is considered highly enjoyable, but also because an experienced and active shaman always welcomes any opportunity to chant to his *hekula*. No matter how many shamans may be chanting and/or dancing at one time (I have often seen sessions with four to six shamans taking part and two or three actually dancing at any one time), this is never done in unison. Each shaman proceeds with his own series of chants and his dances are quite unsynchronized with those of the other shamans.

The sessions of group hunting shamanism, which are an integral part of any "Festival for the Dead," are always performed by day, using snuff. Individual hunting shamanism, on the other hand, is likely to be a solo nighttime performance, without the use of snuff.

On two occasions we also witnessed sessions of group shamanism by day, using snuff. It was insisted that these sessions were for no specific purpose, but simply for the pleasure of it. Both times, at the Kadimani village, this was the project of older shamans from the Mamugula village some distance to the south. They brought with them a supply of the *palalo* type of snuff, which is not available in the vicinity of Kadimani. These sessions were referred to by the term *polemo* ["to make like a jaguar"] rather than by the common generic term *ōkamo* used for the usual types of shamanism for specific purposes. Regular afternoon snuff-taking, with shamanism and /or chest-pounding duels, as Barker (1953:453), Zerries (1964) and Chagnon (1968:90–91) have described for the Yanomamɨ subgroup, is not practiced by the Sanumá of the upper Auaris. This may be related to differences in the supply of the snuff. Not all known varieties are locally available, and in this area there is no domesticated or semi-domesticated source of snuff, such as Chagnon et al. (1971) have described for at least some of the Yanomamɨ villages (cf. Biocca 1971:146–148).

I have only limited information as to the content of the shamanism chants. The language used is not that of everyday speech, but a distinct, possibly archaic, form reserved for this use. What is definite is that for each *hekula* called, the same tune is sung many times over, and each time it is what might be considered a different "verse" of the total chant. It seems to be the case that, depending on the nature of the *hekula* in question, the content of the chant is either an account of the events surrounding the death of the animal or person involved, or a recounting of the myth, or a myth, associated with the being whose *hekula* is being called.

In curing shamanism, soon after he has begun his performance, the shaman may go through a sometimes lengthy and elaborate period of "diagnosis." This may or may not involve questioning the patient as to his signs and symptoms, and often entails the recognition by the shaman — intoxicated by the snuff, and receiving information from the *hekula* — of the precise procedures, movements, approach and departure routes of the spirit responsible for the illness. In curing, the interludes between the "verses" of the chants involve the vigorous massaging or rubbing of the patient's body, typically from the head downwards, ending with a clap of the hands and a throwing movement. This is all part of ejecting the illness and is accompanied by loud growling, gargling noises, and rapid-fire recitative-like speech, as distinct from the chanting proper. Certain illnesses, when duly diagnosed, require the sucking out of pathogenic objects inserted in the patient's body by ghosts (*ni pole bi dibi*) or evil spirits (*sai dibi*), to cause the illness. This is best done by a *lala de* [anaconda] shaman, whose dangerous and rare anaconda *hekula* is expert at this task. Other shamans who are not *lala de* shamans say that they can also do this, using other spirits, but not well.

In general it seems that shamans are duty bound to perform cures and to ward off evil, without receiving any kind of payment or remuneration, in material goods, for these services. In terms of social status and prestige, on the other hand, they do receive considerable advantage from their shamanism. When people are visiting in another village, the shamans among them will very commonly be asked by their hosts to take part in any group curing sessions which may become necessary. Important shamans may be asked to go to another village to try to cure a very sick individual. A sick person who is able to travel will, on occasion, make a special visit to another village to ask an important shaman to perform for his or her benefit.

Types of Hekula

The *hekula* used in shamanism are of the following different kinds:
(1) animal,
(2) human,
(3) mythico-ancestral (to animal species),
(4) mythico-ancestral (to human kin groups),
(5) Sky People (humanoid, animaloid, and celestial phenomena),
(6) *sai dibi* [evil spirits],
(7) plants, and
(8) artifacts.

The most important and constantly used *hekula* are those of the first five categories. Only a very few plants and artifacts have *hekula*. These seem to be items acquired (or known about) as a result of culture contact with other Indian groups, or with whites. Regardless of the nature of the object, being, or spirit in question, its appearance as a *hekula* is always humanoid. *Hekula* look like miniature men, from ten inches to three feet or so in height.

ANIMAL HEKULA. When a shaman takes an animal *hekula* (almost invariably he takes a pair of brothers), they go to live inside his chest until he either dies or passes them on to a novice or friend. During the day they sleep in their hammocks inside his chest. At night (which is daytime for them) they are awake and alert for any approaching supernatural danger.

If evil spirits or enemy-sent *hekula* do approach, they strum on the strings of the shaman's hammock to waken him so that he will shamanize to avert the danger.

HUMAN HEKULA. The spirits of dead people are already humanoid in form, but they do somewhat correspond to the *uku dubi* phase of an animal's existence in being also disposed to harm living people. Such spirits are known as *ni pole bi dibi* [ghosts]. The ghosts typically do harm to their own surviving relatives, usually in revenge for some offense committed during their lifetimes, though it is often many years after their death before they find an oportunity to take this revenge. Ghosts can also attack their killers if ritual seclusion after the killing is not correctly observed. Disposal of the dead is normally by cremation. If the body of a dead person is incompletely cremated, his ghost can be especially dangerous: *ni pole bi dibi* are said to live in a home far off to the south in what is nowadays unoccupied territory (De Barandiaran 1965: 2–3).[6] They can be called from there to become a shaman's *hekula* and also to live in his chest.

MYTHICO-ANCESTRAL HEKULA. The mythical ancestors of both animal species and human kin groups, after turning into animals and humans, as recorded in the myths, evidently continue to exist in spirit form and can also be used as *hekula*. They live in the forest, far to the south, where the events described in the myths are believed to have taken place.

SKY PEOPLE HEKULA. The *hudomosi liuwi dibi* [Sky People] live on the level-above-earth (*hidi hendua*) of the universe.[7] This level-above-earth has as its lower surface the visible sky.

Certain of the Sky People have humanoid bodies, e.g. Omawi, the creator twin and Salagazoma, his wife; some are celestial phenomena, e.g. sun, moon, sky, stars; others are animaloid, e.g. the white vulture, the (celestial) buzzard, the *koliomoni*, a large cranelike bird. These celestial birds appear from time to time on earth. I have myself seen celestial buzzards, and once a *koliomoni*, and heard hunters speak of a dead tapir that a white vulture was feeding on.

All Sky People, whatever kind of bodies they may have, have humanoid "souls," which can be called by shamans to act as *hekula*.

SAI DIBI [EVIL SPIRITS] HEKULA. Some, possibly all, of the *sai dibi*, which live on this level of the universe and exist to do harm to human beings can, nevertheless, be used as *hekula* in shamanism. Young shamans are afraid

[6]   Note that this does not agree with Chagnon (1968:48), who reports for the Yanomami that the *ni pole bi dibi* go up to *hidi hendua*, the level-above-earth of the universe.
[7]   Cf. Chagnon (1968:44–45), but note that while, for the Yanomami, the scheme of four layers of the universe is identical, the inhabitants of these layers are not entirely the same as for the Sanumá.

to do this, but an experienced shaman has always at least a few such *sai dɨbɨ* that he can control in his shamanism and make to operate on his behalf as *hekula.*

The Relationship Between the Shaman and His Assistant Spirits

It is clearly the case that the shaman-faunal *hekula* relationship benefits the shaman and his people. The *hekula* protect, and cure the sicknesses of, his friends and, in the case of certain types of *hekula*, obligingly kill his enemies. The human beings derive considerable benefit from and, in fact, are in several ways entirely dependent on the help of the *hekula.* It seems reasonable, then, to ask what benefit the *hekula* derive from the arrangement.

Sanumá informants do indicate that the *hekula* enjoy and approve of the relationship, specifying two aspects of this approval. They say that *hekula* like the house inside the shaman's chest and also that they much enjoy the hallucinogenic snuff (*sagona*) which they have ready access to when this is taken, in part on their behalf, by the shaman. Several authors speak of the use of the snuff as indispensable for the shaman's establishment of contact with the *hekula* (e.g. Chagnon 1968:24, 52; 1971:2; Goetz 1969:41; Biocca 1971:45). Among the Sanumá, at least, this is by no means the case. I have personally observed numerous sessions of curing shamanism — both at night and by day — in which no snuff was used, but a long list of *hekula* were called to assist the shaman. What does seem to be the case, however, is that the *hekula* which are thus willing to operate without snuff are those which live in the shaman's chest. These include, of course, the faunal *hekula* I am discussing.

Chagnon goes so far as to speak of a symbiosis between shaman and *hekula*, "For man cannot destroy the souls of his enemies without the aid of the *hekura*, but the *hekura* cannot devour the souls without the direction of men" (1971:3).[8] Unfortunately, he does not specify to which category or categories of *hekula* this applies. He later mentions one particular *hekula, hedumisiriwä*, which is used "to destroy the souls of the [enemy] babies with fire." The name of this *hekula* is cognate with the Sanumá *hudomosi liuwɨ*, which means both the *hekula* of the sky, and also the inclusive category of "Sky People" *hekula* (see above). The specific *hekula* mentioned in my data as used by the Sanumá, or against the Sanumá, in enemy-killing shamanism are:

(1)   the *hekula* of the sun;

(2)   the *hekula* of the white vulture (considered a supernatural being which lives in *hidi hendua* (the "level-above-earth"); and

[8]   I am much indebted to N. A. Chagnon for kindly providing me with a soundtrack transcript of his film *Magical death.*

(3) the *hekula* of the *sanuna* jaguar.

The first two of these are Sky People; and the third, while from our point of view probably only an exceptionally large jaguar, is for the Sanumá not a game animal (*salo a*), but an inedible and dangerous being. None of the three, then, is a faunal *hekula*. It should also be noted, however, that all of these three enemy-killing *hekula* are also regularly used in curing shamanism.[9] They do not specialize exclusively in the killing of enemies. Thus, the particular symbiosis (or aspect of a symbiosis) which is mentioned by Chagnon — in which the *hekula* benefit by being enabled to devour human souls — does not seem to apply in the case of the faunal *hekula* category. But, as I have pointed out, these are the *hekula* which are particularly cooperative in their relationship with human society.

THE NATURE OF THE MYTHOLOGICAL BEINGS

In mythological times, those beings which were eventually to be the ancestors of present-day fauna had the appearance of human beings. In the myths they are described as behaving just as do the present-day Sanumá. For example, the myths tell of them hunting animals, chopping wood, going on visits, dancing and singing, etc. The looked and acted like human beings and, also like human beings, they had solid bodies and immaterial, humanoid spirits. Like the other beings of mythological times, they were potentially immortal. At this stage of existence they were not distinguished from other mythological beings, including the ancestors of present-day human beings. They were simply human like all of their contemporaries and lived in harmony with the other (human) beings of that time.

In fact, they were ancestral beings and destined to become the first animals. Instead, then, of continuing in existence unchanged (and able to enjoy their immortality) something went wrong and they were transformed (*išwanižo*) into the fauna of the present day.

The other beings of mythological times still exist today, some of them quite unchanged, though they now no longer live in human territory. Many of them live on the level-above-earth of the cosmos, the *hidi hendua*; these are the Sky People discussed above.

The characteristics common to all mythological beings are, then,
(1) humanity,
(2) corporeality,
(3) indestructibility.

[9] Cf. De Barandiaran (1965), where of a list of forty-one *hekula* used in curing, eight are Sky People *hekula*. Of these, one is the *hekula* of the sun and one that of the white vulture.

THE TRANSFORMATION OF THE ANCESTORS

When the animal ancestors were transformed into the original animals of the normal present-day type, their humanoid "soul" components separated to continue an immortal spirit existence. These spirits form one of the eight categories of *hekula* available for use in shamanism. Thus when certain Yanoama myths speak of the origin of *hekula*, it is *hekula* of this particular type that they refer to.[10] The corporeal component of the ancestral being was transformed into the animal. All present-day animals have mortal animal bodies and potentially destructible animaloid spirits.

The transformation of animal ancestors is always referred to by use of the verb *išwanižo*.[11] *Išwanižo* also occurs in a different but related context. In the case of certain of the faunal food prohibitions (see Taylor 1971a, 1972), the penalty for nonobservance of the prohibitions involves the attack of the animal's ghost or animaloid spirit (*uku dubɨ*) in a particular sense. This is when the *uku dubɨ* makes the victim (in some cases the eater of the meat; in others, his or her child) become, to a greater or lesser extent, in some way like the animal in question. For example, a pubescent may become "piebald" like the markings of the eaten *amotha* ["paca" or "labba"], or one's child may get a twisted wrist like that of the eaten *šimɨ or saulemɨ* (the two species of sloth in the Sanumá area). Such penalties are referred to as cases of *išwanižo*.

There is reason to suppose that the *išwanižo* transformation is not just a matter of "turning into" an animal, but rather one of an undesirable loss of a preferred condition. This is suggested by the nature of the situations which, in the relevant myths, precipitate the transformation. The number of adequately elaborate versions of animal-origin myths available to me is still quite limited (a total of only sixteen myths,[12] which tell of the origin of forty-one faunal categories[13]).

Nevertheless, I feel that there are strong indications in the common structure of these myths (and of certain other myths which tell of explicitly undesirable happenings of other kinds) that the *išwanižo* transformation to animality occurs as a consequence of behavior which would

[10] For example, in the Yanomamɨ myth as recounted in the film *The myth of naro* (Asch and Chagnon 1971), where the origin of *hekula* is referred to without distinguishing the particular category of *hekula* involved.

[11] On one occasion when a very old man went somewhat berserk and developed the habit of wandering off alone into the darkness of the night (extremely abnormal behavior by Sanumá standards), this was also spoken of as *išwanižo*. One other application of the term is in the case of cotton thread or threaded beads becoming snarled up. I am indebted to Mr. Donald M. Borgman, missionary at Auaris, for first pointing out this usage to me, and for his comments on the meaning of *išwanižo*.

[12] The sources of these myths are: Borgman (n.d.) for the majority, with corroborating versions in my own field data and other authors; Chagnon (1968); De Barandiaran (1968); Wilbert (1963); and Becher (1959).

[13] Some of these are species, but several appear to be higher level categories, e.g. that of all macaws, parrots and parakeets (*ala bɨ*).

be judged incorrect by present-day standards. This, of course, is also true of the food prohibition penalty usage of *išwanižo*, where it is explicitly the nonobservance of the prohibition which leads to the *išwanižo* experience. In one of the myths this is also expressed quite explicitly: "Because a woman was forcibly led out [to dance] while she was menstruating, the [mythical ancestors] said, 'We're becoming dehumanized' " (Borgman n.d: "The Waikas who go underwater"). In fourteen of the sixteen myths there are instances of such "incorrect behavior" explicitly or implicitly precipitating the transformation of mythical ancestors into animals.[14]

The mythological *išwanižo* transformation does not, then, occur as an arbitrary, inexplicable development. In most, perhaps (with more complete versions of the myths) all, cases it is directly preceded by behavior which would, nowadays, be considered at the least improper, if not in fact prohibited. In the myth of the origin of man's access to fire, for example, as discussed by De Barandiaran (1968), the alligator-man from whom the fire is stolen is, thereupon, transformed into animal form, becoming the first alligator. This alligator-man had been keeping the fire for his own exclusive use, guarding it in his mouth. A party was thrown with the purpose of making him laugh, so that the fire in his mouth could be stolen. With some difficulty, this was eventually done and the fire was carried to the top of a tree of the type which is used by Sanumá in making fire by the fire-drill technique.

De Barandiaran does not discuss those elements of the myth which represent what I am calling "incorrect behavior." These are possibly three. First, the alligator-man is stingy[15] in his keeping the fire exclusively for his own use. Second, when he is eventually made to laugh and thus to open his mouth, the fire is stolen (rather than requested in trade) from him. Quite apart from the fact that these two offenses appear somewhat to cancel each other out, they are less dramatically incorrect than the third. This has to do with the way in which the alligator-man is finally made to laugh — by the *hăsimo* bird-man exploding a discharge of feces in his face. By present-day standards this is truly inconceivable behavior. While it is true that the Sanumá are extremely casual about where they urinate, defecation is always an extremely private and concealed act,[16] and it is considered most objectionable to have to see someone else's feces. Thus the *hašimo*-man's behavior was outrageous and the

---

[14]   Compare, for example, Wilbert (1970) where in thirteen of fourteen Warao animal origin myths (those in his index under "Punishment: transformation into animal" and "Creation of animal life") the transformation occurs following incorrect behavior. See also Lévi-Strauss (1970), where twenty-five of twenty-seven animal origin myths follow the same pattern.
[15]   See Chagnon (1968:48) *re* the undesirable afterlife to be expected by someone who is stingy. In trading situations, Sanumá are afraid to be stingy as a disappointed visitor can be expected to retaliate by using magic to attack his stingy host.
[16]   Cf. Goetz (1969:108).

alligator-man's experience was deeply shaming. In fact, the version of the myth presented by De Barandiaran does say, without specifying why, that the alligator-man, *avergonzado* [shamed], went to live in the water and become animal.

A particularly elaborate animal-origin myth is the one Borgman (n.d) has called "The fall of the possum."[17] In this myth the transformation into animals of some fifteen faunal categories (see Note 13) and, in the process, their acquisition of distinctive anatomical features of taxonomic significance, is described. I have elsewhere discussed how this and other similar myths present an explanation of faunal "taxonomic features" (Taylor 1972:178–183) and shall here concentrate on the question of the "incorrect behavior" precipitant of the *iswanižo* transformations described.

The myth tells of how the possum-man, the mythological ancestor of one or possibly both of the two species of possum (*pumodomi* and *pumodomi tanama*)[18] known in the upper Auaris region, kills a bee-girl (*samonama* species — *yamonama* in the Yanomami dialect) who has offended him, precipitating the origin of the *samonama* bees. The possum-man is then chased into hiding at the top of a tree (a mountain in the Yanomami version). After much effort, a large gathering of animal-ancestors manages to chop down the tree (mountain) and the possum-man falls to his death.

At this point, appropriate behavior — by present-day standards — would involve the cremation of the body by the dead person's relatives and ritual seclusion (*kanenemo*) by the killers. In the myth, however, the killers and others with them proceed to desecrate the dead body by using its blood, brains (and feces in the Yanomami version) to paint their bodies as if for a festival. They immediately *iswanižo* into animals, with colored plumage, hair, etc., in accordance with the body-painting selected by their respective ancestors.

The other instances of "incorrect behaviour" are: three cases of taboo-breaking by a menstruating woman; two cases of personal insults; one of stingy behavior; one of throwing away food in a fit of temper; one of deceiving a mother-in-law by giving blood instead of honey (cf. Goetz 1969:30 *re* horror of rare or bloody food); one of disobedience to a father-in-law; one of wife-stealing; one of making a nursing infant go

---

[17] I refer to six different versions of this myth: three recorded at Auaris, and kindly made available to me, by Don Borgman; another I recorded myself at Auaris (all four from different informants); one I recorded at Kadimani; and the Yanomami version shown in the film *The myth of naro* (Asch and Chagnon 1971). I am much indebted to N. A. Chagnon for kindly providing me with a transcription of the soundtrack of the film.

[18] Chagnon was so kind as to show me *The myth of naro* in New York, November 1971, at which time we discussed the similarities and differences between this Yanomami version and the Sanumá versions. Chagnon has since confirmed that *naro* is indeed the Yanomami word for one species of possum, the other being *daraima* (personal communication).

hungry; one of nonobservance of visitors' etiquette; and one of general disorderly conduct leading to expulsion from the village.

THE PRESENT-DAY CYCLE OF ANIMAL EXISTENCE

For the Sanumá, all normal present-day fauna pass through a series of possibly three phases of existence. These are:
(1) *salo bɨ* [edible fauna],
(2) *uku dubɨ* [animaloid spirits], and
(3) *hekula dɨbɨ* [humanoid spirits].

SALO Bɨ [EDIBLE FAUNA]. The living fauna are hunted, fished for, or collected to be eaten as food. Once an animal is killed and carried home to village or camp it will, if large enough to warrant eventual distribution and consumption beyond the hunter's immediate household, be butchered in a set manner by someone other than the hunter himself, typically by an older brother. Once butchered, the portions of the animal are distributed around the village according to set procedures. Overlying this system of distributing meat as food is the food prohibition system which requires the avoidance of this food by the members of specified subsets of society.

UKU DUBɨ [ANIMALOID SPIRITS]. All animals, birds, snakes, fish, etc., and also all human beings have inside them, while alive, an *uku dubɨ* spirit. This is a miniature of, and has exactly the appearance of, the living being. At death this is released from the body and is free to move and act as a fully sentient and autonomous being. It is thus rather similar to our Western concept of "ghost." Unlike all other spirits of the Sanumá belief system, the *uku dubɨ* of animals can be destroyed. It should be noted that all other corporeal beings have humanoid spirits, even the corporeally animaloid Sky People (celestial buzzard, etc.), and that these spirits are in all cases indestructible. The destruction of an *uku dubɨ* spirit will, however, only occur as the end result of the chain of events which begins with the breaking of a food prohibition by a human being.

As I have described in detail elsewhere (Taylor 1971a, 1972) all locally edible animals are prohibited to the members of one or more of the ten "population segments" of Sanumá society. Young children, for example, should not eat kinkajou meat or they will become lazy; pubescents should avoid jaguar meat for fear of getting a sore back; the parents of a nursing infant should not eat capybara meat or the child may be drowned; middle-aged people will get pains in the rectum if they eat the meat of toads. In each case, the undesirable result or "penalty" is produced by an attack by the *uku dubɨ* spirit of the animal in question.

When such a situation develops, i.e. when someone does break a food prohibition and, as a result, the animal's *uku dubɨ* does attack and harm the offender (or his or her child), one's recourse is to shamanism. A shaman will be asked to arrange for some of his *hekula* to dispose of the *uku dubɨ* in question and also to remove the signs and symptoms of the patient's condition. The *uku dubɨ* being animaloid and the *hekula* humanoid, those *hekula* which can dispose of the particular *uku dubɨ* involved in any given case are always those equipped with weapons and/or skills appropriate for the purpose of hunting and killing, on the model of the hunting procedures of living human beings. For example, when the prohibition on anteater meat is broken and the *uku dubɨ* of the dead anteater inflicts the "stroke" penalty on the offender, the *uku dubɨ* has to be (1) tracked, (2) chased into ambush, and then (3) killed. The *hekula* of a *honama* (a grouselike bird which feeds on the ground and can run very quickly) searches for the tracks, hunts, and then chases the anteater *uku dubɨ*. The *hekula* of a *kulemɨ* bird (long-legged and a fast runner), of an *amu una* [fast-flying species of bee], and of an *uemigɨgɨ* [fast-moving snake] all chase the anteater *uku dubɨ* into an ambush where the *hekula* of the *maitaliwɨ* [arrow-head bamboo] and *managaitili* [mythical ancestors of a specified distant group of Yanoama] are waiting to kill it with bow and arrow. If necessary, a *paso* [spider monkey] *hekula* can then deliver the coup-de-grâce with its quarter-staff.

When someone is bitten by a poisonous snake and the snake has been killed, shamanism is used to cure the snakebite. The snake *uku dubɨ* is first (1) found, then (2) killed. Following this, (3) the venom is removed from the patient, and (4) the patient is relieved of pain. The *hekula* of certain small songbirds locate the snake *uku dubɨ*, which is then killed, with their staffs, by *paso* [spider monkey] *hekula*. Otter, capybara, egret, and cormorant *hekula* then wash away the snake's venom with the river water they carry in their mouths, and a *kobali* [large hawklike bird] *hekula* gets rid of the pain by massaging the patient with its smooth downlike feather arm-bands, held in its hands for the purpose.

When killed in this way, the *uku dubɨ* are considered to fall to the level-below-earth (*hidi kuoma*) of the universe, where they are eaten by the *oinan dɨbɨ* dwarfs. Thus twice-over hunted, killed, and eaten, they are totally destroyed.

HEKULA DɨBɨ [HUMANOID SPIRITS]. If all prohibitions are correctly observed, the *uku dubɨ* will then (without in any way molesting human beings and thus avoiding the risk of its own total destruction) leave the forest and "go home" to the house of the humanoid *hekula dɨbɨ* spirits of its species for that particular hunting territory.

These *hekula* houses are typically in mountains, waterfalls, rivers, but not simply "in the forest." On arrival, the *uku dubɨ* will metamorphose into a *hekula*, a spirit with the appearance of a miniature human being. It is then available to be taken as one of his assistant spirits by some Yanoama shaman, necessarily someone living a considerable distance away in a totally different part of Yanoama territory. On its metamorphosis to humanoid form, the animal spirit acquires a miniature weapon or weapons (*lasɨwɨ gɨgɨ*), similar to those used by human beings. These are the metamorphoses of distinctive body parts of the living animal. Using these spirit-weapons, faunal *hekula* can attack and kill or chase off the supernatural beings which cause illness and death.

The worst that can happen to a *hekula*[19] is that, if it is sent to attack a human being, other *hekula* may defend its human victim by attacking and chasing it away. The extreme form of such an attack involves actual dismemberment of the *hekula*'s body. But this is only a way of establishing dominance and does not destroy the dismembered *hekula*, which will put itself back together again and withdraw.

On undergoing metamorphosis from its *uku dubɨ* to its *hekula* phase, the being in question has regained a state of indestructibility.

THE REGAINING OF THE MYTHOLOGICAL CONDITION

The sequence of phases of mythological and postmythological faunal existence, and the corresponding changes in the incidence of the three basic mythological characteristics, can be shown as in Table 1.

Table 1.   Phases of faunal existence

	Mythological ancestor	Animal	*uku dubɨ*	*hekula*	Incorporated *hekula*
Humanity	+	−	−	+	+
Corporeality	+	+	−	−	(+)
Indestructibility	+	−	−	+	+

When the mythological ancestors were transformed into animals, they lost both humanity and indestructibility, retaining only one of their three characteristics, that of corporeality. When an animal dies or is killed (as when hunted by humans), even this corporeality is lost and its *uku dubɨ* (animaloid) spirit does not have any of the mythological characteristics. When it then metamorphoses into a *hekula*, the being in question regains

---

[19]   On the model of human birth and the relation between ghosts (*nɨ pole bɨ dibɨ*) and the living, it may be the case that these *hekula* are also available for reincarnation in newly-born animals. I do not have information on this point, but will be able to check it out in the field in the near future. The particular relevance of this possibility is that it would mean that the *hekula* in question would thus revert to *uku dubɨ* status and be reexposed to the risk of annihilation.

indestructibility and humanoid appearance. But it is still only an immaterial spirit, living apart from human beings and with no direct relationship with them, as yet.

When a faunal *hekula* becomes one of the assistant spirits of a shaman — going to live in his chest, to be incorporated into his body — it then also achieves a substitute for the corporeality of its long-lost mythological condition. It is also reintegrated into the life and interactions of human beings. Its corporeality is, by all means, only a pseudocorporeality, since the body in question belongs to the human shaman and not really to the *hekula*, but at this stage in the game it is the best available possibility. At this point the faunal being has regained, in the most complete way that postmythological circumstances permit, all three of the characteristics of its mythological ancestor. It is at a possible end point in the series of transformations, metamorphoses, etc., of its existence. Closing the circle in this way, it has, in a sense, returned to its starting point. With luck, it will be able to remain in this state indefinitely, but this depends on its future as a chest-dwelling assistant spirit.

To begin with, there is the possible lifetime of the shaman in question. In addition there is always the possibility of being passed on to another shaman as an act of friendship on the part of the first shaman involved. Beyond this, there is the possibility of being transferred to a young novice as one of the set of first *hekula* which he has to receive from the stock of *hekula* of an experienced, older shaman. In this way the pseudocorporeality of a given animal *hekula* may continue for a long time.

The desirability of this pseudocorporeality is explicit in the fact that there are always some of a given shaman's *hekula* which he neither received as a novice nor called to himself once established as a shaman. These other *hekula* simply appear and offer themselves to the shaman, saying that they much admire the "*hekula*-house" inside his chest and would like to come and live there. Not only does the shaman at times have need of the particular skills of these *hekula*, but these are among the category of chest-dwelling *hekula* which will help him handle an emergency, even when there is no hallucinogenic snuff available. The *hekula*, on the other hand, are entirely dependent on the shaman for their pseudocorporeality in what is, in this way, indeed a symbiotic relationship.

The harmony of mythological times, when all beings were human, was lost when the ancestors were transformed into animals, etc. The subsequent phase is one of hostility between animals, and their animaloid spirits, and human beings. This is resolved, and harmony is restored, when the humanoid *hekula* are incorporated into the body of a shaman, becoming assistant spirits, i.e. collaborators in his shamanism, for the benefit of his kinsmen, neighbors, and allies.

REFERENCES

ASCH, TIMOTHY, N. A. CHAGNON
1971   *The myth of naro*. Film. Somerville, Massachusetts: Documentary Educational Resources.
BARKER, JAMES
1953   Memoria sobre la cultura Guaika. *Boletin Indigenista Venezolano* 1:433–489.
BECHER, HANS
1959   Algumas notas sobre a religião e a mitologia dos Surara. *Revista do Museu Paulista* n.s. 11:99–107.
BIOCCA, ETTORE
1971   *Yanoáma: the narrative of a white girl kidnapped by Amazonian Indians*. New York: E. P. Dutton.
BORGMAN, DONALD M.
n.d.   "Collections of Sanumá myths: transcriptions and translations." Unpublished manuscript.
CHAGNON, N. A.
1968   *Yanomamö: the fierce people*. New York: Hold, Rinehart and Winston.
1971   *Magical death*. Film. Waltham, Massachusetts: Center for Documentary Anthropology, Brandeis University.
CHAGNON, N. A., P. LE QUESNE, J. M. COOK
1971   Yanomamö hallucinogens: anthropological, botanical and chemical findings. *Current Anthropology* 7(1):3–32.
DE BARANDIARAN, DANIEL
1965   Mundo espiritual y shamanismo Sanema. *Antropológica* 15:1–28.
1968   El fuego entre los indios Sanema-Yanoama. *Antropológica* 22:1–64.
GOETZ, I. S.
1969   *Uriji jami!* Caracas: Associacion Cultural Humboldt.
LÉVI-STRAUSS, CLAUDE
1970   *The raw and the cooked*. New York: Harper and Row.
MIGLIAZZA, ERNESTO
1972   "Yanomama languages, culture and intelligibility." Unpublished doctoral dissertation, University of Michigan, Ann Arbor.
RAMOS, A. R.
n.d.   "How the Sanumá acquire their names." Unpublished manuscript.
1972   "The social system of the Sanumá of northern Brazil." Unpublished doctoral dissertation, University of Wisconsin, Madison.
TAYLOR, K. I.
1971a   "Sanumá (Yanoama) implicit classification and derived classification." Revised text of paper presented at the Annual Meetings of the American Anthropological Association, San Diego, 1970.
1971b   "Sanumá (Yanoama) shamanism and the classification of fauna." Paper presented at the Annual Meetings of the American Anthropological Association, New York, 1971.
1972   "Sanumá (Yanoama) food prohibitions: the multiple classification of society and fauna." Unpublished doctoral dissertation, University of Wisconsin, Madison.
WILBERT, JOHANNES
1963   *Indios de la región Orinoco-Ventuari*. Caracas: Fundación La Salle de Ciencias Naturales.

1970   *Folk literature of the Warao Indians.* Los Angeles: University of
       California, Latin American Center.

ZERRIES, OTTO
1955   "Some aspects of Waica culture," in *Proceedings of the XXX International Congress of Americanists, Cambridge, 18–23 August 1952,* 73–88. London: Royal Anthropological Institute.
1964   *Waika.* Munich: Klaus Renner.

A Peruvian Curandero's Séance: Power and Balance

DOUGLAS SHARON

Northern Peru has long been reputed to be a major region for *curan-derismo* [shamanistic folk healing] as practiced by mestizo *curanderos* [folk healers] in night healing séances involving the use of hallucinogens, elaborate and culture-specific psychotherapy, and syncretistic religious symbolism in which Indian beliefs and folk Catholicism are functionally blended. Since the 1960's such practices have been attracting increasing attention from scholars (cf. Friedberg 1959, 1960, 1963; Chiappe 1967, 1968, 1969a, 1969b; Dobkin de Rios 1968, 1968–1969, 1969a, 1969b; Seguin 1969, 1970; Rodríguez Suy Suy 1970; Sharon 1972). This paper is meant to contribute to our growing knowledge of northern *curan-derismo* by concentrating on the dynamics of the night séance of one *curandero*. It is based upon ethnographic data gathered during two field seasons (summer 1970, and fall 1971) of apprenticeship to the *curandero* Eduardo Calderón. The focus will be on the central goal of Eduardo's séances, balance of power, as expressed in the symbolism of his curing rituals.

Studies by Gillin (1945), Cruz Sánchez (1948, 1950), Friedberg (1960, 1963), Chiappe (1968), Dobkin de Rios (1968), and Sharon (1972) have independently verified that the focal point of all northern Peruvian night healing séances to cure witchcraft is the *mesa* [table], an altarlike arrangement of power objects laid out on the ground. Eduardo also works with a *mesa*. As with other *curanderos*, the power objects of his *mesa* have all been acquired under special circumstances during his years of practice as a *curandero*. Each object has a personal significance to him and embodies a special "account" or story representing a projection of his own inner psychic power. This account becomes activated together with the accounts of the other power objects on the *mesa* whenever they are manipulated at night under the catalytic influence of the psychedelic

San Pedro cactus, imbibed in liquid form (mixed with black tobacco juice or alone) by the *curandero*, his two assistants, patients, and accompanying friends. Taken as a whole, the *mesa* symbolizes the duality of the worlds of man and nature — a veritable microcosmos duplicating the forces at work in the universe.

Eduardo's *mesa* is divided into two major (though unequal) zones, called *campos* [fields], which are kept apart by a third neutral *campo* between them. The left, and smaller, side of the rectangular *mesa* is called the *Campo Ganadero* [Field of the Sly Dealer (Satan)]. It contains artifacts associated with the forces of evil, the underworld, and negative magic, mainly fragments of ancient ceramics and stones from archeological ruins, along with cane alcohol, a deer foot, and a triton shell. This zone is covered by Satan, whose negative powers are concentrated in three staffs, called Satan's Bayonet, Owl Staff, and the Staff of the Single Woman. These are placed upright in the ground behind the artifacts of the *Campo Ganadero*. A sorcerer would use this negative zone for witchcraft or curing for gain; a benevolent curer needs it for consultation in cases of witchcraft, adverse love magic, or bad luck, because this is the realm responsible for such evils, and consequently it is also capable of revealing their sources. The number thirteen is associated with this zone.

The right, and larger, side of the *mesa* — called the *Campo Justiciero* [Field of the Divine Judge, or Divine Justice] — contains artifacts related to the forces of good or positive magic, including images of saints, crystals, shells, a dagger, a rattle, three perfumes, holy water, wild black tobacco, sugar, sweet lime, and a five-gallon can of San Pedro infusion. This zone is governed by Christ — considered as the center or axis of the *mesa* and Lord of all three fields — whose positive powers are focused in the crucifix at the center of the *mesa* as well as in eight staffs (called Swordfish Beak Staff, Eagle Staff, Greyhound Staff, Hummingbird Staff, Staff of the Virgin of Mercy, Sword of St. Paul, Saber of St. Michael the Archangel, and Sword of St. James the Elder). These staffs and swords are placed upright in the ground behind the artifacts of the *Campo Justiciero*. The sacred number twelve (for the twelve apostles and the signs of the zodiac) is associated with this field. The crucifix is the focal point for the 12,000 accounts of the *Campo Justiciero*, as well as for the sacred number seven (the "perfect" number of Christianity and the symbol of seven "justices" or miracles of Christ).

The Middle Field (*Campo Medio*) between the other two fields contains artifacts of a neutral nature in which the forces of good and evil are evenly balanced. This zone is governed by St. Cyprian (a powerful magician who was converted to Christianity), whose neutral powers are focused in a Serpent Staff, the Staff of Moses. The neutral or balanced objects are: a bronze sunburst, a stone symbolizing the sea and the winds, a glass jar containing magic herbs that Eduardo considers to be his spiritual alter ego, a statue of St. Cyprian seated on a deck of Spanish divining cards with divinatory runes at his feet, a "fortune stone," and a crystal "mirror" with a cat amulet on top of it. The sacred number twenty-five — i.e. twelve plus thirteen — is associated with this Middle Field. The artifacts of the Middle Field are symbolic of forces in nature and the world of man which can be used for good and for evil, depending on the intention of the individual. For Eduardo, who is a "white" shaman, the emphasis is on good, in accord with the pact he made when he was initiated. This commitment is further emphasized by the fact that the *Campo Justiciero* is the largest field of the *mesa*. Here is how Eduardo explains what the concept of balance governing the *Campo Medio* means to him:

> The *Campo Medio* is like a judge in this case, or like the needle in a balance, the controlling needle between those two powers, between good and evil. The *Campo Medio* is where the chiefs, the guardians, those who command, those who govern, present themselves since it is the neutral field — that is, the dividing field between two frontiers where a war can occur over a dispute. That is the place where one has to put all, all, all his perseverence so that everything remains well controlled.

The Middle Field represents the core of Eduardo's philosophy, for the opposing forces of the universe — as manifest in this microcosmos known as a *mesa* — although giving birth to the struggle between good and evil in the world, are not conceived of as irreconcilable. Rather, they are seen as complementary, for it is their interaction which creates and sustains all life. The Middle Field, in addition to symbolizing the concept of balance or the complementarity of opposites, also provides guidance for practical action because it is the focal point of the *curandero*'s supernatural vision or sixth sense, which is activated by the San Pedro infusion. It is this vision or capacity to "see" that distinguishes the *curandero* from other men and permits him to divine and cure. The Middle Field, as a neutral, balanced area, helps focus the *curandero*'s supernatural faculties on the problem at hand, thus making possible his therapy.

A night healing session is the event which provides the proper environment for the focusing of the *curandero*'s vision and the manipulation of the forces of the *mesa* in order to solve the patients' problems. There are two parts to the session: ceremony and curing. The ceremonial division lasts from about 10 p.m. until midnight and consists of a series of prayers, rituals, and songs or chants (including whistling) performed to the rhythmic beat of the *curandero*'s rattle. At periodic intervals a mixture of boiled San Pedro cactus and wild black tobacco juice is taken through the nostrils by the *curandero* and his two assistants. Nasal imbibing is called "raising," which Eduardo defines as a libation, offering, or tribute to the cosmos intended to "clear the mind." The first division of the seance terminates with the drinking (at midnight) by all of a cup of pure San Pedro infusion. The purposes of the ceremonial division of the session are to invoke the forces of nature and guardian spirits, to balance the opposing forces operating within man and the cosmos, to make the patient susceptible to therapy, and to focus the *curandero*'s vision on the problems at hand. The following are the phases of the ceremonial division of the séance as observed by the author and later explained by Eduardo from taped replays:

1. Opening of the account of the entire *mesa*. Between invocations to the forces of nature and the "four winds and four roads" — i.e. the cardinal points — the *curandero* orally sprays the *mesa* twelve times with substances from the *Campo Justiciero*. This same phase is repeated at the end of the entire séance to close the account.

2. Prayers addressed to God, the Virgin Mary, Christ, and the saints of the Roman Catholic faith.

3. Invocations to sacred hills, lagoons, archeological shrines of pre-Columbian Peru, the ancients, and other *curanderos*, alive and dead.

4. "Raising" the seven justices of Christ and the 7,000 accounts. The *curandero* nasally imbibes seven servings of boiled San Pedro cactus mixed with wild black tobacco juice. Each time he holds his dagger, rattle, and the crucifix from the center of the *mesa* over his head. The *curandero*'s two assistants "raise" the same mixture once only, and do not handle the crucifix. These acts activate the center or axis of the *mesa*.

5. Chant addressed to the personages of the Christian tradition — i.e. Jesus, the Virgin Mary, the apostles, saints, angels — and to miraculous events in their lives, sung to the rhythmic beat of the rattle and interspersed with whistling.

6. "Raising" the 12,000 accounts of the *mesa*. The *curandero* nasally imbibes four servings of San Pedro and tobacco. His assistants imbibe one serving. These acts activate the *Campo Justiciero*. Twelve symbolizes the eleven faithful disciples of Christ plus Paul, who replaces Judas.

7. Chant relating the life of Christ (birth, deeds, death, and resurrection). It is intended to invoke his presence in spirit.

8. Imitation of the mass. The *curandero* lifts a mixture of perfume and holy water above his head and then drinks it.

9. "Raising" the 25 and 250,000 accounts. Only the *curandero*'s two assistants perform this operation, imbibing one portion of San Pedro and tobacco each. Twenty-five in *curandero* symbology is obtained by adding the twelve disciples of Christ (the eleven faithful plus Paul) to thirteen — i.e. the eleven faithful plus Paul and Judas. In this act the two assistants activate not only the Middle Field governed by the sacred number twenty-five but also the *Campo Ganadero* governed by the number thirteen. However, the negative accounts of the *Campo Ganadero* are carefully balanced by the Middle Field.

10. Chant addressed to all the forces of nature and the "ancients"

(Indian and Christian). This chant is addressed to the activate collective forces of both *campos, Justiciero* and *Ganadero*.

11. "Raising" the San Pedro remedy. The two assistants nasally imbibe three servings of San Pedro and tobacco in the name of the San Pedro brew. Each portion is literally raised along the side of the container of San Pedro. Then the sign of the cross is made over the brew before it is imbibed. After the assistants have "raised" the brew, everyone else present must perform the same operation. The *curandero* abstains from this operation.

12. "Raising" and purification of the *curandero* and San Pedro brew. The *curandero* stands up, holding the herb jar — his alter ego from the *Campo Medio* — as well as his dagger, rattle, and a cup of pure San Pedro — all from the *Campo Justiciero*. Then his two assistants raise individual portions of San Pedro and tobacco from his feet to waist, waist to neck, and neck to the crown of the head before imbibing. While this is being done, the *curandero* chants a song in his own name.

13. "Raising" the San Pedro remedy. This is performed once only, and by the *curandero*. He then drinks the first cup of pure San Pedro brew. When he is finished, everyone else present is allowed to drink the pure brew. The two assistants are the last ones to drink.

14. Cleansing of all present. While one assistant holds his seat before the *mesa*, the *curandero* steps out in the open beyond the staffs at the head of the *mesa*. One by one, all present must be rubbed down with the *curandero*'s rattle. Finally the *curandero* rubs himself. The stage is now set for the curing acts.

In sum, opening prayers and invocations lead to the activation of the center or axis associated with the number seven — i.e. the crucifix. Next, the right side of the *mesa*, associated with the forces of good and the number twelve, is activated. Then the neutral Middle Field, associated with the number twenty-five, is activated by the two assistants. In the latter process the smaller left side of the *mesa*, associated with the forces of evil and the number thirteen, is also brought to life through the balanced mediation of the Middle Field. After this the two assistants activate the forces of the San Pedro brew. Then they "center" the *curandero*, which allows him to give the San Pedro brew a final activation and initiate its consumption at midnight. Finally the *curandero* cleanses all participants in the séance, including himself.

A shorthand formula for the numerical buildup of power involved in the activation of the accounts of the *mesa* is: $3+4=7+5=12+13=25$. Eduardo gives the following explanations for these numbers: 3 represents the trinity of Christianity, the three planes of the cosmos (hell, earth, and heaven), the pyramid, the triangle, and the tripartite division of man into body, mind, and spirit; 4 represents the four cardinal points, the "four winds and roads," and the four elements of nature; 7 represents the seven "justices" or miracles of Christ, the seven seas, the seven rungs of Jacob's ladder, the seven virgins, the seven churches of early Christianity, the seven seals on the book of life mentioned in Revelation, the seven angels, the seven planets, the seven martyrs, the seven metals, the seven capital sins, the seven spirits, the seven hours required for the preparation of San Pedro before the session, the seven somersaults performed to exorcise attacking evil spirits in serious crises during the curing acts, the four cardinal points plus the three planes of the cosmos, and the center or axis of the *mesa*, i.e. Christ; 5 represents the five senses of man, and the four corners of the mesa united to a central fifth point (the crucifix) via the "four roads"; 12 represents the twelve disciples (with Judas replaced by Paul), the twelve hours of the day, the twelve signs of the zodiac, the twelve months of the year, completion, unity, and the *Campo Justiciero*; 13 represents the eleven loyal disciples plus Paul and Judas, as well as the *Campo Ganadero*; 25 represents the twenty-five balanced accounts of the *Campo Medio* in which polar opposites are united.

In the ninth phase of the ceremonial acts, i.e. "raising" the twenty-five and the 250,000 accounts of the *Campo Medio*, the balancing of the forces of evil or darkness implied in the number twenty-five involves a skillful power play. According to *curandero* folklore, St. Paul, the great lawyer of Christianity who replaced Judas and thus restored balance to the "incomplete" ranks of the eleven disciples through the "complete" number twelve, gathers the positive forces of the *Campo Justiciero* (particularly the Virgin of Mercy, patron of the military forces of Peru, and St. Michael, the commander of the celestial armies). Then, through the balancing power of the *Campo Medio*, he moves into the *Campo Ganadero* to remove Judas temporarily from the domain of Satan. The rationale behind this process is that Judas, as one who has fallen from grace, has a certain affinity with the forces of light — despite his residence in hell — which makes him the most likely candidate to serve as "informer" regarding the evils performed in the *Campo Ganadero* which he knows so well. But the power of the number twelve, by itself and as part of the number thirteen (i.e. $12+12+1=25$), is required to concentrate enough force to perform this balancing act.

There seems to be an apocalyptic undertone to this numerical symbolism and repetitive increase of sacred power. A review of the mystical experiences of St. John the Divine contained in the Book of Revelation in the New Testament confirms this. For example, the idea of the "four winds" and the four cardinal points, although having Indian antecedents, probably received some reinforcement from the following passage: "And after these things I saw four angels standing on the four corners of the earth, holding the four winds of the earth, that the wind should not blow on the earth, nor on the sea, nor on any tree" (Revelation 7:1). There are also four beasts — a lion, a calf, an animal with a man's face, and a flying eagle — corresponding to the Four Apostles, around the throne of God, which provides a central fifth point, like the crucifix of the *mesa* in relation to the four cardinal points. We also have the Four Horsemen of war, destruction, hunger, and death.

The number seven is found throughout the whole book — i.e. the seven churches of early Christianity symbolized by seven golden candlesticks surrounding Christ, seven stars in Christ's right hand symbolizing the seven angels of the seven churches, the seven seals on the book of life as held by the seventh angel, the seven angels with seven trumpets who usher in the millennium, seven plagues, the red dragon with seven heads and crowns, and the beast from the sea also with seven heads. But the following passage gives us a clear indication of the number's use in association with Christ, the sacrificed Lamb of Christianity: "And I beheld, and lo, in the midst of the throne of the four beasts and in the midst of the elders, stood a Lamb as it had been slain, having seven heads and seven eyes, which are the seven spirits of God sent forth into all the earth" (Revelation 5:6).

Six is found in the number 666 used to mark the followers of the devil on their right hands or foreheads. The following passage may indicate where the idea of multiplying the accounts of the *mesa* by the thousands comes from: "And I beheld, and I heard the voice of many angels round about the throne and the beasts and the elders: and the number of them was ten thousand times ten thousand, and thousands of thousands" (Revelation 5:11).

Twelve is very clearly an important number associated with completion or salvation, for Jerusalem, the holy city in heaven promised to the elect after the millennium, embodies the number: twelve gates (three at each cardinal point) associated with twelve pearls, guarded by twelve apostles, and named after the twelve tribes of Israel; twelve foundations of twelve precious stones named after the twelve apostles; and a wall 12,000 furlongs in length, height, and breadth. In addition, at the end of the book, the tree of life, nurtured by the water of the river of life flowing from the throne of God, has twelve fruits which are replenished every month. A power buildup is associated with the number twelve when it is squared (12×12) in reference to the 144,000 elect. This is the number of servants of God sealed on their foreheads with the seal of the living God by a fifth angel, ascending in the east from among the four angels at the four corners of the earth just before the destruction of the world. Finally, we have twenty-four elders surrounding the throne of God, which provides the central, "balanced" number twenty-five, the sacred number governing the Middle Field.

It is interesting to note the number of times the *curandero* and his assistants "raise" San Pedro and tobacco through their nostrils during the ceremonial division of the seance, as summarized in Table 1.

Table 1. Summary of "raisings" during the séance

		Number of incidences	
"Raisings"		*Curandero*	Assistants
Mesa, 7,000 accounts		7	1
Mesa, 12,000 accounts		4	1
	Subtotal	11	
Mesa, 25 and 250,000 accounts		0	1
San Pedro (by 2 assistants, patients)		0	3
		Subtotal	6
Curandero (by 2 assistants)		0	1
San Pedro (by *curandero*)		1	0
	Total	12 Total	7

From Table 1, it can be seen that the *curandero* is "centered" — that is, he "raises" the symbol of the center seven times early in the session. Then he "raises himself to an incomplete number (eleven, the number of disciples after the betrayal by Judas) or state of imbalance (in terms of completion, or twelve). After performing the mass he maintains the dynamic tension of this imbalance by abstaining from the next two "raising" rites (for twenty-five and San Pedro). Because the herb jar in the *Campo Medio* is the *curandero*'s spiritual alter ego, it is understandable that he abstains from the "raising" of the number twenty-five (symbol of the *Campo Medio*), for in effect he is overseeing the delicate task of "raising" his own soul as well as activating the negative forces of the *Campo Ganadero* and, because the *mesa* is a projection of his own inner powers, those of his own nature, both balanced by the *Campo Medio*. While he maintains this detachment, the assistants also "raise" themselves to an incomplete number (six, the number of the devil in Revelation) or state of imbalance in terms of the center, or seven. They escape this dilemma by imbibing for the seventh time while "raising" the *curandero*'s corporeal self as he holds his activated alter ego, the herb jar. They thus center themselves and establish their capacity to do this for the patients later on in the curing rituals. Now that both his alter ego and corporeal self are "raised," the *curandero* is finally in a position to complete or integrate himself by "raising" the San Pedro infusion and then drinking it at the twelfth hour of clock time, midnight. This climactic culmination of events leads to activation of all his personal powers at the birth of a new day, realized by balancing the opposing forces of the microcosmic *mesa* and of his own psyche.

Thus the ceremonial division of the séance consists of a balanced power buildup. This power is then applied in the second part of the session, which lasts from midnight until 4 to 6 a.m. and consists of the actual curing acts. During the curing division of the séance, each person present must take a turn before the *mesa* while the *curandero* chants a song in his name. Then everyone concentrates on the staffs and swords placed upright in the ground at the head of the *mesa*. One of these artifacts is supposed to vibrate, because it is the focal point of the forces affecting the patient. It is given to the patient to hold in his left hand and over his chest, while the *curandero* chants the song of the staff to activate its account and cause its powers to become manifest. While everyone now concentrates on the patient, the *curandero* begins a long divinatory discourse in which he relates what he "sees." Sometimes others present see the same things as the *curandero*. According to Eduardo, the purpose of the discourse is to get the patient's subconscious to release whatever blockages are causing his problem. Once terminated, two assistants (one behind the patient and one in front) "raise" the patient from foot to waist, waist to neck, and neck to crown with a liquid provided by the *curandero* (usually the San Pedro and tobacco mixture, but other liquids — often a perfume — may be chosen) while he chants a final song. Then the patient must nasally imbibe a liquid provided by the *curandero* while holding the staff by one end over his head. This is called "raising the staff." Finally an assistant or the *curandero* rubs the patient with the staff, sprays it orally with whatever liquid is indicated, and returns it to the head of the *mesa*. After all present have had a turn before the *mesa*, the *curandero* closes the account with a final invocation to the "four winds and four roads" combined with a ritual purification of the *mesa* — performed by spraying it twelve times with substances from the *Campo Justiciero*. Thus the number twelve associated with Christ can be seen as an apt symbol for completion and the saying "I am Alpha and Omega, the beginning and the ending . . ." (Revelation 1:8). Before departing, each person must be orally sprayed with a mixture of water, lye, and white corn flour while the *curandero* makes the form of a cross in the ground where the *mesa* stood and sprinkles the four corners of the area and the outlines of the cross with the same white corn flour mixture.

In conclusion, analysis of the spatial arrangement of power objects on Eduardo's *mesa* and the structure of the curing séance reveal the symbolic expression of his major goal: balance of power. Through ritual and the mediation of the Middle Field, the opposing forces of the *mesa* — and of the *curandero* — are activated and brought into meaningful, balanced interaction. The power generated by the ritual manipulation of power objects is then applied in solving patients' problems. The creative synthesis between aboriginal shamanism and Christian symbology manifest in Eduardo's art seems to be directly relevant to those who seek his services. It appears that shamanism in northern Peru may be more than a colorful relic left over from the Indian past.

REFERENCES

CHIAPPE, MARIO
1967   Alucinógenas nativas. *Revista del Viernes Médico* 18:293–299. Lima.
1968   Psiquiatría folklórica peruana: el curanderismo en la costa norte del Perú. *Anales del Servicio de Psiquiatría* 11. Lima.
1969a El curanderismo con alucinógenas de la costa y la selva del Perú. *Psiquiatría Peruana* 1:318–325. Lima.
1969b El sindrome cultural de "daño" y su tratamiento curanderil. *Psiquiatría Peruana* 1:330–337. Lima.

CRUZ SÁNCHEZ, GUILLERMO
1948   Informe sobre las aplicaciones populares de la cimora en el norte Perú. *Revista de Farmacología y Medicina Experimental* 1:253–259. Lima.
1950   Estudio folklórico de algunas plantas medicamentosas y tóxicas de la región norte del Perú. *Revista de Medicina Experimental* 9:159–166. Lima.

DOBKIN DE RIOS, MARLENE
1968   *Trichocereus pachanoi* — a mescaline cactus used in folk healing in Peru. *Economic Botany* 22:191–194.
1968–1969 Folk curing with a psychedelic cactus in north coast Peru. *International Journal of Social Psychiatry* 15:23–32.
1969a Curanderismo psicodélico en el Perú: continuidad y cambio. *Mesa Redonda de Ciencias Prehistóricas y Antropológicas* 1:139–149.
1969b Fortune's malice: divination, psychotherapy, and folk medicine in Peru. *Journal of American Folklore* 82:132–141.

FRIEDBERG, CLAUDINE
1959   Rapport sommaire sur une mission au Pérou. *Journal d'Agriculture Tropicale et de Botanique Appliquée* 6:439–450. Paris.
1960   "Utilisation d'un cactus à mescaline au nord du Perou," in *Proceedings of the Sixth International Congress of Anthropological and Ethnological Sciences* 2(2):21–26.
1963   Mission au Pérou — Mai 1961–Mars 1962. *Journal d'Agriculture Tropicale et de Botanique Appliquée* 10:33–52, 245–258, 344–386. Paris.

GILLIN, JOHN
1945   *Moche: a Peruvian coastal community.* Smithsonian Institution 3.

RODRÍGUEZ SUY SUY, VICTOR ANTONIO
1970   "La medicina tradicional en la costa norte del Perú actual," in *Actas y memorias del XXXIX Congreso Internacional de Americanistas, 1970.* Lima: Instituto de Estudios Peruanos.

SEGUIN, CARLOS ALBERTO
1969   Psiquiatría folklórica. *Psiquiatría Peruana* 1:154–159. Lima.
1970   "Folk psychiatry," in *World biennial of psychiatry and psychotherapy,* volume one. Edited by S. Arieti, 165–177. New York: Basic Books.

SHARON, DOUGLAS
1972   "The San Pedro cactus in Peruvian folk healing," in *Flesh of the gods: the ritual use of hallucinogens.* Edited by Peter T. Furst, 114–135. New York: Praeger.

Creative Process in Ritual Art: Piaroa Indians, Venezuela

LAJOS BOGLÁR

In 1967–1968, while doing ethnographical fieldwork among the Piaroa Indians in the forests of southern Venezuela, I was able to observe some phenomena at a seasonal rite that may throw light upon certain features of the creative process. The present paper is an attempt to sum up the problems of analysis on this subject.

For the examination of the creative process appearing under ritual conditions it was also necessary to ascertain secular relationships among creators, interpreters, and participants.

In their economic formation, the Indians under examination hardly differ from the other tropical-forest tribes. Besides their horticultural activity other ways of obtaining food — hunting and gathering — also play important roles. As to the social aspect of obtaining food we can establish above all that a clear and consistent division of labor prevails according to sex. The cultivation of plants, and some of the gathering and the preparation of food belong to the women's scope of duties, while the men are chiefly engaged in hunting (Boglár 1971). The economic basis of existence is secured by the integration of the cultivation of plants and the hunting activity — neither branch can be neglected. At the same time, primarily male dominance is typical in their life. A male bias arises from the fact that certain very important ritual functions can be performed only by men.

The fieldwork was sponsored by the Wenner-Gren Foundation for Anthropological Research, the Ethnographical Museum (Budapest), and the Hungarian Academy of Sciences. István Halmos, ethnomusicologist, also participated.

RELIGIOUS SPECIALISTS AND THE PERMANENT RITE

The head of the local group is the religious specialist whose duty it is to perform a series of ritual functions. His most important activity is a partly preventive, partly curative "struggle" against illnesses, but he is also responsible for organizing the ritual ceremonies, such as initiation and masked dance. He is the one best acquainted with mythical traditions and his duty is to prevent their sinking into oblivion. Finally, he is the master of preparation and use of the ritual objects.

According to observations he is also highly respected in everyday life if he fulfills his duties "without fault." This refers particularly to the magical chants concerning mythical animal relations which are performed almost every day. Searching for the sources of the prestige of the *menyerua* [man of the songs],[1] we have to observe, above all, the field which is in the center of his activity, namely, hunting or to be more exact, *the animal which is hunted.* As the animal also carries magical powers, its meat has to be sung "pure" before eating it in the evening, in order that it may not bring "danger" (illness) to those who eat of its flesh. The epic content of the *menye* [magical chants] deals with the killed animal, referring abundantly to the myths.[2]

Clearing up the relations of myths and rites is of utmost importance first of all because of social resonance. It is the questions concerning, first of all, the language, that occur in connection with the magical chants and mythical narratives. I would refer to the fact that besides the everyday language there also exists an esoteric one: the mythical narratives are usually only understood by the initiated, and sometimes only by "the narrators." (The fact that the men hiding behind the masks sing in a changed voice during the dances is also relevant here.)

The role of the prohibition of language is remarkable in other cases, too: the names of certain objects and representations are identical to the denomination of the raw materials. The real or ritual denomination remains hidden. The ritual "instrumental language" is a further step in hiding: by means of a certain instrument it is possible to contact

[1] One of the guarantees of the religious specialist's prestige is a good memory: this particularly pertains to the magic songs performed almost every day. We know an example when the group expelled its *menyerua* because he did not sing the magical chants correctly. This man was a narcotics addict, so his mind became disturbed and because of lapses of memory he could not recite the ritual texts correctly.

A way of learning for the *menyerua* is that he meets highly respected and skilled religious specialists, and he repeatedly listens to their narratives. Even mythology refers to the importance of remembering Wahari, the culture hero. To avoid being forgotten by people he created illnesses, which are carried by animals, so the meat-eating Indian is bound to "remember" the creator day by day.

[2] The central figure of the mythology, Wahari, appears during the creation in the form ("mask") of several animals. After his death his soul went into the tapir, which is under taboo.

the women who are excluded and cannot see the men playing the music.[3]

Concerning the ideology, it is important to clear up the relation of idea and act. It is the religious chief and some chosen who possess the idea (with all its important details). The mythical texts mentioned several times are mostly incomprehensible to the members of the community, but they can hear them and they know that the religious chief "fulfills" his duty. He performs traditionally maintained rites; this is most important for the audience, which reacts with a real social resonance.[4]

According to an informant the chants sung in the hut in the evenings belong together, like "pearls on a necklace." He could hardly have pointed out more correctly and poetically the complexity of the phenomena. Describing the connection of a magical chant (pearl) and the chain of the magical chants (necklace) is not only an example of dialectical thinking but it also allows one to suppose the social need for totality. It casts a light on the problem if we draw our attention to the all-embracing rite of the Piaroa culture: the rite connected with the seasons.

RITUAL "SCHOOL": THE CEREMONIAL CONDITIONS OF CREATIVITY

The *warime* rite is the grandest event of the Piaroa Indians. During the masked rite many concepts of mythology are revealed as well as ritual painting, sculpturing, music, and dance as a chain of manifestations of expressive culture. During the ceremony the mask bearers represent animal spirits or, more exactly, the "lords" of certain animals. These are the peccary, the monkey, and the wild bee. According to the idea of the Piaroa, spiritual identification with the animal makes their relationship with the animal more intimate, and at the same time it induces them to multiply.

During the preparation of the masked rite the members of the local group (summoned from several settlements) under the direction of religious leaders and under ritual circumstances prepare the ritual accessories (masks, musical instruments) while they are initiated into the knowledge of mythology, religious ideas, and activities. Women and girls are forbidden to see the preparations; they do not know the identity of the mask bearers, nor can they see who play the instruments. The organization of the rite is an important task of the religious leader. He has his

---

[3] The *muotsa* [leaf-whistle] made of palm-tree wood is a ritual instrument, an accessory of the masked ceremony. Indians playing this instrument can ask different questions, also related to everyday life. They can play the Piaroa name of palm nuts and fruits favored by birds on another instrument, the *dyaho* flute, which bears the name of the toucan bird.
[4] The situation with nonritual narratives (tales, "true" stories, etc.) is different, as described in an earlier paper of mine (Boglár 1970).

assistants who are to a certain degree acquainted with the ritual "crafts," yet all the responsibilities of organization are his. The masks and the musical instruments are made under his supervision, and he directs the course of the ceremony. In the view of the Piaroa Indians, however, it is not simply a matter of organization and staging; it is another proof that the religious leader is capable of controlling the powers of nature. The oldest religious chief I have met owes his distinguished authority to the fact that in his lifetime he has organized several *warimes*, or masked rites. During the rite and its preparations the .harmony of individual and collective actions also defined from the point of view of relationship is clearly expressed. This dialectic chain of relations can be summed up as follows: the rite results from social needs; the making of ritual accessories is directed by an individual; securing the raw materials is the duty of specialists; the basic operations are done by specialists; the painting is the operation of individuals; although the rite is communal it enhances the prestige of the individual.

IDEOLOGICAL BASES

The basic concept, which is expressed in myths, religious ideas, and acts, is the humanization of nature. In the following I would like to mention identification as an important means of humanization. While examining the world concept of tribal societies it is repeatedly stated that man identifies himself with certain natural phenomena. Several factors — environment, cultural milieu, mentality, etc. — can determine the group of phenomena preferred by a community. It is evident that animals are particularly suitable for such purposes. What factors can play a role in establishing the man-animal relationship with the Piaroa Indians?

This relation is the most striking in the *warime* rite, where the animals are represented by forms, voices, and movements. Representation of the mythical "lords" of animal spirits is not only a formal act, but contextually they are also an animation and direction "from within." (Representation and identification are well conditioned by an intense situation established by the common presence of rhythmical sound and motion.) The figure of the peccary, which is to be found in several myths and magical chants, rises out of the threefold unity of animal spirits, and it is determined by the incestuous relation of Wahari (the culture hero, the Creator) with his sister from which the peccary was born. The myth also explains the origin of the *warime* rite, and makes the community conscious of the "relation" of man and animals which has existed since ancient times.

It is important from the point of view of the identification examined that according to the myth the peccary was born from the sexual act of "humans " Why does the peccary play the role of the "most human" animal? What are the common traits of the peccary, monkey, and wild bee that helped them to play a distinguished role in the masked ceremonies?

Assorting these animals on the basis of their way of life we can establish that:

1. all three animals live in the woods — not on savannahs or clearings;
2. they live in communities — rather than alone, like the jaguar, tapir, etc.;
3. they are plant-eating animals, not beasts of prey.

Since obvious questions pertaining to food acquisition are raised, the basic one for the Piaroa naturally is whether the animal (or plant) is edible or not. It is obvious that the hunting of communal animals is more desirable in the woods (where the Indian hunter feels more at home). It must be mentioned that the animals examined provide the raw materials for some ritual instruments too (tooth, bone, bristle, etc.), and the importance of the wild bee is emphasized by the fact that it supplies honey and wax (honey is not simply food but also medicine in the hands of the religious specialist and a symbolic material for the cohesion of the community; wax is used for several works of the religious specialist, e.g. for making masks, sculptures).

Besides the above facts — which can be verified biologically — the Piaroa also establish some secondary marks which indicate the continuity of identification and which make the relation of man and animal more profound. (The silver lip pendant is like the white beard on the peccary; the tongue of the Piaroa men is pierced at the initiation to make it similar to the tongue of the peccary, which has two natural grooves in it.)

Summing up we can establish that identification with the spirit of the animal not only confirms the continuity of the mythic state, but it also promotes the rebirth "from inside" as the creature being represented and finally helps its multiplication.

THE CREATIVE PROCESS

Studying tribal culture (generally the expressive culture) the investigator has to analyze ready forms and objects. The relation of myths and rites and the idea of identification call our attention to the fact that the forms and objects are the result of a continuous transformation, and their value can be revealed by examining specific cultural surroundings.[5] Now let us

[5] We must agree with d'Azevedo (1958:703), that in anthropological literature, "The processes of art are obscured by an emphasis upon its formal products and their value as a source of information about other things." The paper of Goodale and Koss (1971:190) represents a similar view: "Descriptions of art objects frequently fail to consider the ways in which initial values associated with or achieved in the construction process influence terminal values associated with the finished product."

sum up some thoughts on the subject, mainly to indicate the process of cognition which leads to representation. In the process of preparing the ritual masks we can observe a line of transformation:

1. For realizing an abstract idea (animal spirit, whose "owner" is the religious specialist),

2. they need a concrete model (peccary, monkey, wild bee) and several materials.

3. Under the direction of the chief certain specialists transform and compose the materials so that the representation shall be identical with the model (and to make identification easier for the interpreter during the performance).

4. The identified representation finally gets the attributes from the religious specialists to raise the world of the spiritual beings to a more abstract sphere.

The transforming process of creation can be well observed in the preparation of the *redyo* [wild bee] mask. The *redyo* is a frequent figure of the narratives, a manifold being which can be benevolent as well as malevolent. As to its representation, the Indian sculptor takes a concrete living picture from nature which represents the abstract spirit, namely the wild bee, and its nest on the jungle tree. During the shaping process the sculpture gradually withdraws from the living picture by means of putting different covers (bark, wax, and paint) on top of one another. Meanwhile the elements of the image of nest and wild bee absorbed in each other return from time to time. At the end the white earth-paint used by the Indian sculptor "to alienate" emphasizes that there is a spiritual being present.

Besides the creative process it is very important that the community should see finished forms. It is only the creators, the initiated, the participants of the ritual "school" who can feel and know, that in a mask there is a line, a process registered, and its further life is full of motion and dance, which takes place before the others' eyes. The interpreters remain hidden like Wahari, the culture hero, who has appeared in front of the Indians in an ever-changing form. Not only the hiding is interesting in this case, but also the fact that, similarly to Wahari, the Piaroa Indian also strives to humanize nature. This is a basic tendency of the man who lives within nature and I believe that this is the essence of "the art of the forests."

REFERENCES

BOGLÁR, LAJOS
    1970   Aspects of story-telling among the Piaroa Indians. *Acta Ethnographica*
           19:38–52.

1971   "Besuch bei den Piaroa-Indianern: T.F. Amazonas, Venezuela," in
       Verhandlungen des 38ten Internationalen Amerikanistenkongresses
       volume three, 23–27. Munich: Klaus Renner.
D'AZEVEDO, WARREN L.
1958   A structural approach to esthetics: toward a definition of art in anthro-
       pology. *American Anthropologist* 60:702–714.
GOODALE, J. C., J. D. KOSS
1971   "The cultural context of creativity among Tiwi," in *Anthropology and
       art.* Edited by C. M. Otten, 182–200. New York: Natural History Press.

Not in Ourselves, But in Our Stars

JEAN-PAUL DUMONT

Among the Panare Indians of Venezuelan Guiana, the word *tyakun* means "star." The stars result from the incestuous union of two siblings: *ecexkun*, the sun, who is male, and *wönö*, the moon, his sister. The informants were not clear about the number of stars thus generated; it was either "star" or "all the stars" which were involved. The sex of *tyakun* could not be clarified by the informants.

Only some of the visible stars are named. Among the stars which do receive a name, a group of them is characteristic of the dry season: Orion's Belt is called *pecka* or *kamawö tyakun* "the star(s) of the dry season." Characteristic of the rainy season is Antares (alpha of Scorpio), *tosenpitomunö*, also referred to as *kanokampe tyakun* "the star of the rainy season." As such, Orion's Belt and Antares form an axis, opposed not only as stars of the opposite seasons, but also as "lonely" to "accompanied." In the sky of the dry season, the Pleiades are followed by Orion's Belt. In addition, the Pleiades form a galaxy, and different societies recognize in it a different but precise number of stars. The Panare see six stars which are reputed to be siblings, five men and one woman. One of the men has a daughter, Aldebaran (alpha of Taurus), *yoröinkin* "the child of *yoroö*." The only female among the Pleiades is married to the man *pecka*. They have a son, Sirius (alpha of Canis Major), *peckankin* "the child of *pecka*." It is noteworthy that one of our informants denied the existence of *peckankin*, saying that *pecka* had no child and that Sirius was nothing but a plain *tyakun*. This discrepancy in information does not affect the point of our argument. Indeed, whether Sirius is named or not, several stars are named in the sky of the dry season, and a whole aspect of social life is reflected here in terms of an astronomical code.

On the other hand, the Panare are explicit about the star of the rainy season: "Antares is lonely." This solitude of the only named star of the rainy season is opposed to the cluster of named stars of the dry season: the latter are close together (in terms of location, that is, of residence) and linked together (in terms of kinship). Hence, the correlation of dry season : togetherness : : rainy season : isolation is stated here in an astronomical code.

But a difficulty emerges: the Pleiades and Orion's Belt are not far from each other. That is to say, they are on the same celestial meridian, and the latter's rise takes place somewhat later than that of the former. Consequently, although the "star of the rainy season" has disappeared when the Pleiades appear, the "star(s) of the dry season" have not yet appeared. As a corollary, a reverse alternation happens at the other end of the year. When the Pleiades disappear, Antares is not yet in the eastern horizon while Orion's Belt is still in the western one; Antares will appear after the disappearance of Sirius (the last named star in the sky of the dry season) and of Orion's Belt.

In fact, the opposition between Orion's Belt and Sirius is neutralized. The latter appears as a weakened combinatory variant of the former, since informants disagreed on the mythical status of Sirius but agreed in emphasizing the role of Orion's Belt. If Sirius is named, it is included in the category of "stars of the dry season." It is opposed to Orion's Belt as appearance is opposed to disappearance. In effect, the appearance of Sirius goes unnoticed at the beginning of the dry season; it is the appearance of Orion's Belt which is noticed. At the beginning of the rainy season, it is the disappearance of Sirius which is noticed (and of Orion's Belt for the informant who did not name Sirius). As we can see, the opposition of Sirius and Orion's Belt is redundant with the opposition of appearance of dry season star and disappearance of dry season star; the former opposition can be suppressed without affecting the structure. In other words, Orion's Belt and Sirius, as signs, do not have the same form (they are not the same stars), but they do have the same meaning and are merged in the category of "stars of the dry season."

The matter is entirely different with the Pleiades, which are not thought of as "stars of a season" but "stars of a year." We are therefore confronted with a contradiction. The Pleiades in their movement mark the change of season, but there is a brief overlap in each season of the stars conceived of as belonging to the opposite season. The contradiction results from the noncoincidence of two axes, represented as diameters of a yearly cycle in Figure 1. The appearance and disappearance of the Pleiades determine a diameter in the circumference of a yearly cycle; the appearance of the stars of the dry and rainy seasons determines another diameter of the same circumference. The Pleiades diameter represents the peaks of the seasons, since it marks the change of seasons. The smallest arcs formed on the circumference mark the two interseasons from rainy season to dry and from dry season to rainy.

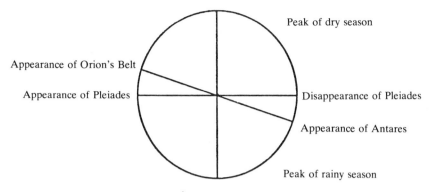

Figure 1. Remarkable star movements in yearly cycle

This is the astronomical frame within which the structural oppositions and correlations of the yearly cycle will be organized. A simple examination of this frame reveals a major *formal* opposition between dry season and rainy season. From a strictly formal viewpoint, there are two ways to interpret the length of the seasons: (1) the dry season proper extends from the appearance of Orion's Belt up to the disappearance of the Pleiades, while the rainy season proper extends from the appearance of Antares up to the appearance of the Pleiades; or (2) the dry season extends from the appearance of the Pleiades up to the appearance of Antares, while the rainy season extends from the disappearance of the Pleiades up to the appearance of Orion's Belt. In the first case, the two seasons do not constitute a whole yearly cycle; in the second case, the two seasons overlap. For the moment, there is no way to decide in favor of one rather than the other reading. It is, however, certain that the Panare, in using two axes, conceptualize the change of season as a distinct time period, namely, the duration of the interseasons, which in themselves form an opposition to the seasons proper. While the seasons proper are congruent to the presence of stars, the interseasons are delimited by four movements of stars. From the rainy season to the dry season, *yoroö* and then *pecka* appear; from the dry season to the rainy season, *yoroö* and then *pecka* or *peckankin* disappear. The movement of *tosenpitomunö* itself is not used to conceptualize the interseasons; only its presence, not its movements, are relevant during the rainy season.

We are therefore confronted with a major series of congruent oppositions, such that seasons : interseasons : : star presence : star passage : : duration : moment. Further, each term of the first major opposition may be subdivided in turn into a pair of minor oppositions. We could have easily established the opposition between dry season and rainy season. The interseasons are similarly opposed, such that from-dry-season-to-rainy-season : from-rainy-season-to-dry-season : : star disappearance : star appearance.

We turn now toward the examination of astronomical sexuality, where we discover its social implications as well as further developments in the preceding oppositions. If we are to understand the logic of this sexuality, we have to begin with the shortest time cycle, the twenty-four-hour period, which involves only two elements. Despite its apparent simplicity, this should hold our attention for a while.

Within the daily periodicity, the alternation of day and night is congruent with the alternation of two celestial bodies, the sun and the moon. It has been mentioned that the sun is male and the moon female, which may seem surprising at first sight. If day : night : : sun : moon : : male : female, then this is in flagrant contradiction with what ethnographic observation of daily life has established, i.e. that men : women : : night : day. Such a relation is evidently reversed by the sexes of the sun and the moon. But it should not be difficult to understand why.

The moon and the sun are an incestuous pair of siblings. In other words, through intemperate sexual behaviour, they have reversed their kin status into an affinal role. Such antisocial behavior has provoked their astralization. By behaving like animals, i.e. mating naturally and not culturally, they become supernatural beings. This tends to establish that the cultural order (expressed in the present case by the normally expected behavior) mediates between nature and supernature, while its natural transgression leads to a supernatural effect.

In order to understand the involved conceptual logic, we must first discuss the Panare theory of incest. The mere idea of incest provokes a strongly emotional reaction among the Panare. They say *arkon monkay usotnö* [to have sex like monkeys], meaning by this that incest is essentially natural, not cultural. Interestingly, one informant had a very revealing *lapsus linguae*, saying *arkonya usotnö* [to have sex with monkeys], which would be equally distant from cultural behavior. Such a slip of the tongue tends to indicate that, in the subconscious of its author, incest as hyperbolic endogamy and bestiality as hyperbolic exogamy, were similarly conceived of as equally deviant from the cultural norm. We would need more than this simple example to draw any conclusions about bestiality. The Panare are not shepherds and do not indulge in bestiality at all, and little emotional response is involved in its discussion, which may merely serve to provoke laughter.

Although the Panare have, of course, a rule for the prohibition of incest, there is a radically different reaction to the discussion of incest, since its eventuality is not ruled out. The Panare are horrified by the very idea of incest. I have neither observed nor been told about any actual case of incest, and therefore could not check whether or not the sanction reserved for those who commit it was ever enforced. But everybody agreed that the guilty couple would be beaten to death, and emphasized that the punishment was absolutely mandatory if the case were to occur within the range of a nuclear family. The corpses of the victims would then be buried as are the corpses of people who die "normally." The informants, however, failed to remember an actual occurrence of such an event; indeed, with a slightly outraged tone of voice, they indicated that no incest case had ever occurred in their settlement.

Whether enforced or not, the penalty is strongly stated. Whatever the case, incestuous individuals are cultural mishaps who behave too naturally. The threatened cultural order reacts violently to reassert itself. In fact, the only way through which those who have strayed into the natural order can be brought back into the cultural one is by being killed. This is so for two reasons: (1) were the incestuous couple to escape before being put to death, they would wander like animals in the forest, die, and be transformed into dangerous spirits, that is, they would reach the supernatural order and escape completely the competence of culture to deal with them; (2) on the other hand, by being killed through cultural channels, those who have committed incest are thereby recovered by the cultural order, and their corpses are then processed culturally, that is, buried. Such a cultural burial leads to the separation of the body, which rots in the tomb, from the soul, which then glows in the Milky Way.

To sum up at this point, an overly natural behavior (incest) has one of two consequences. Either the incestuous couple, without any active participation of culture, escapes into nature (forest) and becomes incorporated into supernature (spirits) or, due to the intervention of culture (clubbing and burial), they rot naturally (in the tomb) while their souls glow supernaturally (in the Milky Way). The first case is unfortunate because culture has been unable to mediate between nature and supernature, whereas in the second case, it has succeeded in doing so. When mediation takes place, it is good because everything happens according to cultural norms; nature and supernature remain separated and under control. The absence of mediation, however, results in the collusion of nature with supernature, which has serious consequences: spirits are to be feared.

Incest is by definition anticultural and it has natural as well as supernatural consequences for its authors, whether they are killed or manage to escape. We are confronted then with a new problem. It is understandable that incest as an overly natural behavior might have either a natural end result or a supernatural one. But why both? Is it not because incest is not only too natural but at the same time too supernatural? By being marked as behavior which is maximally removed from culture, incest would therefore necessitate natural as well as supernatural consequences, that is, consequences equally removed from culture.

It is precisely such a collusion of nature with supernature which the cultural order attempts to prevent; this can be shown from the Panare conceptualization of the solar eclipse. The word *towömuku*, which means both "eclipse" and "incest" is revealing in this respect. From such mere linguistic evidence, it can be seen that to commit incest is to participate in the supernatural order to which the sun and the moon belong. Indeed, a solar eclipse is linguistically expressed as renewed sexual intercourse of these two celestial bodies and such recurrence of the natural behavior of supernatural beings threatens the cultural order by provoking epidemics. Although these epidemics have a supernatural cause, they have the most terrible of natural consequences: the death of many individuals. The Panare do not conceive of diseases in general (*a fortiori* of epidemics) as a natural process, but as a supernatural one, although they recognize the natural effects of such supernatural causes.

As indicated linguistically, a solar eclipse is the incestuous behavior of celestial bodies, which does not mean that the latter is the cause of the former. In fact, solar eclipses result from "a bad dance." A bad dance is a cultural mishap, a cultural failure of the group, since dance is a ritual, performed at night, aimed at reaching supernature at the peak of the dry season. Hence, a bad dance is a manipulation of the supernatural in which supernature has not been adequately controlled, so that celestial incest may happen again. In a similar but opposed way, in human incest, two individuals fail to behave according to the cultural patterns and succeed too well in behaving according to nature. In the same incestuous movement, but secondarily, the celestial pair participates in natural behavior (like monkeys), the human pair in supernatural behavior (like the sun and the moon). In both cases, what should have remained disjoined (day and night, brother and sister) has been conjoined. As we have seen, the same is true for nature and supernature.

Since day : night : : nature : supernature, on the one hand, and since men : women : : night : day, on the other hand, we can say now that day : night : : female sibling : male sibling : : nature : supernature. But again, it follows therefore that the moon, star of the night, should be male, and the sun, star of the day, should be female. To think in these terms would be to overlook the fact that the norms have been reversed in the incest case and in the solar eclipses. As night appears in daytime, as two consanguines mate, and finally as nature and supernature become associated in both cases, we can understand that other reversals can take place. Among the sexualized celestial bodies, the moon and the sun are the only "misfits," so to speak; their sexuality is out of place. The correlation can be written sister : brother : : sun : moon, since they have inverted the norm. It follows that within supernature, the moon is "very" supernatural, while the sun is "rather" natural. This should not surprise us: (1) a parallel ranking can be observed in the structure of the inhabited space, that is, in the domain of culture; and (2) ceremonies are performed at night, not before sunset or after sunrise.

Solar eclipses and human incest both result from a cultural fault, the former through a defective manipulation of supernature (bad dance), the latter through an excessive manipulation of nature (violation of incest taboo). Both have deadly consequences: a solar eclipse leads to the outbreak of epidemics in the group; human incest provokes the killing of the guilty pair by the group. In both cases, the group is confronted with an accident, a contingency, which should have been prevented by "a good dance" and by "incest taboo," that is, by preventions aimed toward supernature and away from nature, respectively. When inadvertently confronted with these "bad" events, the group will actively "remedy" (*mediate* and *mediate again*) the intemperate anticultural collusion of nature and supernature, i.e., their "im-mediation."

Incest and eclipses are both perceived as death threats for and by the group. Incest announces social death, since without its prohibition, no society can last as such. In provoking epidemics, eclipses announce the physical death of the group. In both cases, therefore, the cultural order has been subverted, and the group in self-defense will culturally disjoin what in the first place should never have been conjoined. In order to accomplish this, the culture resorts to a homeopathic treatment of death. In both cases, the group uses a metonymy of death as prophylactic, although not the same one for human incest as for solar eclipse.

To prevent the outbreak of epidemics, the group practices self-flagellation, that is, it inflicts on itself a short-term common painful mistreatment. This external mithridatization, although cultural *par excellence*, uses a natural means toward a supernatural end: natural, since animals are freely tortured in Panare culture while physical violence toward human beings is generally avoided; and supernatural, since, again, epidemics come from supernature. Through symbolic killing of the animality, the Panare are "reencultured" by flagellation in the same way that the killing of a natural animal transforms it into a cultural food supply. Yet this ritual is, by definition, aimed at supernature. It is efficient only insofar as the cultural order is able to operate the mediation between nature and supernature which it had missed. Flagellation culturally "remediates" the duality of nature and supernature.

On the other hand, the incestuous human couple is supposed to be clubbed to death. A technique similar to flagellation is employed, and the Panare say *ötnyepa ipumowon* (which includes the root *ipumo* 'club') meaning "to club the Panare" for both cases. This tends to prove that they do not conceptualize both events differently, and indeed both rituals have the same function. But the incestuous pair is eventually killed; in other words a metonymic substitute of the group is actually killed, while the flagellation is a metaphor of death, self-inflicted by the group. Now the individuals are in turn "reencultured," which is obvious since (1) they have twice severed themselves from culture in committing incest and need to be relinked (in a religious way, ritually) to culture, and (2) they are culturally buried, and have therefore recovered their culturality. The killing in this case is again a treatment for natural beings and the killing is ritual, that is, oriented toward supernature. The cultural order, in this case as well, has been able to reestablish its balance between nature and supernature which had been "im-mediated." If the couple escape, nothing is done at all, which is understandable since they are out of reach and no longer under the control of the cultural order. By their violent death, the killed individuals are brought back into the cultural bosom and can be buried while the fugitives, of course, would not be.

This burial is what leads us back to the sky, with which we started the present analysis. In the burial process, what culture performs is the mediation as well as the disjunction of nature and supernature. The fugitive pair will live in the forest (naturally) and be transformed into spirits (supernaturally), which is the fate reserved for nonburied people. The buried ones, on the contrary, rot (bodies) in their tomb (naturally) and burn (souls) in the Milky Way (supernaturally). In other words, nature and supernature are disjoined through the cultural mediation of the burial process.

Here it is time to recall that the Milky Way is itself made up of stars. Each star of the sky is called *tyakun* whether it is in or out of the Milky Way. However, we are confronted with a double origin of the stars. On the one hand, all stars, including the stars of the Milky Way, result from the incestuous union of the sun and the moon; on the other hand, the stars of the Milky Way, exclusively, are the burning souls of the dead. No contradiction is involved here. In effect, we have already established the congruence which exists between human or celestial incest, and death. In addition, incest is a sexual union which is the opposite of procreation. The human incestuous couple not only fails to beget offspring as a result of their embrace, but receives death from the group. The incestuous celestial bodies are hardly more fecund, giving birth to asexual *tyakun*, that is, sterile beings which consequently are social misfits. What could be a better expression of the fact that sexual life, without incest prohibition, cannot last for long? Incest, in reversing the sexual norms, leads directly to asexuality: the spirits, the souls, and the *tyakun* have no sex. The Panare believe in an afterlife which is not very different from the earthly one, except that it is quite dull — there is no sex after death.

From this discussion of incest and death, we can see that the sexuality of the moon and the sun has been displaced due to their incestuous behavior. It is a male celestial body which appears in the daytime and a female one which appears at night. The latter is accompanied by asexual offspring which are themselves the by-product of an inversion: either normal death as opposed to the continuation of physical life, or incest as opposed to the perpetuation of social life. In fact, there is a supernatural ranking. The ultimate future of the individuals is to reach, as souls, the status of supernatural beings. (But at the same time, dead human beings accede to the supernatural order as asexual offspring of an incestuous union; they accede to a supernatural minus.) In effect, there is a ranking from superior male to inferior female. This ranking continues as sexuality is superior to asexuality. It can be easily established that asexuality is congruent with early childhood. Consequently, during the short periodicity of the day, the relevant celestial bodies which originate from a reversal have either a reversed or suppressed sexuality. The latter case is evidently a modality of the former. At the same time, being reversed, they are "abnormal," so to speak, insofar as incest and death are not "normal." But they are supernatural.

Therefore, the fact that the sun appears during the daytime while the moon and the Milky Way appear at night conforms perfectly to a dialectical logic: all are ambiguous celestial bodies. The sun is a superior male, but reversed as incestuous; "he" appears in the female daytime, and therefore "supernaturalizes" the daytime in the same way as the daytime "desacralizes" him. The moon is an inferior female, but reversed as incestuous; "she" appears in the male night, and therefore enhances and weakens the sacredness of the night. But it is under the condition of being asexual souls that human beings can accede, almost furtively, to the supernatural, humbly glowing in a weakened night.

There is one remaining difficulty which must be examined before we exhaust the structure of daily periodicity. The Milky Way is more often visible during the dry season. If such is the case, the Milky Way is not only marked in the short periodicity of the day, but also in the long periodicity of the year. However, the short mark is undoubtedly primitive, the long one derivative, since (1) the Milky Way is made up of the offspring of the sun and the moon, and (2) it does not appear exclusively in the dry season, only more often. The Milky Way glows at night but also more often during the dry season, the supernatural aspect of the Milky Way is reinforced; indeed, it provides the ultimate access of culture to supernature. At the same time, the frailty of this cultural access is emphasized by the asexuality of the souls.

What is opposed, if anything, to the Milky Way? What would appear during the daytime and mainly during the rainy season? It is obviously the rainbow, *manataci*, the Panare demiurge. While the souls burn in the sky, *manataci* appears only associated with the rain. Consequently, the most supernatural of all beings appears at the least supernatural moment. Moreover, it reveals itself only irregularly, whereas the Milky Way is present (actually or potentially) every night. The most natural is therefore opposed to the least supernatural in ever respect since *manataci* manifests its supernatural strength (and simultaneously its distance from culture, of course) in appearing at the most profane time.

This leads us to wonder about the sexuality of the rainbow. In this respect, the rainbow is similar to the Milky Way in that it has none, although rather by excess than by defect. Indeed, I first thought that my inquiries had not been understood, since the questions, "Is it male? Is it female?" were both answered by "yes." The answers obtained about the sex of the celestial bodies are presented in Table 1. In response to my question whether the sex of the moon, the sun, the rainbow, the Milky Way and the stars in general (the two latter separately) were *apo* [male] or *wunki* [female], the answers were either *aye* [yes] or *cika* [no]. Although a number of informants answered *tinca pwi yu* [I don't know], none contradicted the data presented in Table 1.

Table 1.   Sex of celestial bodies

	Male	Female
Sun	*aye*	*cika*
Moon	*cika*	*aye*
Star(s)	*cika*	*cika*
Milky Way	*cika*	*cika*
Rainbow	*aye*	*aye*

From the table, it can be seen that there is a major opposition between the sun and the moon, on one hand, and the Milky Way and the rainbow, on the other. Moreover, the rainbow and the Milky Way are themselves opposed, just as the moon and the sun are opposed. The correlation, rainbow : Milky Way : : sun : moon, is fairly obvious; the rainbow and the sun both appear during the day and have a "strong" sexuality (quantitatively for the rainbow, qualitatively for the sun), while the Milky Way and the moon both appear at night and have a "weak" sexuality (quantitatively for the Milky Way, qualitatively for the moon). In addition, while the sun and the moon are at the same supernatural level (they have to meet if they are to mate), the Milky Way is above, the *ne plus ultra* of supernature, and the rainbow is below, the *ne minus infra* of supernature.

These four celestial bodies, apart from being supernatural, share their "abnormality" since they occupy marked positions, either ambiguous (the sun and the moon) or extreme (the rainbow and the Milky Way). For one reason or another, each of these four celestial bodies is displaced: the sex of the moon and of the sun has been reversed in the daily periodicity; and the less supernatural Milky Way appears in the most sacred time (night and dry season), while the most supernatural rainbow appears in the most profane time (day and rainy season). Thus, we can write the correlation, day : night : : rainy season : dry season : : sun : moon : : rainbow : Milky Way. This is important since we can now establish the logical transition between the conceptualization of the short periodicity of the day and the long periodicity of the year that we had earlier abandoned but to which it is now appropriate to return.

The stars characteristic of the year-long periodicity are also sexualized. But their sexuality is, so to speak, "straight," in opposition to both the reversed sexuality of the stars of the day-short periodicity and the ambiguous sexuality of the Milky Way and of the rainbow. The moon and the sun represent a reversed transformation of social life. In a similar but opposite way, the Milky Way and the rainbow represent a reversed transformation of biological life. Both aspects are further linked since we have already established the congruency between incest and death as opposed to socially acceptable sexuality and biological life, as well as to the rainbow, i.e. the demiurge *manataci*.

Manataci does not represent socially acceptable sexuality, nor human life. Doubtless, *manataci* is a principle of life, but it represents its excess, its hyperbole, and this is why "it" is sexually displaced. In effect, *manataci* is a bisexual being who is also fecund since "it" is at the origin (the present shape) of everything and everyone. An androgynous being who is also self-impregnated, *manataci* is therefore located not so much outside of but rather beyond the scope of the social order, of culture.

In addition, while *manataci* represents the excess of life, the asexual stars represent its defect, death. Thus by following a sexual code, when we pass from the rainbow to the Milky Way, we observe a reversed transformation in terms of sexuality: through excess for the former, and through defect for the latter, both equally depart from human sexuality. Still following the same sexual code, when we pass from the sun to the moon, we observe a reversed transformation, this time in terms of sex: as an incestuous being, the sun is, as it were, a *faux-frère*, a "false brother" who behaves as an affine, i.e. the reverse of a brother; in the same way, and for the very same reason, the moon is a "false sister." For having exchanged sex (socially) which they should not have done, the sun and the moon have also exchanged their sexual attributes (biologically).

According to the sexual code which is presently examined, the sun and the moon have been socially excessive, and remain so after their transformation into celestial bodies only when there are eclipses. In this respect they are like *manataci*, who is biologically excessive. *Manataci* in turn is "themselves," so to speak, opposed to the Milky Way which is biologically defective. Let us recall that *manataci* is not excessive socially (indeed *manataci* is quite isolated socially) and that the Milky Way is not defective socially (except for sex, the souls of the dead follow the same "life" as earthly Panare).

For the moment, we have to account for a final transformation of the major opposition between the sun and the moon, on the one hand, and of the rainbow and the Milky Way, on the other hand. In so doing, we shall be able to get rid of a seeming contradiction. We have already indicated that the moon and the sun were at the same "altitude," and that the rainbow was located above, with the Milky Way below. This "vertical" conceptualization contradicts the empirical observation that the moon passes in front of the Milky Way. In fact, the conception exactly reverses perception: the rainbow is an atmospheric phenomenon; the sun and the moon are, with the earth, parts of the solar system; and finally, the stars of the sky are even more distant. The inversion of perception and conception can be perfectly understood once it is grasped that the four elements of this astronomical conceptual system sexually reverse the Panare cultural norm, either biologically or socially, either by excess or by defect. In this process, the rainbow and the Milky Way have exchanged their respective positions while the medium pair (moon and sun) has remained in place.

Indeed, the Panare know that during an eclipse (seen, of course, from the earth), it is the moon which passes below the sun and not the reverse. Both are therefore "straight" in their copulation when compared to the favorite Panare technique for sexual intercourse in which the man stands above the woman. The woman lies on her back in her (rather than his) hammock. The man stands up, the hammock passing between his legs. The legs of the woman pass over the arms of the man where elbow and knee can clinch together. The woman lies horizontally and is below the man who stands vertically and is above the woman. Since the Milky Way and the rainbow have commuted along a vertical axis, the moon and the sun should have done the same and . . . the moon should pass behind the sun!

Of course, what has been forgotten is that this opposition is neutralized along this vertical axis, because the transformation has already taken place along a horizontal axis. In effect, the moon and the sun, stars of the diurnal periodicity, are a pair of siblings who copulate, that is they are *par excellence* contemporaneous. Their spatial conjunction causes their disjunction which is expressed in terms of time, as they mark the alternation of days and nights. This transformation into time alternation is correlative of a sexual transformation. The sun and the moon can be represented along a horizontal axis (as in any kinship diagram), along which they have been transformed; this inhibits, by neutralization, their vertical transformation.

Yet we have also said that there was a vertical ordering of the sun and the moon, as a pair, lying between the rainbow and the Milky Way. Diagram 2a of Figure 2 shows clearly that when the vertical poles commute, the horizontal poles remain unaffected and vice versa. This vertical neutralization of the sun and the moon was already implied when we established, on the one hand, that the moon is very supernatural and the sun rather natural and, on the other hand, that the moon is an inferior female and the sun a superior male. At that point, every effort was made by Panare thought to put the sun and the moon in the same conceptual framework.

But further examination of the kinship relations manifested in this astronomical system is necessary. *Manataci* is the "parents" *par excellence*, and therefore of the moon and the sun, among others. In addition, the sun and the moon are the parents of the stars, including the stars of the Milky Way. In Diagram 2b (which complements Diagram 2a) of Figure 2, the transformations are indicated by double arrows. While the horizontal axis represents alliance and collaterality on the same genealogical level, the vertical axis represents filiation in the succession of genealogical levels. The vertical axis is therefore oriented.

Several points have now been established. While the transformation of the sun and the moon is reciprocal, the transformation of the rainbow and the Milky Way is oriented and dynamic, following the flow of the time. On the one hand, the sun and the moon are used to express, through the periodicity of their alternations, a mechanistic conception of time. On the other hand, the rainbow and the Milky Way are used to express a dialectic conception of time. Repetitive time and cumulative time coexist and mediate one another. By means of an astronomical code, the Panare — excellent philosophers ready to reconcile Zeno and Heraclitus — express the paradox of time. Consequently, two conceptions are involved: one deals with a closed repetitive or cyclic time, in other words, with rhythms; the other one deals with open or cumulative time, in other words, with melodies.

In this structure of an ill-tempered astronomy, all the relations of time are expressed in terms of space: separation of the moon and the sun who have been too close to each other and who are responsible for the diurnal periodicity; and reversal of location (from percept to concept) for the rainbow and the Milky Way who are responsible for the flow of time. Therefore, starting from time categories, we are sent back to space categories.

But, on the other hand, the structure under consideration is not only concerned with astronomy but with sexuality as well. What does it mean? According to the rather complex form of a sexual code, the meaning of the message is, in fact, disturbingly simple: not only does incest generate death mythically and actually, but sexual frenzy, passing through incest, leads to death which itself leads nowhere. In other words, a sexual departure from the cultural norm leads to death. All sexual excesses lead to death since it is the final point in the dynamics of the structure: the sexual frenzy of the rainbow and its subsequent hyperfecundity; the incest of the moon and the sun and the subsequent sterility of their offspring; the asexuality of the unnamed stars (of the Milky Way) and their subsequent sterility — all are essentially anticultural. Only the cultural way is compatible with the perpetuation of life, and androgyny and asexuality are biologically excluded as much as incest is socially excluded. Sexual excesses are conceptually "restraightened" through the reversed transformations that we have just studied, and in the same logical way two processes are guaranteed: the regularity of the alternation of day and night, and the proper progression from birth to death, just as the conjunction of the sun and the moon provokes the catastrophic eclipse, and as the Milky Way above the rainbow provokes the precedence of death over life. In both cases, life would be reversed into death.

It is precisely to avoid this reversal that the Panare conceptualize it as happening outside of them. In such a conceptualization, they attempt to prevent a disruption of their cultural order which maintains its frail balance between two threatening disorders: nature and supernature. Only through their astrosexuality can the Panare make sense — in opposition to absolute abnormality (and relative nonsense) — of what is hyperbolically outside of them: celestial bodies. In viewing the triumph of the antinorms as far from them as in the sky, they assert nothing but the justification of their norms and the ideological impossibility of the disruption of such norms.

At this conceptual price, the Panare order, cultural order *par excellence*, is established and its negation is prevented, as it is rejected in the infinite distance of the named celestial bodies. Hence, culture has gained, both spatially and conceptually, the security of its own norms since the "abnorms" exert their force not only apart from us, but beyond us — "not in ourselves, but in our stars."

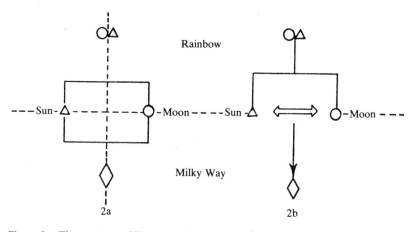

Figure 2.   The structure of ill-tempered astronomy

Biographical Notes

ENRIQUE ARANETA (1925–   ) is a physician and Professor of Psychiatry, University of Florida, Gainesville, and Assistant Chief, Psychiatric Services, Veterans Administration Hospital, Gainesville, Florida. He was born in the Philippines and was educated both in the Philippines and in the United States. He is a Diplomate of the American Board of Psychiatry and Neurology and Adjunct Professor of Behavioral Sciences (Psychiatry), Allport College of Human Behavior, Oakland University, Rochester, Michigan. He served as Head of all Mental Health Services, Ministry of Health, Guyana, South America.

MIGUEL ALBERTO BARTOLOMÉ. No biographical data available.

LAJOS BOGLÁR (1929–   ) was born in São Paulo. He studied Ethnology and Archaeology at the Budapest University (1949–1953). He received the degree of Candidate of Historical Sciences and his Ph.D. in 1969. Since 1953 he has been Curator at the Ethnographical Museum, Budapest, and since 1969 Head of the Department of Ethnology. His field-work has been in South America and Brazil (1969), and in Venezuela (1967–1968, 1974).

DAVID L. BROWMAN (1941–   ) was born in Montana. He recieved his B.A. from the University of Montana in 1963 in Math and Physics; an M.A. from the University of Washington in 1966; and a Ph.D. in Anthropology from Harvard in 1970. He is currently teaching Anthropology at Washington University, St. Louis. Research interests include general New World prehistory, but particularly Andean archaeology and ethnohistory. Recent articles include "Pastoral nomadism in the Andes" (1974), "Trade patterns in the central highlands of Peru in the first millennium B.C." (1975), and "Demographic correlations of the Wari Conquest of Junín" (1976).

JEAN-PAUL DUMONT (1940–   ) was born in France and has been a resident of the United States since 1966. He recieved a Licence ès-Lettres from the Sorbonne in 1964 and, after two years of fieldwork in Venezuela and Guiana (1967–1969), a Ph.D. in Anthropology from the University of Pittsburgh in 1972. Since 1975, he has been Assistant Professor of Anthropology at the University of Washington. His publications include *Le foetus astral: essai d'analyse structurale d'un mythe cinématographique*, written in collaboration with Jean Monod (1970) and *Under the rainbow: nature and supernature among the Panare Indians* (1976).

JOSEPH A. GAGLIANO (1930–   ) was born in Milwaukee, Wisconsin. He studied at Marquette University, where he received his B.S. in 1954 and his M.A. in 1957. In 1961, he received his Ph.D. in Latin American History at Georgetown University. He is Professor of History at Loyola University of Chicago, where he has taught Latin American history since 1962. His special interests include Andean history and Latin American social history.

H. WILLIAM HARRIS, JR. No biographical data available.

SOLOMON H. KATZ (1939–   ) received his Ph.D. in Physical Anthropology from the University of Pennsylvania in 1967. He is currently Associate Professor of Anthropology at that university. His primary research interests are in the areas of human biology and adaptation.

E. JEAN LANGDON (1944–   ) received her B.A. at Carleton College, Minnesota, her M.A. at the University of Washington, Seattle, and her Ph.D. at Tulane University, Louisiana. She is a cultural anthropologist interested in ethno-medicine, hallucinogens, and Latin American cultures. She is currently editing a volume on South American mythology. She is also working on hallucinogenic art of South America.

JOHN MCDANIEL (1942–   ) received his undergraduate degree from Washington and Lee University and his M.A. and Ph.D. in Anthropology from the University of Pennsylvania. He is currently Assistant Professor of Anthropology at Washington and Lee University. His major research interest is the relationship between culture and disease and his research has been done in Latin America.

JAMSIE NAIDOO (1900?–   ) has retired as a sugar estate plantation worker in Albion, Guyana. He is the *Pujari* of the Kali Mai church in

Albion, Guyana, and has been a Visiting Professor of Behavioral Sciences (Indigenous Healing) at the Allport College of Human Behavior, Oakland University, Rochester, Michigan. His area of specialization as a healer is "kali work" (or functional disorders) as distinguished from "doctor work" (or organic disorders). His parents came to Guyana from South India as indentured laborers. In Guyana, he is presently continuing to supervise Allport College Oakland University students doing field-work in traditional healing. In the past, he has also supervised medical students and psychiatric residents from the Albany Center Medical Hospital, New York. His illiteracy proved no bar to his cooperation as coauthor of the chapter in this volume.

ANTONIO QUINTANILLA (1927–) was born in Peru. He studied Social Sciences and Medicine, received his M.D. degree in Lima in 1957, and did postgraduate studies in New York and Chicago. He has taught at the Catholic University of Lima, the Planning Institute of Lima, and the University of Arequipa Medical School. At present he is Associate Professor of Medicine at Northwestern University, Chicago.

ALVARO RUBIM DE PINHO is currently Head of the Department of Neuropsychiatry and Professor of Psychiatry of the Faculty of Medicine at the Federal University of Bahia, Brazil. He is a former President of the Brazilian Psychiatric Association and has numerous publications in his field. His main current research interest is cultural influence in the treatment of mental disease.

RONALD A. SCHWARZ (1939–) received his B.A. in Philosophy from Colgate University, and his Ph.D. from Michigan State University. He has done post-doctoral studies at Tulane University, School of Public Health and Tropical Medicine. He is currently affiliated with the Department of Behavioral Sciences, The John Hopkins University, School of Hygiene and Public Health. He also works as a freelance consultant on development projects in Latin American and Africa. He previously taught at Colgate University, Williams College, and Instituto Norte Andino de Ciencias Sociales, Colombia. His research interests include social organization, social change, aesthetics and the medical system of the Guambiana Indians of Colombia, primary health care practitioners, midwives, and drug addiction in South American and the United States. He is coeditor (with David L. Browman) of two books: *Peasants, primitives, and proletariats* and *Spirits, shamans, and stars* and is currently working on a book on environmental health and development for the American Public Health Association.

DOUGLAS SHARON (1941–) was born in Quebec City. He worked in archaeological exploration (Mexico and Peru) with the Andean Explorers Club from 1957 to 1967. He studied Cultural Anthropology at the University of California, Los Angeles, where he received his B.A. (1971), an M.A. (1972), and a Ph.D. (1974), the latter with a dissertation on north Peruvian shamanism. He is currently a Postdoctoral Scholar at the Latin American Center, UCLA, and Member of the editorial board of *Folklore Americas*. His special interests include shamanism, symbolic anthropology, comparative religion, ethnohistory, and ethnographic film. Recent publications are: "The San Pedro cactus in Peruvian folk healing" (1972), "Eduardo the healer" (1972), and "Shamanism in Moche iconography" (1974), and *Wizard of the four winds*.

PHILIP SINGER (1925–   ) is Professor of Anthropology and Behavioral Sciences at the Allport College of Human Behavior, Oakland University, Rochester, Michigan, and Member of the International Committee on Traditional Medical Therapy. His special interests include medical anthropology, ethnopsychiatry, community development, and pharmacognosy. He has worked for the United Nations and the Albany Medical Center Hospital and College, New York. His fieldwork has been conducted in America, India, Guyana, and Nigeria.

KENNETH I. TAYLOR (1934–   ) was born in Glasgow, Scotland. He received his B.Sc. in Architecture from the University of Strathclyde in 1961, and his M.S. and Ph.D. degrees in Anthropology from the University of Wisconsin, Madison, in 1967 and 1972, respectively. As a Ford Foundation Consultant, he taught one semester in the Graduate Program in Social Anthropology of the Federal University of Río de Janeiro (Museu Nacional) in 1972, and since August 1972 has been Assistant Professor at the University of Brasília. He has done fieldwork among Eskimos in northwest Greenland and Kodiak Island, Alaska, and with the Sanumá Indians of north Brazil. He is currently Coordinator of the Perimetral-Yanoama Project of the Fundação Nacional do Índio (FUNAI), a program of assistance and supervision of Indian-white contact in connection with the construction of the Perimetral Norte highway. His special interests are ethnoscience and structuralism, and food prohibitions and shamanism.

S. HENRY WASSÉN (1908–   ) has been Professor, Director emeritus of the Gothenburg Ethnographic Museum, Sweden, since September, 1973. He received his academic training at the University of Gothenburg and held the positions of Assistant, Curator, and Director at the Gothenburg Ethnographical Museum since 1930. He did repeated seasons of fieldwork in South America and Central America. His special interest is in Americanistic research and his speciality is Latin America's Amerindian cultures, including use of medicines and hallucinogenic drugs. Bibliographies of his scientific publications can be found in the *Årstryck* [Annual Reports] of the Göteborgs Etnografiska Museum since 1930.

JOHANNES WILBERT currently holds the positions of Professor of Anthropology and Director of the Latin American Center at the University of California at Los Angeles. He also holds the position of Guest Professor at the University of Vienna. From 1956 through 1966 he served in Caracas variously as Director of Anthropology for the Society of Natural Sciences, Director for the Caribbean Institute of Anthropology and Sociology, and Chairman of Anthropology for the same organization. In addition to his teaching responsibilities Dr. Wilbert is editor of the Venezuelan journal *Antropológica* and of the "Latin American Studies" monograph series.

Index of Names

Index of Subjects